Patrick Dahmen

Multi-Channel Strategies for Retail Financial Services

GABLER EDITION WISSENSCHAFT

Patrick Dahmen

Multi-Channel Strategies for Retail Financial Services

A Management-Framework for Designing and Implementing Multi-Channel Strategies

With a foreword by Prof. Dr. Walter Ackermann

Deutscher Universitäts-Verlag

Bibliografische Information Der Deutschen Bibliothek
Die Deutsche Bibliothek verzeichnet diese Publikation in der Deutschen Nationalbibliografie; detaillierte bibliografische Daten sind im Internet über <http://dnb.ddb.de> abrufbar.

Dissertation Universität St. Gallen, Schweiz, 2004

1. Auflage Oktober 2004

Lektorat: Brigitte Siegel / Sabine Schöller

Der Deutsche Universitäts-Verlag ist ein Unternehmen von Springer Science+Business Media.
www.duv.de

Umschlaggestaltung: Regine Zimmer, Dipl.-Designerin, Frankfurt/Main

Gedruckt auf säurefreiem und chlorfrei gebleichtem Papier

ISBN-13:978-3-8244-8191-0 e-ISBN-13:978-3-322-81828-7
DOI: 10.1007/978-3-322-81828-7

To my Parents

Foreword

The retail financial services industry, especially the insurance industry, is undergoing fundamental changes. Prior to and in the aftermath of the deregulation of the insurance industry at the beginning of the 1990's, insurers have continued to focus more on stability and security rather than on efficiency and profitability. The capital market crisis, the deregulation, the gradual break-up of the traditionally integrated value chain coupled with the emergence of new players in the market as well technological advancements have all led to a fundamental shake-up of the financial services industry. Nevertheless, the cultural consequences of the regulated period are still visible today: in some insurance companies changes in the distribution of financial services can seldom be implemented without the acceptance of its tied agent channel, although experience from neighbouring industries, for example retail banking, clearly illustrates the necessity to align the distribution system with new trends in consumer behaviour, i.e., with the general wish for more convenient shopping opportunities anywhere, anytime and in any way.

Financial services are characterised by a high degree of interactivity with the customer during the entire process of service delivery, while information asymmetries arise as a result of the dominance of credence and experience qualities. The product "financial services" therefore goes far beyond its core product, e.g. risk protection; it covers all other elements of the customer relationship process. Distribution, understood as the management of the exchange processes between the financial services provider and the customer, thus becomes part of the product itself and represents an important source of differentiation. However, such an understanding of the distribution function also implies that distribution tasks cannot be analysed and optimised in isolation, but need to be embedded in the overall strategic, financial and marketing concept of the company.

Managers in the financial services industry consider the distribution function to be one of the most important elements of corporate strategic positioning with high potential for improving company performance. However, the industry is confronted with the challenges of providing customers with more targeted, personalised products and simultaneously ensuring that distribution costs are significantly reduced. Therefore, the general idea of multi-channel distribution is to employ multiple distribution channels in such a way that personalised channels can concentrate on clearly value-adding sales activities, while administrative tasks are relocated to low-cost distribution channels.

Some academic research has already been performed on the general aspects and managerial tasks of multi-channel distribution systems, although no specific references have been made to the services industry, let alone to the retail financial services industry. Therefore, this dissertation analyses the strategic dimensions and operational elements of multi-channel distribution systems with specific and exclusive reference to the retail financial services industry.

In this dissertation, the fundamental rationale of multi-channel distribution strategies is analysed from the point of view of management. The author discusses (i) internal and external conditions under which the company opts for a specific structural type of multi-channel distribution systems and (ii) which internal and external operational elements are required to implement a multi-channel distribution strategy. The author has developed a theoretical framework, enabling practitioners and academics alike to structure their decision-making processes regarding the establishment (configuration) and co-ordination and control of multi-channel distribution systems. Each aspect in the development of this framework is illustrated by a large number of different case studies. Thereby, the author could rigorously link his theoretical findings to "real-life" management topics. The comprehensive use of case studies is a specific highlight of this dissertation and renders the subject accessible both for the academic and professional reader.

Given the academic and professional relevance of the subject, I am confident that this dissertation will actively be read, especially by managers in the industry, who can use the comprehensive framework of this dissertation to structure their decision-making processes regarding the establishment and management of multi-channel distribution strategies.

Professor Dr. Walter Ackermann

Preface

This dissertation combines the recent findings of both academic and professional research on the subject of multi-channel distribution in retail financial services. It is my belief that academic research in the area of management science needs to develop frameworks and rules which are useful to the professional world. I was in a favourable position to tackle this research postulate. On the one hand, I could draw on my professional experience gained during my two-year period as executive assistant to the Chief Executive Officer of AXA Germany, which launched its multi-channel distribution strategy in 2000. On the other hand, I was involved in academic research at the Institute of Insurance Economics at the University of St. Gallen, Switzerland, where I performed an international benchmarking study to ascertain best-practice elements regarding both the strategic positioning and operational implementation of multi-channel distribution strategies in the field of retail financial services.

The constant cross-referencing between the academic and professional worlds is what makes the nature of this dissertation unique. I am therefore especially indebted to both my professional and academic supporters. On the professional side, I would like to express my sincere gratitude to Dr. Claus-Michael Dill, Chief Executive Officer of the AXA Group in Germany, who has actively encouraged me to embark on this research subject and who has helped me with the practical organisation of this dissertation project and the related benchmarking study. On the academic side, I would like to thank my doctoral supervisor, Professor Dr. Walter Ackermann, for his support and his very valuable input as well as his active participation in the benchmarking study. Finally, I would like thank Professor Dr. Christian Belz, who was kind enough to undertake the secondary review of my dissertation.

A large number of people contributed actively to developing the fundamental ideas and concepts of this dissertation in doctoral seminars, workshops and bilateral discussions. Furthermore, I would like to thank Mrs. Maria Odendahl of the library of the Insurance Institute at the University of Cologne, who has helped me to identify all relevant literature. Finally, Ms. Jane Ufton, B.A. (Hons) reviewed the linguistic quality of the dissertation within a short period of time and I am very grateful for her valuable comments.

My utmost thanks go to my wife, Dr. Kristine Dahmen, who has staunchly supported this research project, especially in the more difficult phases, and who was always prepared to grant me the necessary freedom to complete this dissertation. Last, but not least, I would like to express my sincere gratitude to my parents, Claus and Heide Dahmen, who have actively and constantly supported me throughout my entire academic and professional career in every way they could. This dissertation is therefore dedicated to them.

Bonn, July 2004 Patrick Dahmen

Contents

Overview of Figures

List of abbreviations

AMB	Aachen Münchener Beteiligungsgesellschaft (Generali Group Germany)
APE	Annualised Premium Equivalent
AuM	Assets under Management
ATM	Automated Teller Machines
CEO	Chief Executive Officer
CL	comparison level
CTP	Customer Touch Points
CPCU	Chartered Property Casualty Underwriter
CRM	Customer Relationship Management
CM	Client Manager
DVAG	Deutsche Vermögensberatung AG
ed.	editor
eds.	editors
etc.	et cetera
e.g.	for example (exemplia gratia)
et al.	et alii (and others)
HSBC	Hong Kong Shanghai Banking Corporation
HR	Human Resources
i.e.	that means, that is (id est)
IFA	Independent Financial Advisor
IT	Information Technology
K	thousand
mgt.	management
NAPAA	National Association of Professional Allstate Agents
No.	Number
OC	Outcome
OM	Operations Manager
p.	page
PEP	Political Economy Paradigm
P&C	Property and casualty business
pp.	pages (more than one page)
RTL	Radio Television (television programme)
TSB	Lloyds TSB Bank (Trustee Savings Bank Association)

TCA	Transaction Cost Analysis
TECTEM	Transferzentrum für Technologiemanagement (Universität St. Gallen)
TV	television
UK	United Kingdom
v.s.	versus
Vol.	Volume
w. A.	without author (article without indication of the author)

I. Academic and Empirical Relevance of the Research Subject

The first part explains the relevance of the subject from the academic as well as the professional point of view. In the first chapter, the overall importance of the research subject is explained. Subsequently, the research questions, approach and process as well as the structure of the dissertation are laid out. The second chapter then illustrates the overall importance of multi-channel distribution from the specific point of view of the financial services industry. By reading the illustration of the major change drivers for the distribution of financial services, the reader will fully understand the strategic and operational significance of multi-channel distribution systems. Therefore, the first part forms the basis for embedding the subsequent two parts in the overall academic and management context of financial services providers.

1. Research Objectives, Approach, Methods and Structure

The objective of this chapter is to explain the relevance of the subject of this dissertation. Subsequently, the concrete research objectives as well as the research approach and process will be defined. At the end of this chapter, an overview is provided regarding the overall structure of the dissertation to give the reader some guidance regarding the content of each of the three parts and their interrelationship.

1.1 The Relevance of Multi-Channel Distribution and Definition of the Research Questions

The design and management of effective and efficient distribution channels offer significant, frequently untapped, opportunities for firms to create unique, long-term strategic advantages.[1] The traditional source of competitive value - product-based differentiation - is diminishing in importance and is gradually being replaced by differentiation in service and support in the interaction process with the customer, and those differences are all features of the channel.[2] Apart from branding, multi-channel management is one of the few customer-facing differentiators that can deliver true sustainable competitive advantage.[3] A survey among 120 managers in the financial services industry has discovered that the management of distribution chan-

---

[1] Louis, W. and Weitz, B. 1997, p. 823.
[2] Wheeler, S. and Hirsh, E. 1999, p. xxiii.
[3] Stone, M., Hobbs, M. and Khaleeli, M. 2002, p. 43.

nels is considered to represent a fundamental managerial challenge.[4] A separate survey among senior financial services marketers revealed that, after pricing policy, senior managers perceived the interface with customers as the second most important area of marketing activity as well as the area of second highest potential for improving company performance.[5] Similarly, with respect to insurance services, Sherden argues that distribution effectiveness is a major driver of success in insurance because it is the source of new business, involves most of the critical processes of the operation and is a major determinant of the quality and value delivered to the customer.[6] However, decisions regarding the distribution system are of a long-term nature since they require high investments and a strong alignment of the entire sales organisation with the objectives of the distribution strategy.

The **retail financial services industry**, comprising all companies offering products that respond to the financial needs of the private client, is undergoing fundamental changes as a result of a number of different change drivers (e.g. capital market crisis, increased competition, changed customer behaviour, as well as technological advancements)[7]. In terms of the distribution of financial services, the industry is confronted with the challenge of providing customers with more targeted and personalised offerings and simultaneously of ensuring that distribution costs are significantly reduced. Consequently, the dominant distribution approach "one channel fits all needs" should be replaced by more targeted distribution systems, fully aligned with the customer's needs for interacting - sometimes via different communication and distribution channels - with the financial services provider. Therefore, amongst professionals in the financial services industry, it is no longer a question of whether multi-channel distribution should be introduced,[8] but how, given the particularities of the financial services industry, such a multi-channel distribution strategy can be implemented and managed without destabilising the overall distribution system.

In the **academic literature**, the subject of distribution and, more specifically, multi-channel distribution has increased attention since the beginning of the 1990's. Although it is more or less agreed that distribution falls within the general arena of marketing, there is no generally accepted definition of the exact nature, objectives and tasks of the distribution function.[9] Cespedes qualifies distribution as the "neglected side of marketing", which has only received

---

4 Herzog, M. and Panzer, J. 2003, p. 49.

5 McKechnie, S. and Harrison, T. 1995, p. 45.

6 Sherden, W. A. 1992, p. 28.

7 Chapter 2 illustrates the three major change drivers in more details: changes on the supply side, changes of consumer behaviour and changes due to technological advancements.

8 Easingwood and Storey, in a survey of 153 financial product providers, found out that multiple channels accounted for about 85% of channel strategies. Easingwood, C. and Storey, C. 1996, p. 223-242. See also CPCU 1999, pp. 140-1.

9 Rimpler, G. 1995, p. 31.

increased attention from the end of the 1980's onwards.[10] It is discussed whether distribution is merely an instrument of the marketing mix or an important management function within the overall steering framework.[11] In addition, most of today's literature on distribution deals with the distribution of physical goods rather than with the delivery of services.[12]

During the last decade, some general academic research has been undertaken on the aspects of multi-channel distribution without specific reference to the distribution of goods or services. Schögel[13] was among the first to structure the managerial questions of multi-channel distribution strategies. In his framework, he identified two fundamental tasks of multi-channel distribution management: configuration (i.e., establishment of appropriate structures and processes to ensure the internal and external fit of the channel system) and co-ordination (management and steering of the distribution system).[14] Some research has been performed on the analysis of the appropriate co-ordination mechanisms for different structural types of multi-channel distribution systems: one can fundamentally distinguish between market-based vs. rules-based co-ordination mechanisms.[15] Thus, it can be concluded that the existing literature in this field has laid the basis for a general understanding of distribution of goods and services via multiple distribution channels. Emphasis has been placed – implicitly or explicitly – on the distribution of goods rather than services, thus not taking note of the particular characteristics of services. A systematic analysis of the fundamental dimensions of multi-channel distribution systems in the area of financial services has not yet taken place.

Furthermore, the operational design and elements of multi-channel strategies has been neglected in the existing literature on distribution channels. Many managerial aspects relating to the organisation and management of distribution channels have received no attention in empirical research.[16] "In fact, there are few systematic and rigorous investigations into the determinants of multiple channel strategies. This shortfall in literature has persisted despite its being repeatedly noted by many writers in the area of distribution channels."[17] This represents a significant research void, since literature on channel management generally agrees that multiple channels can only be properly managed if there is an understanding of the reasons why such distribution structures emerge: "A prerequisite to the effective management of marketing

---

10 Cespedes, F. 1998, p. 98; Louis, W. and Weitz, B. 1997, p. 824.
11 Cespedes, F. 1988, p. 99.
12 Järvinen, R. 1998, p. 15; Popp, S. 1990, p. 47.
13 Schögel, M. 1997.
14 Schögel, M. 1997, pp. 30-1.
15 Cespedes, F. V. and Corey, R. E. 1990, pp. 72-4; Schierenbeck, H. 1999, pp. 44-5; Schögel, M. 1997, pp. 148-157; Schögel, M. and Tomczak, T. 1999, pp. 28-30; Specht, G. 1992, p. 44.
16 Frazier, G. 1999, p. 226.
17 Easingwood, C. and Coelho, F. 2003, p. 32.

channels is a knowledge of the reasons channels exist, the functions they perform, and the factors that account for the way they are structured".[18]

To conclude, in line with Schögel's fundamental work[19] in this field, multi-channel distribution management pursues two fundamentals tasks: structuring of the distribution system to ensure its internal and external fit (configuration) as well as implementing appropriate instruments to run and control the distribution system (co-ordination and control). Neither in the professional world nor in academic research has the question of how to establish multi-channel distribution for financial services been sufficiently answered to date. Firstly, this requires an analysis of the relevant internal and external dimensions of a distribution system for financial services as well as an understanding of the strategic and marketing objectives which determine the configuration of multi-channel distribution systems. Secondly, once a specific distribution type has been chosen, an analysis of how the different types of multi-channel distribution systems can be operationally implemented and controlled must follow. This conclusion gives rise to the definition of the following two fundamental research questions for this dissertation:

- Development of a **comprehensive theoretical framework for multi-channel distribution systems** enabling financial services providers to structure their decision-making process more clearly by analysing the major internal and external dimensions, relevant to the configuration and co-ordination of multi-channel distribution systems for financial services. Both economic and socio-political dimensions as well as the overall strategic, financial and marketing objectives of the corporation have to be integrated into this framework.
- The second research question refers to the identification of the **constituent elements** required for the **operational implementation and steering of multi-channel distribution systems**. The operational elements of a multi-channel distribution system include internal as well as external aspects, such as pricing, product offering, branding, customer service levels or the channel compensation system, and also the question as to the efficient financial steering of such a distribution system. Rigorous and effective financial control systems are crucial for the management of multi-channel distribution systems. It is believed that different structural types of distribution systems involve different operational implementation plans and control concepts.

---

18 Stern, L. W., El Ansary, A. I. and Coughlan, A. 1996, p. 31.
19 Schögel, M. 1997.

1.2 Definition of Research Approach, Methods and Process

Once the overall objectives of the dissertation have been identified, it is essential to clearly define the research approach as well as the research methods. In line with Ulrich's view on business administration, the author considers business administration as a theory of management, which derives its research questions from the actual problems prevalent in the industry, and which analyses the behaviour of social systems and their interactions rather than focusing purely on the analysis of individual behaviour.[20] Therefore, the overriding criterion for the evaluation of any research project has to be its usefulness (i.e., utility) for the professional industry and its contribution to solving actual economic, social or ecological problems.[21]

Ulrich distinguishes between fundamental and practice-oriented research, which sometimes is also contrasted with 'quasi-natural sciences' and 'quasi-judicial sciences'.[22] Fundamental research is predicated on a set of existing theoretical rules and focuses on the development of rule-based frameworks ('laws') and on the falsification of existing theories within the context of the observed reality. Conversely, practice-oriented research considers the empirical world as the starting point for the exploration of future possible sets of reality in an effort to come up with models, which are useful for analysing and understanding a specific empirical context or enable the practitioner to modify ('shape') the existing reality.

In a practice-oriented research approach, the constant reference to the empirical world also entails complexity, so that the researcher, on the one hand, has to limit the research spectrum to reduce complexity, while accepting, on the other hand, the overall complexity of empirical systems per se. As a consequence the over-simplification of research questions or the use of methods which overly restrict the research spectrum, e.g. ceteris-paribus clauses, is ruled out.[23] Furthermore, Ulrich points out that reality cannot be captured by studying the behaviour of individuals based on the concept of methodological individualism. It is, on the contrary, more important to analyse the behaviour of social systems and to appreciate the overall complexity of social interactions.[24]

Marketing science analyses the behaviour of people and institutions in markets. Since this behaviour is constantly changing, marketing science cannot use rule-based ('nomological') research methods, which explain certain phenomena independent of the specific temporal and local context factors and which derive their hypotheses from a consistent theoretical back-

---

20 Ulrich, H. 1981.
21 Tomczak, T. 1992, p. 77.
22 Gillham, B. 2000, p. 8.
23 Ulrich, H. 1981, pp. 29-32.
24 Ulrich, H. 1981, pp. 17.

ground.[25] Deductive-nomological research methods cannot be applied to the still relatively young theory of business administration, where, due to the lack of a comprehensive theoretical framework, 'ad-hoc' hypotheses are more appropriate.[26] It can, therefore, be concluded that this dissertation pursues a more practice-oriented research approach, intending to provide frameworks and rules for analysing specific social contexts and/or to influence these context factors to achieve a specific future outcome. These frameworks and rules are there to facilitate any decision-making processes for professionals in the financial services industry.

Whereas research aimed at testing theory generally uses quantitative research methods, qualitative research methods are more appropriate for theory building.[27] Qualitative research methods are generally used when the complexities are beyond the scope of more 'controlled' approaches, no theoretical basis exists, and/or where the context of the situation is of particular importance. Given the objective of this dissertation to build up a relevant theoretical framework for structuring the decision-making process for the configuration and coordination of multi-channel distribution system, qualitative research methods seem to be more appropriate. Although a first generic move into the area of multi-channel distribution across all industries has been undertaken, there is, however, no research on the specific application of multi-channel distribution to the financial services sector. In fact, the challenges of the design and implementation of multi-channel distribution systems in the service industry, let alone in the financial services industry, have not been reviewed within the context of a comprehensive theoretical framework. To conclude, due to the complexity of the research problem, the nature of the research questions (primarily 'how?' and 'why?' questions) as well as the development stage of the targeted industry (Financial Services being in a transition period, if not turmoil) a quantitative approach would not lead to the desired outcome, so qualitative research methods will be applied.

The nature of the research questions, i.e., "why are multi-channel distribution systems used?" and "how are they structured and operationally implemented?", is more explanatory and can, therefore, best be analysed via case studies.[28] In fact, broad and complex phenomena that cannot be usefully studied outside their natural context, such as dyadic relationships in distribution channels, are best approached by case study strategy.[29] Patton adds that qualitative inquiry typically focuses on relatively small samples, even single cases, that are selected purposefully. The logic of purposeful sampling lies in selecting information-rich cases for study

---

[25] Tomczak, T. 1992, p. 78.
[26] Tomczak, T. 1992, p. 79.
[27] Galliers, R.D. 1991, pp. 327-345.
[28] Yin, R. K. 1994, p. 7.
[29] Bonoma, T. 1985, p. 202 and 207.

in depth, and the number of cases may vary a great deal, being usually within a range of four to ten.[30]

Case Studies have been selected as the main method because they will "allow an investigation to retain the holistic and meaningful characteristics of real life events such as managerial processes".[31] In fact, case study research is often used to cover 'contextual conditions', which are believed to be highly pertinent to understanding the mechanism of multi-channel distribution strategies.[32] However, traditional concerns about case studies - such as the lack of rigour or basis for scientific generalisation - are fully recognised and the views in this dissertation should be interpreted within such limitations.

The use of a more practice-oriented research approach has clear implications for the **research process**, which, by definition, cannot start in a purely theoretical context, but has to be initiated within the context of the empirical world.[33] The specific research process, which has been chosen in this dissertation, is illustrated in the following figure.

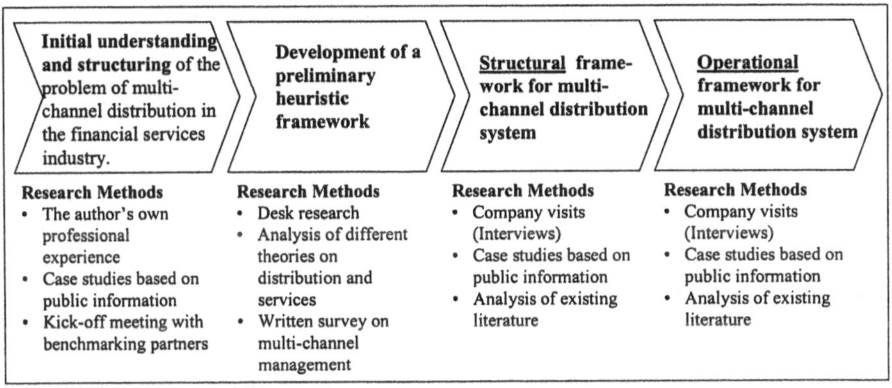

Figure 1: The Research Process[34]

At the start of a research process, the researcher needs to develop an initial high-level understanding of the research problem by becoming immersed entirely in the empirical world. Nevertheless, in order to ensure an inter-subjective validation of the research findings, it is important that the research process is governed by a preliminary theoretical (heuristic) framework which, on the one hand, controls the research process and provides concrete orientation

[30] Patton, M. 1990, p. 169.
[31] Yin, R. K. 1994, p. 3.
[32] Yin, R. K. 1994, p. 13.
[33] Ulrich, H. 1981, p. 19.
[34] Own Illustration.

for subsequent research and, on the other hand, can be reviewed and validated by an external party (validity and reliability of research findings). In this context, Yin further defines the concept of the validity of the research findings:[35]

- Construct Validity: Development of a clear, precise and grounded theoretical framework by referring to different theoretical backgrounds.
- Internal Validity of Results. Use of different research methods (desk research, interviews, etc.) to confirm the results (pattern matching)
- External Validity: Comparison of research results with other research findings

In the first phase, an inter-disciplinary research approach is pursued in a way that combines different theories to come up with a first heuristic framework for the analysis of the research question.[36] This initial heuristic framework will be validated by a constant reference to the empirical world. Tomczak qualifies this process as an 'explorative research cycle', which constantly relates the empirical findings back to the theoretical framework, controlling the research process and giving orientation for solving empirical problems.[37]

Since the author works in the insurance industry, he was able to draw on his professional experience to develop an initial understanding of the major aspects and challenges of the research subject. This experience is complemented by the analysis of appropriate case studies from the US and European markets. Regarding the theoretical grounding, the heuristic framework is primarily based on deliberately different theoretical sources. It is believed that these theories are useful for the identification of all relevant dimensions of multi-channel distribution systems.

- **Theory of the Analysis of Distribution**: here both economic and behavioural distribution theories are analysed. Based on system theory, distribution channels are viewed as systems in the sense of a set of interdependent and interrelated agents and institutions with high dependence on and exposure to other task environments.[38] Furthermore, fundamental research schools, both from the economic field (e.g. transaction cost analysis) or behavioural field (e.g. social exchange theory) are analysed and, subsequently, combined in the Political Economy Paradigm.[39] This paradigm, which constitutes the theoretical founda-

---

35 Yin, R. K. 1994, p. 33-4.
36 Ulrich, H. 1981, p. 19.
37 Tomczak, T. 1992, pp. 83-4.
38 See for example Stern, L. W., El-Ansary, A. and Coughlan, A. 1996, p. 14: "Perhaps most important to the analysis of channel structure is an understanding that channels consist of interdependent institutions and agencies, in other words, that their members are interdependent relative to task performance. A channel can be viewed as a system because of this interdependency - it is a system of interrelated and interdependent components engaged in producing an output."
39 Stern, L. and Reve, T. 1980, pp. 52-64.

tion of this dissertation, assumes that both economic as well as socio-political factors determine the structure and processes of distribution systems. In addition, fundamental research on the structuring and functioning of multi-channel distribution systems has also been analysed.

- **Theory of Services**: The understanding of services and its 'production process' is important for developing a more profound understanding of the service delivery process. It will be revealed that the intangible aspects of services as well as the customer interaction process are important determining factors for the design of a multi-channel distribution strategy for services.
- **Theory of Financial Services**: The academic literature on financial services, especially insurance services, is used to develop an understanding of the central properties of financial services.
- **Theory of Service Management**: Researchers, such as Grönroos[40] or Lehmann[41], have developed a comprehensive theory about the objectives and tasks of service management, which primarily relates to the degree of customer integration as well as to the intensity of the customer relationship. The answer to these two aspects of service management certainly has clear implications for the configuration of the distribution system.
- **Theory of strategic, marketing and distribution management**: The actual configuration of the distribution system is also determined by the strategic and marketing objectives the company intends to pursue. Therefore, the theory of strategic management is analysed to understand to what extent the distribution strategy is defined by the fundamental decisions regarding the corporate strategy. Similarly, the specific marketing approach has clear implications for the design of the distribution strategy. Therefore, the two fundamental and opposing concepts of relationship and transaction-oriented marketing are analysed with respect to their implications for distribution management.

The analysis of these different theoretical sources enables the author to validate and constantly refine the heuristic framework and to develop a comprehensive framework for the analysis of multi-channel distribution systems, which will be used to classify and explain different structural types of multi-channel distribution systems. This overall framework then represents the theoretical basis[42] for the analysis of case studies by providing "the criteria for interpreting the findings of the case study".[43] These case studies are taken both from desk re-

---

[40] Grönroos, C. 1994; Grönroos, C. 2000.
[41] Lehmann, A. 1998.
[42] Yin, R. K. 1994, pp. 27-32.
[43] Yin, R. K. 1994, pp. 25-27.

search, the author's professional experience in the financial services industries, but also from a large-scale benchmarking study on the subject of multi-channel marketing.

The benchmarking study on multi-channel marketing has jointly been organised between the Institute of Insurance and the TECTEM of the University of St. Gallen. The research focus has been defined by a consortium of about 15 participating companies, of which 12 are financial services companies. The following figure further illustrates the process of the benchmarking study.

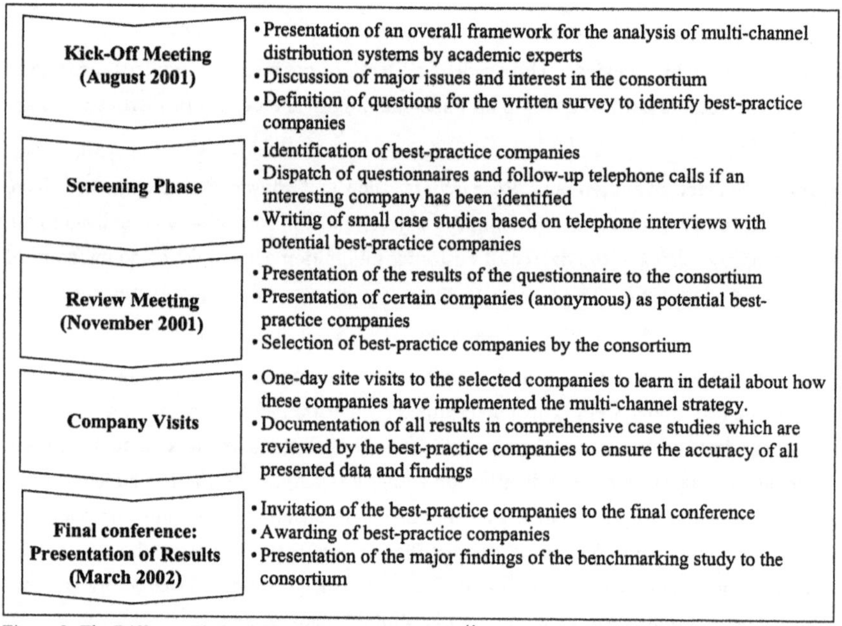

Figure 2: The Different Phases of the Benchmarking Study[44]

The consortium has defined the fundamental areas of interest and the questionnaire used for a survey to identify the best-practice companies. During the first phase (August - November 2001), potential best-practice companies were screened based on a written questionnaire, while in the second phase (November - March 2002) site visits were organised to analyse these companies in more detail. The major findings were documented in in-depth case studies and presented to the consortium at the final conference in March 2002.

---

44 Own Illustration.

In order to validate the hypotheses of the consortium, 110 companies in total were contacted. Based on the return of 38 questionnaires, corresponding to a reply ratio of 35 %, 12 in-depth one-hour telephone interviews were organised and documented; the documentation was validated by the interviewee on each occasion. Finally, 5 companies were selected for one-day site visits in order to develop a profound understanding of all the strategic and operational aspects of multi-channel distribution systems in the specific company. The following figure sums up the entire empirical process of the benchmarking study.

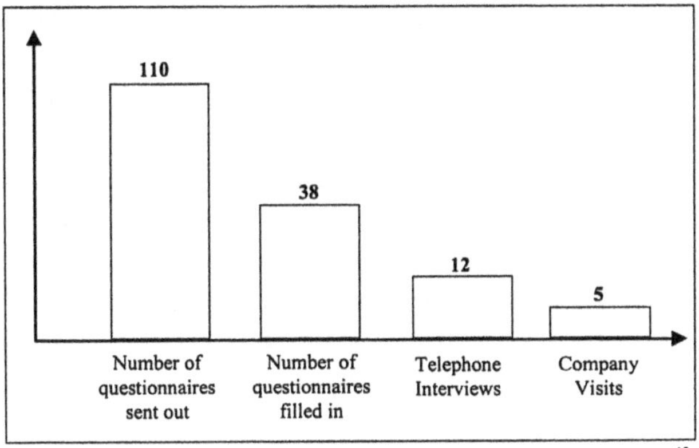

Figure 3: Process in the Benchmarking Study on Multi-Channel Marketing[45]

To conclude, the usefulness of the research for the professional world has been the guiding criterion for this dissertation. Given the complexity and dynamism of the research subject as well as the lack of research in the area of distribution systems for financial services, qualitative research methods, in particular, case studies, have been used to develop a clear understanding of the research subject which is to be analysed in its social context. A number of different theories have been employed to elaborate an overall framework for the analysis of multi-channel distribution systems for financial services. This framework was validated and illustrated by a number of different case studies, since information-rich case studies embedded in the social context are considered to best capture the broad and complex aspects of multi-channel distribution systems. These case studies were developed during a 9-month benchmarking study.

45 Own Illustration.

1.3 Structure of the Dissertation

The research questions as well as the research process also determine the overall structure of this dissertation, which is divided into three parts. In order to develop an initial understanding of the subject of multi-channel distribution, a brief overview of the distribution of financial services, with particular emphasis on Germany, is provided. The aim is to identify the major change drivers, stemming both from the supply and consumer sides as well as from the technological advancements (i.e., Internet, mobile technology). This brief overview enables the reader to develop a clearer understanding of the research issue and the challenges the financial services industry has to face when offering financial services via multiple channels. In other words, the second chapter illustrates the relevance of the subject for the reader from the point of view of the financial services industry.

The second part deals with the development of a theoretical framework for the analysis of distribution systems, i.e., the identification of the relevant analytical dimensions of distribution systems. The second part therefore analyses the existing literature on distribution, services and financial services as well as on service management. These findings are summed up in an overall framework which will be used to analyse the different structural types of multi-channel distribution systems. The framework distinguishes between the internal and external fit as well the degree of customer integration over the entire customer interaction process. In the following chapter, it is then argued that distribution has to be seen in the context of the overall management system, so that distribution management derives its objectives from the financial, strategic and marketing positioning of the company. Furthermore, the financial and strategic positioning of the company equally determine the structural design of the multi-channel distribution system. In the last chapter of the second part, the overall framework for the analysis of multi-channel distribution systems combined with the strategic and financial objectives is used to analyse, in detail, two opposing structural types of multi-channel distribution systems.

While the second part analyses the major economic and socio-political dimensions of distribution systems from a top-down strategic perspective, the third part deals with the operational elements of multi-channel distribution systems. The operational elements necessary for the external (i.e., market perspective) and internal fit (i.e., company perspective) are analysed in two separate chapters. This part is then completed with a review of the current status of the financial steering of these distribution systems. The following figure sums up the structure of the dissertation, which is hence organised in three parts. In addition, it illustrates how the different chapters are connected.

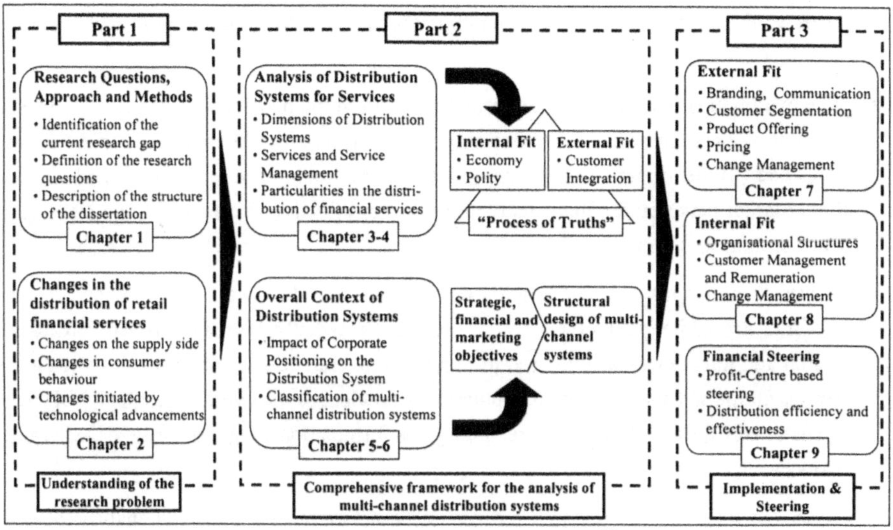

Figure 4: Structure of the Dissertation and Interplay of the different Chapters[46]

The first part defines the overall relevance of the research questions both from an academic as well as industry point of view. Once the research question has been defined, the second part elaborates the overall analytical framework identifying the fundamental dimensions relevant to the configuration and co-ordination of multi-channel distribution systems. While the second part provides the overall framework, the third part describes and analyses its operational elements as well as financial steering mechanisms.

1.4 Conclusion

Among practitioners, distribution is considered to have a high potential for improving the company's long-term performance although in the academic world, distribution has, for a long time, been considered as the neglected side of marketing. There is thus a clear need for more guidance as to understanding the functioning of multi-channel distribution systems. The following main conclusions should be born in mind:

- In the **literature on distribution**, no framework exists for the structuring and analysis or for the identification of the determinants of multi-channel distribution systems for retail financial services. However, a number of studies on the general questions of multi-

46 Own Illustration.

channel distribution systems, with an implicit focus on goods as opposed to services, were developed in the 1990's.

- The two main **research questions** were derived from the benchmarking study: (1) Development of a comprehensive framework for the analysis of multi-channel distribution systems and (2) identification of the major internal (i.e., company perspective) and external (i.e., market perspective) elements required for an effective management and steering of the distribution system.

- **Research approach**: The dissertation will provide useful answers for the financial services industry while qualitative research methods (especially case study research, desk research and interviews) will be used to ensure the overall validity and reliability of the research findings. This dissertation explicitly acknowledges the overall complexity of social systems and thus its limitations regarding the formulation of generic rule-based frameworks.

- **Research Process**: The research process is characterised by a profound analysis of various theoretical sources as well as by the structure of the benchmarking study on multi-channel distribution.

- **Structure of the dissertation:** The dissertation comprises three parts. While the first part illustrates the relevance of the research subject, the second and third parts provide the answers to the two research questions. The second part focuses on the development of the comprehensive framework and the third part identifies and analyses the relevant operational elements.

The following chapter now complements the first, more theoretical chapter by illustrating the relevance of the subject from the point of view of the financial services industry.

2. Changes in the Distribution of Retail Financial Services

To understand the relevance of the subject of this study it is important to give an overview of the current fundamental changes which have affected the retail financial services industry. Hereafter, retail financial services include all products, which are sold to the mass market which, by definition, excludes private or public corporations or any other institutions and which address certain financial or insurance-related needs (i.e., savings, investments or protection of one's own assets or personal health).[47] While, in the past, in literature and in practice, a clear separation was made between banks, mutual funds and insurance companies, this separation is no longer possible, particularly on the distribution side where the retail customer asks for overall financial solutions.[48]

2.1 Challenges in the Distribution of Retail Financial Services

No consistent definition of the term financial services exists in practice or in the academic world. The concept of financial services has been present in the US since 1970. In Germany, financial services comprise all services provided by banks, insurance companies, building societies, security houses, finance companies as well as leasing companies. Bühler defines financial services as those services which are offered by companies to fulfil the financial needs of the private retail and commercial market.[49] This definition of financial services no longer requires the existence of a specialised financial institution, but focuses exclusively on the financial needs of the market. Therefore, so-called non-banks, e.g. Internet Providers, would also fall under the category of financial services if they offered products which respond to the financial needs of the customers.[50] Similar definitions are provided by Haller/Ackermann or Farny, where financial products include both insurance and banking products.[51] Haller believes that the separation between banking institutions and insurance companies has become obsolete and, in the near future, a comprehensive integration in terms of all-finance will take place, where the customer is at the centre of all service activities and not the individual financial institution.[52] Hereafter, retail financial services include all products which respond to the

---

47 It is interesting to note that the AXA Group has defined its corporate mission as "Financial Protection", which explicitly includes both savings and investments products as well as all insurance-related products, which are also necessary to protect the overall asset position of the individual customer.

48 HSBC 2002, p. 5.

49 Bühler, W. 1992, p. 2 (Quote taken from Salmen, S.-M. 2002, p. 86).

50 Salmen, S.-M. 2002, pp. 87-88.

51 Haller, Ackermann 1992, section 9, p. 12; Farny, D. 2001, pp. 38-42.

52 Berghe, Van den L.A.A., Verweire, K. and Roelandt, P. 2001, p. 116; Ehrler, B. 1999, pp. 94-5 and 106-115; Haller, M. 1992, pp. 34-6.

financial needs of the private mass market and are provided in a complex interaction process between the service provider and the customer.

The distribution of retail financial services has undergone fundamental changes in recent years.[53] The deregulation of both the banking and later the insurance industry, the advent of the Internet, the weakening of financial strength as a result of the capital market crisis, the emancipation of the consumer, the migration of banks into the arena of insurance companies (bancassurance) as well as the countermove of insurers into the banking world (e.g. the acquisition of Dresdner Bank by the Allianz Group) and the emergence of new players (e.g. Tesco Supermarket offering banking products) have all resulted in a fundamental shake-up of the distribution landscape for retail financial services.[54] The customer has largely benefited from this development, as he can now choose from a wider and more transparent offering via multiple distribution channels. Over the years, the retail financial services market has changed from a seller's to a buyer's market[55], where the customer ultimately decides which distribution models will persist in the future. As a result of this development, financial markets become more efficient and these efficiency gains lower the security and stability of the market.[56]

As a result of this development, financial service providers need to constantly develop and defend their competitive advantages while the optimal positioning vis-à-vis the financial intermediaries and retail clients represents the most important differentiating factor in the market place. In this respect, financial service companies are confronted with the following strategic dilemma. On the one hand, they need to interact with the customer in a more personalised manner via different distribution channels depending on the customer's specific situation[57], while, on the other hand, there is a clear necessity to increase the efficiency and productivity of the distribution channels in order to lower distribution costs. Therefore, the fundamental strategic and operational distribution challenge refers to the question of how to combine more customer-oriented, personalised distribution strategies with a significant reduction in overall distribution costs. One way to achieve these two targets is to employ different distribution channels for different customer groups or services depending on the profit potential of each customer or product group, e.g. low-margin business or administrative tasks are to be shifted towards low-cost distribution channels while more expensive channels can concentrate on the delivery of more value-adding services (e.g. advisory services). In fact, the

---

53 Ackermann, W. 2001, pp. 67-82; Ravara, C. 2001, p. 109.
54 In Germany, even the public saving banks start to set up branches inside supermarkets. The savings bank in Aachen calls this concept "S-Shop" See Dohmen, C. 2004.
55 HSBC 2002, p. 5; Hypovereinsbank 2001, p. 29.
56 Ackermann, W. 2001, p. 68.
57 Salmen, S.-M. 2002, pp. 58-79.

optimal channel mix needs to be identified to balance off the two competing targets of effective cost management and optimal customer access.[58]

Multi-channel distribution strategies may also enable the financial services provider - at least to some extent - to escape from the ongoing quest to find more efficient modes of service delivery; these modes can range from improved service and quality orientation, via linear product innovation initiatives up to a stricter focus on the core competence of the company. However, all these evolutionary steps will not enable the financial services provider to escape from the 'efficiency trap', since this would require the definition of new, innovative business models, which are different from those of competitors. A business model defines the fundamentals of the strategic corporate architecture, i.e., the way the company positions itself in the market to create value on a sustainable basis. In fact, distribution, or more specifically multi-channel distribution, i.e., the way the financial services provider interacts with the customer, is one way to develop new business models and thus new, sustainable profit patterns.[59]

Since multi-channel providers may be able to develop new business models at attractive distribution costs, this ability to open up or manage multiple distribution channels (so-called 'multi-channel distribution ability'[60]) constitutes an important competitive advantage. In addition, it is a way of dealing with the environmental uncertainty regarding the future distribution landscape. In fact, the acquisition of Dresdner Bank by the Allianz Group has, among other reasons, been justified by the intention to diversify distribution since customer's future consumption behaviour towards financial products is difficult to anticipate, and it is therefore important to have a well diversified distribution system.[61]

However, the operational implementation and management of the multi-channel distribution systems represents a fundamental challenge. In this context, special attention needs to be paid to the prudent management of the socio-political factors, relating to the distribution of power and to the coherence of objectives (i.e., co-operation or conflict). This particularly applies to the German insurance industry, which is still dominated by the tied agent channel; this channel traditionally opposes all attempts to take away revenue streams from its channel and direct it to more cost-effective distribution channels. This major risk can well be illustrated by the following statement from a financial analyst: "The main barrier to insurance companies using alternative distribution channels has been the concern that this could weaken their major source of revenue: tied agents" (Fox-Pitt, May 2000).

---

58 Bonnes-Valkyser, R. and Engels, C. 2003, p. 42, Hientzsch, R. and Bormann, S. 2003, p. 745; Hypovereinsbank 2001, pp. 31-6.

59 Ackermann, W. 2001, pp. 70-81; Porter, M. 1996, pp. 62-3.

60 Heinsen, A. 2001, p. 41.

61 Hypovereinsbank 2001, p. 58.

To conclude, the transition towards multi-channel distribution can be regarded as part of the overall strategic shift that has taken place in the financial services sector, whereby a movement has been made from a product-oriented (seller's market) to a customer-oriented multichannel strategy (buyer's market).[62] From the company's point of view, multi-channel distribution strategies may allow more effective management of the customer exchange process and, simultaneously, of the distribution costs. Ultimately the overall positioning of a company via multiple distribution channels via-à-vis the end customer is one way to develop new profitable business models which enable the company to escape from the efficiency trap. Regarding the operational implementation, special attention has to be paid to the socio-political stability of the system. Multi-channel providers, therefore, need to (i) define the right channel mix, (ii) embed the channel mix in the existing organisation as well as (iii) solve potential conflicts between the individual distribution channels.[63]

2.2 Changes in the Supply Side

Financial services providers can generally decide whether to set up their own sales force, which is either employed by the company or legally and financially tied to the company, or whether to co-operate with entirely independent intermediaries. Reliance on intermediaries is a strategy that many companies pursue to gain wider market access without committing substantial resources. A company that uses intermediaries incurs higher variable costs but lower fixed costs and captures the expertise that the intermediaries have accumulated over time. Flexibility towards environmental change is also likely to be higher because external arrangements are usually easier to re-scale. However, the lack of ownership implies that the benefits of integration are lost and the financial service company has less control over the concrete service levels in the third-party distribution channels.[64]

In addition, in the past, one of the fundamental differences between bank vs. insurance-oriented sales channel has been the commission concept. While insurance channels, particularly in the life insurance business, receive high acquisition commission upon inception of a contract, bank distribution channels receive annual sales targets on the overall financial assets under management. Consequently, insurance distribution is more focussed on new business rather than on an ongoing management of their portfolio of contracts, whereas banks concentrate more on their existing portfolio. However, new compensation systems in the insurance

---

62 Diepen, T. 2000, pp. 37-8.
63 Schnetzer, R. 1999, p. 15.
64 Easingwood, C. and Coelho, F. 2003, p. 34.

channels as well as pressure in the banking channel to grow via new business volume have clearly started to change this distinction in sales orientation.[65]

The following figure[66] serves to position the most important distribution channels along two dimensions. The first dimension refers to the origin of the distribution channel, i.e., whether the distribution channel has traditionally been used by banks/fund distributors or insurance companies. However, in today's market companies which own customer relationships (e.g. retail supermarkets) or which offer particular Services (e.g. Internet Services) represent a third important and new distribution channel.[67] The second important dimension relates to the product offering of the distribution channel. While in the past each product provider had its own distribution channel, this integrated value chain has been broken up into product providers and distribution specialists; this trend is also known under the term 'open product architecture'. Consequently, distribution channels can now also be classified by the number of different product providers a distribution channel can offer to its customers.

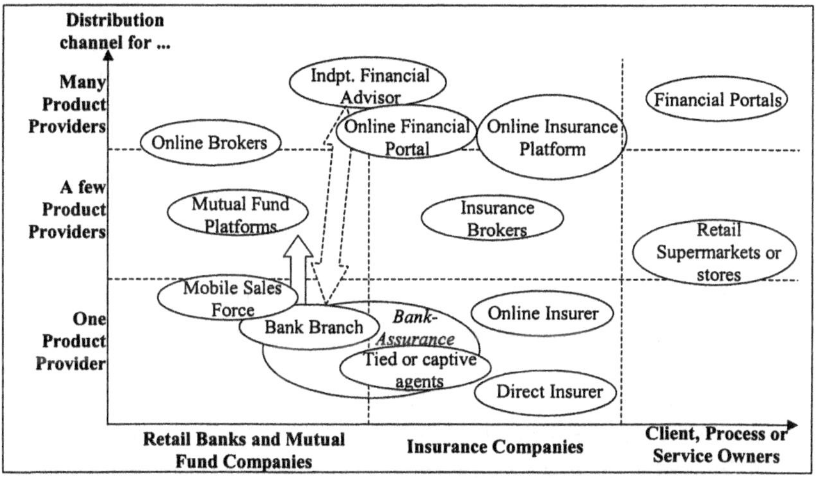

Figure 5: Distribution Landscape for Retail Financial Services[68]

65 Hypovereinsbank 2001, pp. 12-3.
66 Classification grid has been taken from HSBC 2002, p. 6.
67 Ehrler, B. 1999, p. 115-124; Benölken, H. and Wings, H. 2004, p. 44.
68 Classification grid partially based on HSBC 2002, p. 6.

Tied (or captive) agents are legally independent but tied to one specific insurance company, which means that these agents exclusively sell the financial services products of one company. In addition, there are also so-called part-time tied agents who are tied to one insurance company, but their sales activities represent only a part-time job (in addition to their main profession).[69] In Germany, tied agents still represent the dominant sales channel, especially in the retail property and casualty (P&C) business. In Switzerland, the agent channel is even more dominant with a market share of 90% in P&C and 90% in life.[70] The tied agent distribution channel has so far successfully maintained its market position. In Germany at the beginning of the 1990s, this distribution channel was expected to decrease significantly in importance, e.g. a market share of 30% by 1998 was predicted although the overall (i.e., Life and P&C) market share still amounts to 66% (2000 figures). However, market consensus predicts a continued decline of market share for the tied agent channel, which may end up with a market share of only 30 % by 2010.[71] Tied agents in Germany are particularly confronted with the increasing customer demands for qualified advice in the structuring and management of their financial assets. Therefore, the independent financial advisors (so-called IFAs) represent a serious competitor for the tied agent channel. In a survey among US CEOs of life insurance companies, 87% of these executives indicated that a sales process via tied agents would continue to dominate the distribution of insurance services in the US. The challenge is to make this type of distribution as cost-effective and productive as possible.[72]

One of the primary obstacles to integrating the agency-based sales channel into a distribution system was that the insurer traditionally saw the agent as the end customer. In fact, the agent received considerable attention because the agent was at the centre of an information flow and acted as an information gatekeeper for both the insurer and the insured. Consequently, insurers tended to use technology to support transactions between themselves and their agents rather than designing business processes, products and related distribution and information systems to meet end customer's needs.[73] As a result of the eroding market share in the tied agents distribution channel, insurers need to concentrate on two issues in this channel: increasing the professionalism of their sales organisation in terms of customer servicing and relationship as well as optimising the cost structure.[74]

Retail banks in Germany are increasingly confronted with the need to reduce operating costs combined with the customer's demand for more differentiated and personalised service offer-

---

69 Umbau, G. 2003, pp. 3-4.
70 Goldman Sach 2003, p. 39-40.
71 Surminski, M. 2002, pp. 447-8.
72 Bennett, D. and Salazar, C. 2003, p. 36.
73 Arnold, P., Wheeler, B. and Abernathy, C. 1999, pp. 140-152.
74 Hoock, R. and Lüer, C. 2002, p. 980.

ings, so that the classical branch concept 'one-size-fits-all' is increasingly being replaced by more focussed types of branches. As of today, a distinction can be made between three types of branches: (i) technology or direct branches, (ii) service branches and (iii) advisory branches. These three separate categories often exist inside the traditional bank branch, but are considered as separate distribution channels. This separation of bank branches is supported by studies, indicating that about 80% of bank transactions can be undertaken by the customers themselves if appropriate IT support is available and the cost savings are passed on to the customer in the form of financial incentives.[75]

> **Citibank Germany** is considered to be the new reference for modern bank distribution. Citibank installed its Express Terminals in its branch entrances, where customers could perform all of their banking themselves. A welcome desk then manages all remaining customer contacts and, if necessary, refers customers to the 'service bank', where qualified bankers advise their customers on etremely standardised products. This branch concept is supported by direct channels, such as Internet and Call Centre, which either take over administrative tasks from the branches or generate sales leads for the branch offices.

German retail banks have also started to build up **mobile sales forces** to offer a more advice-focussed distribution channel to their profitable retail customers.[76] In life insurance, German retail banks now account for 24% of new business (APE).[77]

> **Deutsche Bank** has increased its mobile sales force up to 1,100 advisors and this number is supposed to increase up to 1,500 advisors by mid 2005. The German Postbank has acquired two financial advisor companies from Credit Suisse and started with about 100 advisors at the beginning of 2003. Citibank and Commerzbank have also set up their own mobile sales force distribution channel while regional savings banks expand into this distribution channel.

German retail banking is in the midst of a fundamental consolidation and restructuring phase. Compared to other countries, German banks are less profitable and Germany is overbanked (i.e., the number of residents per bank branch is almost twice as high as in France and three times as high as in Great Britain).

> **Deutsche Bank** has responded to this development and has rigorously reduced its branch network to lower distribution costs both in terms of the number of bank branches as well as overall workforce. As illustrated in the following figure, the number of bank branches in Germany decreased by 26% between 2001 and 2003, while the workforce was cut by 19%. As a result of strong cost pressure, the distribution strategy of German banks is currently being reviewed since financial income and distribution costs are no longer balanced in the retail customer segment. Banks need to review how they can include direct, less costly channels in their channel mix.[78]

---

[75] Pauluhn, B. 1999, p. 138-140.
[76] Hientzsch, R. and Bormann, S. 2003, p. 744.
[77] w.A. 2004, pp. 127.
[78] Goedeckemeyer, K.-H. 2004, pp. 26-7.

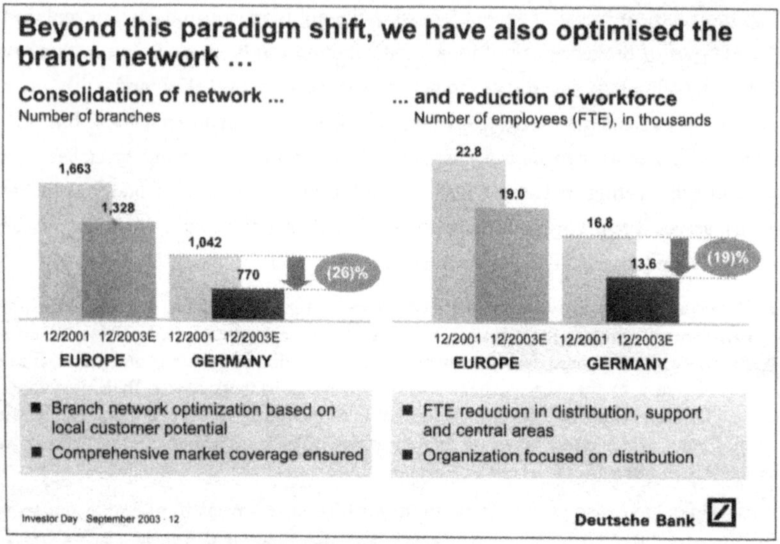

Figure 6: Consolidation Efforts of the Deutsche Bank[79]

However, at the same time the business model was reviewed with a stronger separation of the back-office and administrative tasks from the core business of distribution, i.e., advisory services. Consequently, the number of clients per bank branch increased by 36% while revenues per employee increased by 19% between 2001 and 2003. In addition, the consolidated and thus larger bank branches allowed a higher degree of specialisation.[80]

In the past, banks have traditionally sold their proprietary products. However, in recent years, more and more banks have opened up their product portfolio, particularly in the field of mutual funds, and have thus reacted to the customer demand for a wider product choice. This trend is designated by the term 'open product architecture'. About 64% of mutual fund assets in Germany are distributed via bank branches. This share, however, is expected to decrease in favour of independent financial advisors and the direct distribution channel of mutual fund companies. In addition, unit-linked life product's will become increasingly important.[81]

Citibank Germany has identified advice and sales as their core competence in retail banking and was one of the first banks to introduce the open-product architecture concept for mutual funds. In many areas, e.g. mutual funds sales or insurance, they distribute third-party products. Consequently, non-proprietary funds represent about 80% of the entire mutual funds sales.[82]

---

79 Neske, R. 2003, p. 12.
80 Neske, R. 2003, pp. 12-3.
81 HSBC 2003, p. 6.
82 Buschbeck, P. 2003, p. 472.

The term **bancassurance** or the 'all-finance concept' refer to the distribution of either insurance products via bank branches or vice-versa. The fundamental objective is to leverage both the significant distribution potential inherent in the customer portfolio of the large banks as well as the higher distribution productivity of the agent channel. Bancassurance concepts have been developed particularly in the area of life insurance, where bank employees are supposed to complement their product offering by also advising their clients on life insurance contracts. Alternatively, insurance specialists have their offices inside bank branches to advise these clients on insurance products. While bancassurance concepts are starting to develop in Germany (e.g. AMB and Commerzbank, HypoVereinsbank and Ergo or Dresdner Bank and Allianz), such co-operative ventures between banks and insurance companies are far more developed in other European countries. In France and Italy, bancassurance represents the dominant and still growing channel for the distribution of life products: more than 60% of life insurance products in France and 72% in Italy are sold by banks.[83] Nevertheless, the most prominent example of a significantly large bancassurance transaction has taken place in Germany: the acquisition of the Dresdner Bank by the Allianz Group, which is presented hereafter to illustrate the fundamental rationale of bancassurance concepts.

The **acquisition of the Dresdner Bank by the Allianz Group** has been justified - from the point of view of retail distribution - by the direct access of the Allianz to the bank distribution channel for the distribution of life insurance products, especially unit-linked products as well as mutual funds. In addition, Allianz believes that most of the value, e.g. in the case of a unit-linked product, is created by the distribution function, so that any financial services provider can improve its earnings capacity via the acquisition of new distribution channels. In addition, they believe that the sales productivity of the bank and tied agent channel is expected to increase by special distribution arrangements. Furthermore, on the life insurance side, it is expected that the reinvestment rate, i.e., the amount of money from maturing contracts to be reinvested in other saving vehicles of the same insurer, will be improved, since special investment offers will be arranged via the Dresdner Bank.[84]

By 2003, around 1,000 agents had been placed in the bank branches of Dresdner Bank, while about 300 bank specialist now work in the insurance agencies of the Allianz Group. Consequently, the share of the Dresdner Bank in the new business of Allianz Life has risen from 8 to 12%. Allianz has defined the objective to increase the productivity per bank advisor in terms of new business in life insurance from €62,500 to €143,000 by 2006. At the same time, the tied agent channel is expected to annually sell at least four banking products per client. Furthermore, Allianz customers are expected to invest about €19 billion resulting from maturing contracts in investment products at the Dresdner Bank.[85]

However, by the end of 2003, tied agents had focussed primarily on the distribution of investment funds managed by the Dresdner bank asset manager DIT. The Allianz group has now launched a new one-day training concept for all its agents. It is expected that at least half of their 11,000 tied

---

[83] Goldman Sachs 2003, p. 24 and 32.
[84] Hypovereinsbank 2002, pp. 58-9.
[85] HSBC 2003, p. 44.

agents should advise their clients on standardised banking products, ranging from current accounts, securities accounts or consumer loans. The Allianz agents have direct access to the IT portal of Dresdner bank. This initiative is accompanied by an interesting commission scheme for the Allianz agents.[86] However, one month later Allianz declared that their bancassurance concept would no longer be actively promoted in Bavaria, where for the past 70 years Allianz had maintained a very successful distribution agreement with the Bavarian co-operative banks. 6.6. % of Allianz's life insurance company policies stem from the Bavarian co-operative banks, while the Dresdner Bank accounts for 11% of total life policies. Therefore, Allianz decided to step back from its bancassurance concept in Bavaria in order not to destabilise their successful co-operation with the Bavarian co-operative banks.[87] This decision underlines the importance of the 'soft factors' in the design of multi-channel distribution strategies.

In Germany, the term **broker** includes a number of different sales people, and what they have in common is that they work together with several insurance companies and are legally and financially independent. Brokers and so-called 'multiple agents' represent several insurance companies in each line of business and receive up-front commissions as sales compensation.[88] Small and medium-sized brokers normally join so-called **broker pools**, which in addition to the advantage of more favourable agreements with product providers, offer IT support as well as other services (e.g. training) to these brokers. For smaller brokers, it is the only way they can finance the increasing cost of IT investment and administrative tasks as a result of rising customer demands. It is expected that about two to three major broker pools will survive and may be positioned as 'umbrellas brands' in the market.[89]

Independent Financial Advisors (IFAs) represent specialised brokers and are expected to be one of the big winners in the retail financial arena, since their core competitive advantage is the provision of independent advice regarding the management of the customer's financial assets.[90] Most of the major IFA companies in Germany, e.g. AWD, DVAG or OVB, had their origin in so-called pyramid sales force organisations. These sales organisations are characterised by a very elaborate hierarchy where the superior levels of the system participate in the commission income that sales people on the lower levels of the distribution system receive. The specific commission scheme with the payment of high, up-front acquisition commissions has facilitated the set-up of these organisations.[91] In Germany, the rather opaque IFA market is dominated by a handful of larger players: the 7 major IFA organisations represent about 83% of overall commission income in the IFA market.[92] In the UK, the IFA channel has tra-

86 Reim, M. in Süddeutsche Zeitung, 21.01.2004. See also Die Welt, 15 March 2004.
87 Fromme, H. 2004.
88 Umbau, G. 2003, pp. 4-5.
89 HSBC 2003, pp. 10-1.
90 Benölken, H. and Wings, H. 2004, p. 44; Bormann, S. and Hientzsch, R. 2001, pp. 1730-2.
91 Umbau, G. 2003, p. 6.
92 Bormann, S. and Hientzsch, R. 2001, pp. 1730-2.

ditionally been the dominant channel for distribution of life products with a market share of about 60%.[93]

One of the key success factors for these large distribution companies is to have a well diversified product portfolio of various product providers, so that any decline in one product category can be compensated by other product categories. In fact, in 2003 all major independent financial distribution companies were hit by the continuous decline in the capital markets, which clearly affected commission income from capital market linked products, especially unit-linked life insurance products. In addition, it is expected that these distribution companies will also look for co-operations with bank channels in order to round off the product portfolio, but also to have access to more sophisticated financial planning concepts, which banks normally have developed for their private banking clients. This strategy is pursued by DVAG.

The **DVAG** is the largest independent financial distribution company. DVAG has a strong and successful distribution agreement with the AMB group. In 2002, DVAG contributed about 38% to the total new business of the AMB Group. In 2002, DVAG also signed a distribution agreement with Deutsche Bank and positioned itself as the mobile sales force of Deutsche Bank in Germany. All Deutsche Bank products will also be distributed through the DVAG network. The co-operation already has already shown its first signs of success: 17% of the new money flowing into the fund company DWS of the Deutsche Bank, was generated by the DVAG.[94] It remains to be seen whether Deutsche Bank also sees this distribution agreement as a possibility to further reduce the density of their own retail bank branches.

Direct insurance companies whose sales activities focus on e-mail, direct-response advertising and telephone calls have been set up by insurers. The aim is to avoid high commission costs and provide their customers with an alternative distribution channel in response to an observed change in consumer behaviour with regard to financial services. However, sizeable investments are required to set up the necessary infrastructure, and the costs of marketing to attract customers are substantial. These large expenses eat up the savings made by not having to pay out commissions. Consequently, direct insurers in Germany have only a negligible market share of around 3%.

With the advent of the Internet, the concept of direct insurers has been taken further. **Online insurers** try to outsource as many functions of the insurance value chain to third party providers as possible and concentrate instead on the management of this network of service providers, as illustrated by the example of Ineas.

Founded in 1996, **Ineas** was the first pan-European online insurer to offer P&C insurance. Ineas employs less than 50 people and has a very lean, flexible network organisation. Ineas considers the overall management of online business processes as their core competence, so all other functions of

---

93 Goldman Sachs 2003, p. 20.
94 HSBC 2003, p. 9.

the insurance value chain (i.e., IT, call center, claims handling, marketing) have been outsourced. Ineas offers its customers insurance products at very competitive prices as well as additional supplementary services, for example online access to the accounts and online status tracking of the claims handling process.[95]

Banks also started to set up direct banks, which very quickly developed into **direct brokerage banks**, offering the entire bank product portfolio, but they normally do not offer any advisory services. In Germany, the direct brokerage banks were founded by the big four retail banks, but - with the exception of Deutsche Bank - they are not integrated into the existing distribution network. Some direct brokers started to co-operate with larger IFA organisations, in order to offer a very compelling value proposition of low-cost transaction services with high-quality advisory services.

Due to increasing margins requested for the distribution of funds, some fund companies decided to set up their own **fund distribution platforms**, enabling not only brokers or financial advisors but also retail customers to directly manage their fund-based saving plans.[96]

Fidelity Germany has two major distribution channels. On the one hand, the wholesale distribution channel (90% of business) for servicing the major wholesale clients, such as insurance companies, banks and independent financial advisors. On the other hand, Fidelity also maintains a direct channel (10%), which can be accessed via Internet, Mail and Call Centre, in order to address those customers, who do not consult IFAs or banks. This direct channel also enables Fidelity to remain more independent of market changes. In addition, Fidelity Germany also plans to set up a fund supermarket, in which they can open up their product portfolio to third party funds.[97]

An imminent threat to the distribution of financial services is also posed by **virtual financial portals** and info intermediaries. Contrary to pure online insurance platforms, info intermediaries aggregate the product range of various financial services providers and enrich the offering by proprietary software tools, which enable consumers to actively manage their own financial affairs. These, online infomediaries specialise in providing market transparency for a well-defined target group.[98] Well-known examples are quicken.com, moneyextra.com or aspect-online.de, which have very powerful engines for price comparisons. Financial portals, or more generally the Internet, also open up the markets for software providers or related industries to access the retail financial services market. One example is the German company Finanzscout24, which belongs to a wholesaler, the Metro Group.[99]

---

95 Berghe, Van den L.A.A., Verweire, K. and Roelandt, P. 2001, p. 106.

96 HSBC 2002, p. 7.

97 http://www.finanzplatz.de/internet/fplatz3/fplatz3.nsf/main/main-gte-case-study3+e?opendocument [January 2004].

98 Salmen, S.-M. 2002, pp. 15-18.

99 In 2003, Finanzscout decided also to complement its online business model by setting up a mobile sales force. In 2003 and 2004, they intend to recruit about 100 financial advisors each year. Their strategic objective is to be among the five leading IFA companies. See Handelsblatt, 7 May 2003.

In addition, companies owning customer relationships (e.g. retail supermarkets), are also moving into the area of financial services.[100] For example, Tesco, the UK supermarket chain, has entered into a co-operation with the Royal Bank of Scotland, which distributes standardised banking products and services in the supermarkets. Tesco Personal Finance may acquire more than 3 million customers in the next few years.[101] In Germany, the AXA Group has also started a similar distribution partnership with the well-known retail store Tchibo.[102]

It can, thus, be concluded that the retail financial market is characterised by a number of very different distribution channels. Since the distribution landscape is rather unstable, there are various initiatives both by the product manufacturers (i.e., banks or insurers) as well as distributors, to identify potential ways of co-operation between distribution channels; the bancassurance model is certainly the most prominent example. All these efforts are fuelled by the fundamental distribution challenge to simultaneously reduce costs and strengthen the customer relationship.

This diversity of distribution channels can partially be explained by differing customer requirements as well as by fundamental differences in the products. Life products normally require a higher degree of advice and expertise as well as a long-term investment horizon. The distributor normally spends a significant amount of time selling these contracts to the customer, whereas in subsequent years, there is rarely any contact with the customer. For property and casualty products (P&C products), the product is relatively simple, so price represents a more important buying criterion. However, service aspects, particularly with respect to the claims handling service, are also important, since, over the course of time, there are various interactions between the distributor and the customer, mainly initiated by an increase in premium or by the filing of a claim.

The following figure illustrates the expected changes in the distribution landscape for P&C and life insurance products in Germany. These changes partially reflects the changes, as mentioned before.[103]

---

[100] Ehrler, B. 1999, p. 115-124; Benölken, H. and Wings, H. 2004, p. 44.

[101] Hientzsch, R. and Bormann, S. 2003, p. 745.

[102] AXA Germany comments this development in its 2003 annual report: "In the area of co-operative ventures, we have continued to expand our co-operation with Tchibo. The sales of motor-vehicle insurance policies saw considerable growth, particularly in the run up to the end of 2003. This success confirms our co-operation strategy, which we shall be pursuing consistently in 2004 both in the banking section and also with other service providers." See AXA Germany 2004.

[103] Heinsen, A. 2001, p. 43; Surminski, M. 2002, p. 448.

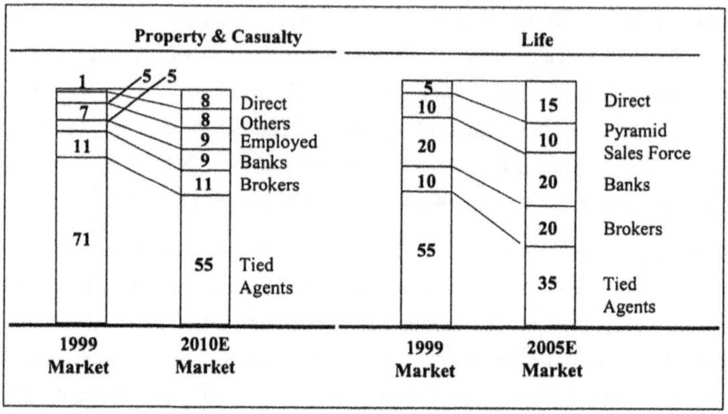

Figure 7: Evolution of Channel Mix in the German Insurance Market (in percentage)[104]

As shown in the figure above, in Germany the tied agent channel is expected to significantly lose market share both in P&C and Life. In the P&C retail business, it is assumed that by 2010 the tied agent channel will have lost almost 20 % of its market share, while the direct channel (telephone and Internet) will still not have increased its market share significantly. The development of the tied agents channel is even worse regarding the distribution of life products. Tied agents are expected to remain at a level of 35% in 2005 and at about 30 % after 2010.[105] Conversely, banks and especially independent financial advisors (brokers) are expected to increase in importance, as they offer independent advice based on a wider scope of different product providers (open-architecture). In a survey by Tillinghast, banks and independent advisors with their emphasis on 'independent advice' are expected to increase in importance in the distribution of life insurance contracts.[106] In 2002, banks accounted for 24% of new business (APE) in the Germany life insurance market. Conversely, due to the lack of offering advisory services the direct Internet channel plays no significant role in the distribution of life insurance policies.[107]

However, in these projections the increasing pressure on the product manufacturer, both in banking and insurance, to reduce administration and commission expenses may change the projected future distribution scenario since the product manufacturer may in future analyse the cost efficiency of the individual distribution channels more intensely. The following figure provides an overview of the direct distribution costs of life contracts for selected distribution channels.

---

104 Data Monitor, Own Estimates, Estimates by McKinsey und Tillinghast.
105 Heinsen, A. 2001, p. 43; Surminski, M. 2002, p. 448.
106 Tillinghast-Vertriebswege Survey 2001, Frankfurt a. Main, May 2002; w. A. 2004, p. 128.
107 w. A. 2004, pp. 127-8.

	Acquisition Commission (in % of sum insured)			Follow-up Commission (portfolio) (in % of regular premium)		
	Minimum	**Maxiumum**	**Average**	**Minimum**	**Maxiumum**	**Average**
Financial Advisors (large)	5,5	6,8	**6,2**	1,8	3,0	**2,5**
Financial Advisors (small)	4,5	6,0	**5,2**	1,8	3,0	**2,5**
Broker	2,5	4,8	**4,0**	1,5	2,5	**2,0**
Banks	2,5	4,3	**3,5**	0,0	0,3	**0,0**
Tied Agents	1,5	3,5	**2,5**	0,2	1,5	**0,6**

Figure 8: Comparison of Commission Costs for Life Insurance across Distribution Channels[108]

This figure clearly indicates that the independent financial advisor channel, e.g. MLP or AWD, is among the most expensive distribution channels for life products. Therefore, one could expect that the large product providers will either try to change those commission arrangements or will re-visit the possibility of focussing more on the tied agent or bank channels, which are less expensive and can be more easily controlled and managed in terms of their distribution activities. These differences in costs also imply that in a multi-channel distribution the correct pricing of the products in the different channels plays an important role, since significant differences in distribution costs cannot be ignored and represent an important value driver.

Significant changes are also expected in the distribution of mutual fund assets in Germany., as illustrated in the following figure. Banks represent the most important distribution channel for mutual fund assets. However, as illustrated by the following figure, IFAs and third-party distribution companies will increase their share in mutual fund assets from 16% in 1998 to about 26% by 2005, while banks are predicted to lose about 18% in market share.

---

[108] HSBC 2003, p. 12.

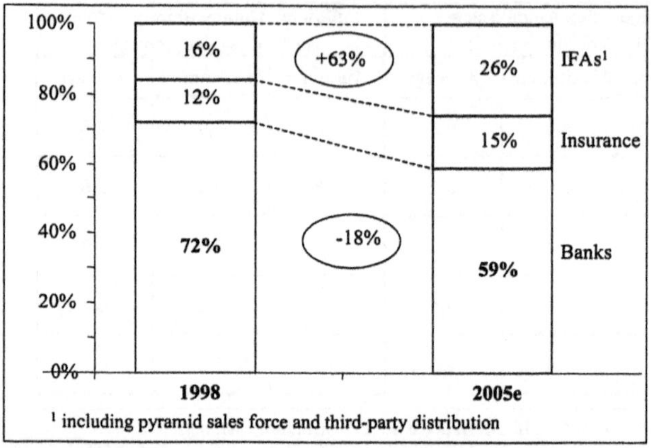

Figure 9: Break-down of Retail Mutual Fund Assets by Distribution Channels[109]

Once the expected landscape in the distribution of financial services has been described, the extent to which changes in consumer behaviour will also contribute to the changes in the distribution landscape will be reviewed in the next section.

2.3 Changes in Consumer Behaviour

The fundamental changes which are currently affecting the financial services industry go hand in hand with a certain consumer emancipation: today's customers ask for high service levels at competitive prices. In addition, easy access via the Internet to detailed product and pricing information not only increases transparency in a traditionally opaque market, but also increases customer's competence in handling complex financial services themselves. Internet-based demand aggregators increase the buying power of the consumer even further. As a result, consumers no longer accept off-the-shelf mass products, but ask for individual product solutions. Products are expected to be perfectly tailored to meet the customer needs, so the identification of the 'right' customer needs becomes the major competitive success factor.[110] Heinsen[111] concludes that, in future, the decision-making process for the purchase of insurance products will be determined by primarily the following factors:

- Competence in solving problems in the area of financial protection and pension schemes
- Individual and flexible product offering

[109] Bormann, S. and Hientzsch, R. 2001, pp. 1730-2.
[110] Salmen, S.-M. 2002, pp. 26-7.
[111] Heinsen, A. 2001, p. 22.

- Coverage of all risks at competitive prices
- Improved product and service offering
- Confidence in quick and uncomplicated claims handling services.

This list of customer requirements clearly indicates that traditional channels are not able to fully respond to these customer requirements on their own. Banks and insurance companies need to establish personal links with the customer across several distribution channels to reduce the risk of customer defection. In fact, the financial services providers are being confronted with diminishing customer loyalty.[112] The association for consumer research in Nuremberg discovered that the proportion of customers loyal to a specific insurance brand decreased from 67% in 1984 to 61% in 1999 while customers had, on average, about 15 contracts with seven different insurers.[113] Since customer profitability increases in the course of the business relationship, both banks and insurance companies make every effort to increase customer loyalty. Distribution will, therefore, undergo a major transformation from an approach of mass customisation to a distribution system which is more aligned with the needs of the individual customer segments. This trend may even culminate in a one-to-one market approach, since customer segments are not homogenous and change over time.[114]

The Internet presence also has an important impact on consumer purchasing behaviour: 48% of consumers state that their online search activities clearly influence their 'offline' purchase decisions.[115] Nevertheless, McKinsey believes that despite the growing acceptance of remote channels, a significant majority of customers in most personal financial services sectors will continue to use traditional face-to-face distribution channels in the foreseeable future.[116] In fact, this hypothesis is supported by a number of different surveys. Although 40% of online customers say they would consider opening an account with an online-only banking institution, some 70% say they would open an account with a bank which also has physical outlets. Similarly, only 28% of brokerage customers say they would open a purely online brokerage account, 42% say they would open an online account if the broker also had physical locations.[117] In a study on consumer behaviour undertaken by Credit Suisse First Boston, about 86% of mass affluent customers in the UK, Germany, Italy and Spain prefer face-to-face contacts regarding questions on financial management and financial planning.[118] These results are also confirmed by a study of retail banking in Germany, where 90% prefer the face-to-

112 Koch, G. and Köhne, T. 2000, p. 98; Salmen, S.-M. 2002, pp. 23-4.
113 CSC Ploenzke 2000, p. 13.
114 Krings, M. 2002, p. 416.
115 Stummeyer, C. 2002, pp. 154-5.
116 Flur, D., Mendonca, L. and Nakache, P. 1997, p. 123.
117 Bekier, M., Flur, D. and Singham, S. 2000, pp. 76-80.
118 Study undertaken by Credit Suisse First Boston in 2000.

face distribution channel as the primary interface while appreciating the existence of other communication channels.[119]

In addition, consumers who are given the choice of using multiple distribution channels will also use them: In the US, the National Retail Federation found that 68% of catalogue shoppers had also shopped at the company's stores, and among a retailer's online shoppers, 59% had also made purchases in the store and 43% from its catalogues. In addition, these multi-channel shoppers are also more valuable: Jupiter Research estimates that these multi-channel shoppers spend about one third more than their single-channel counterparts.[120] Similarly, in the spring of 2002, Forrester Research revealed in a survey that multi-channel consumers spend about 30% more than consumers who use just one distribution channel. Furthermore, about 50% of consumer use online and offline distribution channels to the same extent.[121] These research conclusions represent one fundamental justification for the implementation of multi-channel distribution strategies, where the customer can choose between various distribution channels depending on the specific situation.

The reason why consumers no longer want to stick to just one distribution channel can be explained by their **hybrid consumption habits**; i.e., consumer behaviour is characterised by the parallel existence of opposing, partially contradictory consumption habits (so-called bipolar consumption habits)[122] Therefore, consumers want to decide for themselves how, when and where they want to establish contact with their retail financial services provider. According to the concept of component life-styles,[123] consumer attitudes and behaviour vary by purchase situation and they are no longer constrained by social customs and standards. This means that the same customer may ask for face-to-face, comprehensive advice for financing his retirement and, at the same time, buy his standard motor policy via a direct insurer.[124] Consequently, consumers can no longer be assigned to specific customer segments based on traditional economic or socio-demographic criteria.[125] A second aspect fostering hybrid consumption habits is the fact that the consumer is confronted with an increasing differentiation of

---

119 Salmen, S.-M. 2002, p. 20.
120 Lipke, D. 2000, pp. 41-43.
121 Walser, M. 2002, p. 53.
122 Eggert, U. 1997, p. 157; Fuchs, H. 1998, p. 136-7; Krings, M. 2002, p. 414; Muthers, H. and Muthers-Haas, H. 2001, p. 20; Salmen, S.-M. 2002, p. 31; Schüller, S. and Riedl, M. 2000, p. 828; Schramm-Klein, H. 2003, pp. 38-9; Wings, H. 1999, pp. 22-4.
123 Bermann, B. 1996, pp. 63-4.
124 Heinsen, A. 2001, p. 51.
125 Kühlmann, U. et al. 2000, p. 11; Kurtenbach, W., Kühlmann, K., Käßer-Pawelka, G. 1995, p. 113; Salmen, S.-M. 2002, p. 31.

product offering and, thus, with an abundance of options to choose from – Gross qualifies this trend as the 'multi-option society'.[126]

The multitude of options also refers to the entire value system (value pluralism), which breaks up and become unstable, undergoing constant changes. This change in the value system was initiated by a shift in the value system from a society focussed on discipline, work and diligence (workers' society) to a more open society, seeking a work-life balance, autonomy and fun (event society). This shift from 'working to survive' to 'living to make discoveries and enjoy life and to find self-fulfilment' also has implications for the way customers want to interact with the financial services provider.[127] For example, because customers wish to spend less time on financial affairs, they demand a high degree of convenience and accessibility.[128] Convenience shopping refers to the phenomenon that customers prefer distribution channels which are easily accessible and convenient in a way that the consumer can decide when, where and how he wants to do his shopping.[129] [130]

This new trend in hybrid consumption habits as well as the increased demand for convenience is also reflected in the use of the different distribution channels in retail banking. While today the majority of people still use the branch as the dominant distribution channel, this situation will change significantly in the future. In fact, it is expected that only 10 % of retail customers will use either bank branches or electronic channels exclusively and 60% will use a mix of distribution channels.[131] Similar studies from Booz, Allen and Hamilton on retail banking confirm that about 60 to 80 % of customers use about three distribution channels, i.e., branches, Internet and telephone.[132]

---

[126] Gross, P. 1994.
[127] Salmen, S.-M. 2002, pp. 29.
[128] Berghe, Van den L.A.A., Verweire, K. and Roelandt, P. 2001, p. 115; Mols, N. 1999, p. 296; Stone, M., Hobbs, M. and Khaleeli, M. 2002, pp. 42-3.
[129] Schögel, M. and Tomczak, T. 1999, p. 15.
[130] Fidelity Germany, Thomas Balk President Mutual Funds Europe and Olaf John Executive Director Institutional Business: "The key is to provide a more convenient service. The client will ask for a one-stop-shopping-solution, where he will be able to obtain all of the information he needs in one place. Example: buying funds from several different companies will become more attractive when the customer receives a single statement. Transparency and service are the primary factors for a successful online- business!", http://www.finanzplatz.de/internet/fplatz3/fplatz3.nsf/main/main-gte-case-study3+e?opendoc-ument [January 2004].
[131] Holmsen, C., Palter, R., Simon, P. and Weberg, P. 1998, p. 84; Pauluhn, B. 1999, pp. 150-2.
[132] Salmen, S.-M. 2002, pp. 21-2; Schierenbeck, H. 1998, p. 43; Schüller, S. and Riedl, M. 2000, p. 832.

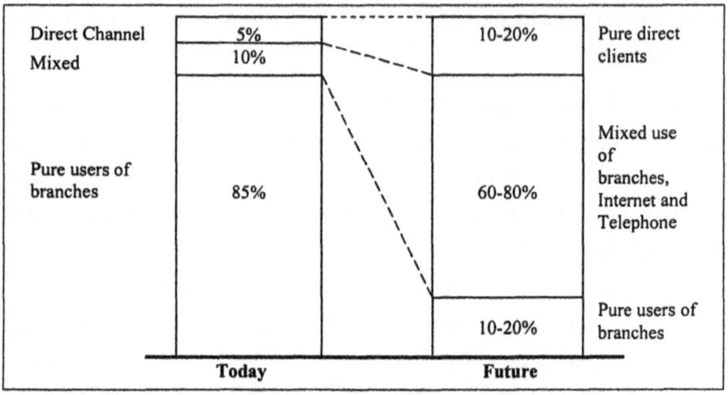

Figure 10: Shifts in the Use of Distribution Channels in Retail Banking[133]

Similar trends can be observed in the insurance industry: customers may want to contact other direct distribution channels in specific cases (e.g. inquiry about a claims settlement), but they still ask for face-to-face advice once they have finished gathering information.[134] It is, therefore, not surprising, that a survey revealed that around 80% of consumers would like to use different distribution channels for their purchases and around 50% think that companies with several distribution channels have a competitive advantage.[135] It can thus be inferred from these findings that it is certainly no longer possible to clearly assign customers to one specific distribution channel.

To conclude, thanks to easier access to information via the Internet and the increased transparency of the retail financial market, consumers are better informed and expect far more tailor-made product solutions. Distribution strategies need to further customise their distribution approach towards the needs of the individual customer segment. In addition, consumers are characterised by hybrid behaviour in a multi-option society and have a general demand for convenience shopping. Their behaviour is determined by the actual environment and situation, so their consumption behaviour may vary between pure price, event or convenience orientation. No single distribution channel can fully serve these varying consumer habits, so a multiple-channel distribution system seems to be the appropriate response to such consumer behaviour.[136] Given the described customer behaviour, it is not surprising that about 50 % of experts in retail banking attribute a high importance to the development of integrated distribution systems.[137]

---

133 Booz, Allen & Hamilton, 1999; McKinsey 2000.
134 Arnold, P., Wheeler, B. and Abernathy, C. 1999, pp. 140-152.
135 Hesse, J. and Huckemann, M. 2002, p. 63.
136 Schramm-Klein, H. 2003, p. 40.
137 Wings, H. 1999, p. 230.

2.4 Technological Changes: Impact of the Internet on Distribution

Today, technology plays an important role in the design and implementation of strategies in retail financial services.[138] In fact, the Internet influences the future distribution channel structure in two ways. Firstly, it represents a distribution channel with an extremely interesting cost structure as well as an interesting service level regarding the exchange of information. Secondly, the Internet influences consumer behaviour because the Internet increases market transparency so customers become better informed and demanding in their interactions with the financial services provider.[139]

The true potential of the Internet as a distribution channel can best be illustrated by describing the major characteristics of this channel[140]:

- The ability to inexpensively store vast amounts of information at different virtual locations.
- The availability of powerful and inexpensive means of searching, organising, and disseminating such information.
- Interactivity and the ability to provide information on demand
- The ability to provide perceptual experiences that are far superior to a printed catalogue, although not as rich as personal inspection.
- The ability to serve as a transaction medium
- The ability to exchange intangible goods, e.g. financial services. Indeed, all information goods can easily be distributed through the Internet. It can generally be stated that to the extent that the value proposition is intangible, the greater the frequency of purchase or the use of a good, the greater the advantage of the Internet as a transaction and distribution medium.
- The ability to ease the often severe time and place constraints. No longer will services be offered primarily at the convenience of the seller.[141]

A survey among insurers has revealed that the majority of insurers believe that technology will drive significant, even revolutionary, change in the industry. 91% of the respondents believe that change will be dramatic.[142] Based on semi-structured interviews in four financial services companies in the UK, it has also been confirmed that the Internet represents a strong force for change. Major impacts will result from the ability to efficiently provide information and services directly to customers as well as from the possibility of automating transactions and services. Potentially, there should be significant changes in the way the relationship between the organisation and the customer is managed.[143] The Internet may intensify competition in two ways: (i) new players can more easily access the financial services industry, and (ii) established users will effectively leverage the Internet in their business model to develop a

---

[138] Benölken, H. and Wings, H. 2004, p. 42.
[139] Mols, N. 1999, p. 295-6; Porter, M. 2001, p. 67.
[140] Peterson, R., Balasubramanian, S. and Bronnenberg, B. 1997, pp. 333-4.
[141] Sheth, J. and Sisodia, S. 1997, p. 17.
[142] w. A. 2001, p. 119.
[143] Hughes, T. 2001, pp. 221-231.

clear competitive advantage. Both aspects will be analysed more deeply. In fact, market entry barriers are reduced for new market players, leading to the emergence of new business models and structural changes,[144] which are illustrated by the following trends:[145]

- **Establishment of new players and competitors**: New players come into the market place thanks to the diffusion of the Internet. Any client owner, e.g. department stores or process owners, e.g. Internet providers, can potentially use the Internet to offer financial services.[146] New business models, such as online financial services supermarkets or online insurance companies, can be set up.
- **Disintermediation**: The Internet can establish direct contacts between the product manufacturer and the end customer while circumventing the traditional distribution intermediaries. This trend can be observed in the case of mutual fund companies which have set up their own mutual fund supermarkets where customers can purchase their financial services directly. There are clear indications both in banking and insurance that a massive deconstruction of the value chain is about to take place. In a World Insurance Leader Panel, the unbundling of the value chain was put forward as one of the most dramatic challenges.[147]
- **Intermediation**: Although certain intermediaries are replaced, new forms of intermediation come into play. Internet or software providers whose core competence refers to the management of the underlying Internet technology can set up their own financial portals and thus own the client relationship, e.g. quicken.com.[148]

The established financial players need to respond to these competitive threats by fully leveraging the Internet technology to re-engineer the entire value chain. The Internet can be used to re-engineer the entire business processes or to outsource some parts of the value chain, e.g. claims processing in the case of insurance companies or transactional services for brokerage services. In addition, given the intangible and process-oriented nature of financial services, the Internet can unfold its true potential in the area of distribution, where exchange processes between financial services providers need to be managed on a constant basis. In fact, the Internet was designed to deliver such information efficiently and to foster connectivity.[149]

The Internet has opened up a new road towards managing the interaction processes between the financial services provider and the customer.[150] More particularly, the idea to combine dif-

---

144 Müller-Hagedorn, L. and Kaapke, A. 1999, pp. 25-6.
145 Porter, M. 2001, pp. 65-70.
146 Ehrler, B. 1999, pp. 115-124.
147 Berghe, Van den L.A.A., Verweire, K. and Roelandt, P. 2001, p. 117.
148 Ehrler, B. 1999, pp. 115-124.
149 Heinsen, A. 2001, p. 54; Peterson, R., Balasubramanian, S. and Bronnenberg, B. 1997, p. 334.
150 Schramm-Klein, H. 2003, p. 32.

ferent distribution channels via a multi-channel distribution system requires first and foremost the possibility of exchanging data across these channels. The Internet, which has been designed to foster this (inter-)connectivity, is, therefore, an important technological prerequisite for the implementation of a true multi-channel distribution strategy. In addition to enabling and strengthening the interaction processes, the Internet can be used to increase the efficiency and productivity of sales channels by transferring any non-value adding activities to less labour intensive distribution channels.

It is important to understand that the true potential of the Internet in the financial services area is not captured by its capacity to sell financial products to customers online, but more comprehensively by its capacity to initiate, facilitate and support long-term interaction processes between the customer and the financial services provider. In other words, the actual potential of the Internet for financial services is not only reflected by the 'online' premium volume, but also by the volume of products which are online-induced (i.e., the customer gets information via the Internet) and are concluded 'off-line' (i.e., in the traditional distribution channels).[151] This potential was assessed for insurance services in Germany by McKinsey in 2001. While the purely online purchase volume amounts to 0.6 million, the online-induced sales volume is significantly higher at about 3 million.[152] These figures are also confirmed by the US market, where Forrester Research has found out that the online- induced sales volume significantly exceeds purely online sales volume.

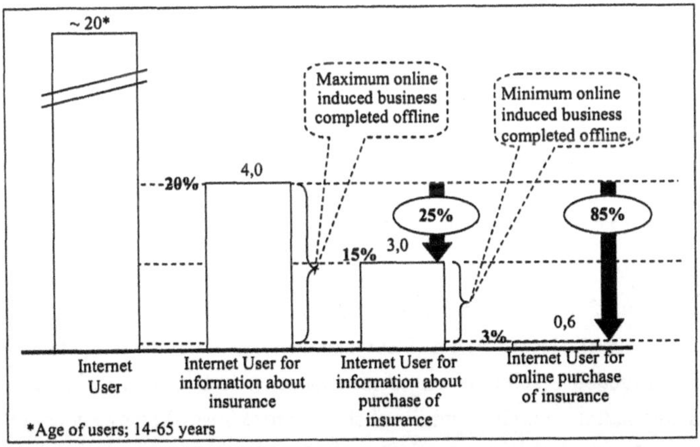

Figure 11: Use of the Internet in Germany for Insurance-Related Issues (in millions, Forecast 2001)[153]

---

[151] Rasch, S. Lintner, A. and Mogelvang, S. 2003, p. 115.
[152] Numbers estimated by McKinsey & Company in 2001.
[153] JPMorgan, McKinsey Analysis, 2001.

This fundamental conclusion that the highest sales potential of the Internet lies in 'online-induced' business is also confirmed by other studies from the retail sector. The example of Charles Schwab illustrates how the online distribution channel can be leveraged effectively.

> **Charles Schwab**, the US financial services retailer, acquires 70% of new customers and 50% of assets via the traditional branch network, while 80% of all stock exchange transactions are carried out online. In addition, it has been revealed that 'offline' acquired customers offer higher potentials: accounts opened in a branch have, on average, three to four times higher assets than online accounts. Therefore, Charles Schwab continues to open up branch outlets. In fact, Charles Schwab intends to increase its branch network by 15% to 25% a year over the next few years.[154]

The reasons why the Internet cannot unfold its 'true' online sales potential can best be explained by a consumer research study undertaken by Forrit in 1999. The lack of face-to-face contact as well as the only limited level of advice are quoted as reasons for not purchasing insurance online. One of the reasons for not buying insurance online is worry about data security.

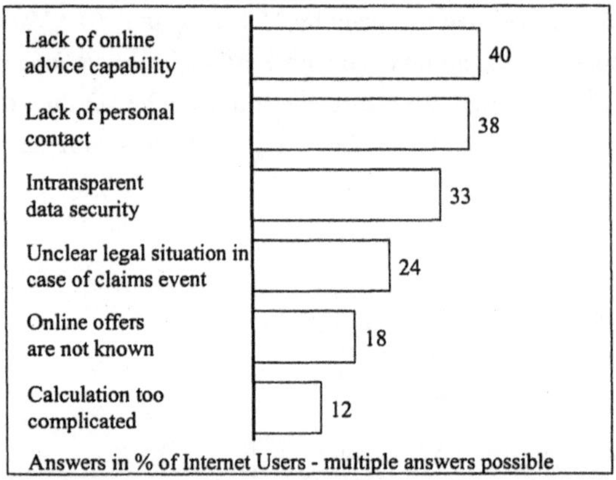

Figure 12: Reasons against the online Purchase of Insurance Products[155]

The Internet not only facilitates exchange processes, but it also exerts fundamental cost pressure on the entire value chain of financial services companies, as is clearly illustrated by the example of the insurance industry. In the case of insurance services, cost savings potentials stem primarily from the reduction or elimination of commissions paid to intermediaries as well as from a rigorous automation of underwriting and claims processes, whereby paperwork and staff numbers can be reduced. According to a 1998 study by Booz, Allen & Hamilton, the

[154] Bekier, M. and Flur, D. 2000, pp. 76-80; Lindstrom, M. 2002, pp. 22-3.
[155] Forrit Study 1999, taken from Heinsen, A. 2001, p. 40.

Internet has the potential to be the most cost effective delivery channel for insurance companies. The study estimates that it costs between $15 and $54 for insurers to sell insurance products directly via the Internet while it costs between $10 and $22 when an intermediary, e.g. InsWeb, sells the same product via the Internet. The study predicts that costs will decline even further as Internet usage becomes more prevalent.[156] If one takes these fundamental differences in the economics of the different distribution channels into account, it is clear that in a multi-channel strategy these differences in cost structure need to be included in the cross-channel pricing decisions.

To conclude, the Internet is a fundamental change driver for the financial services industry as it will pressure companies to re-engineer and streamline their entire business processes by using Internet technology. On the distribution side, the Internet will increase transparency as well as convenience for the customer and will lower transaction prices since the Internet clearly discloses fundamental differences in distribution costs and efficiency. In economic terms, the Internet will certainly reduce operating and distribution costs. By facilitating sales initiatives, it will also generate additional direct or - what is even more important - indirect (so-called online induced) revenue or fee income. Furthermore, easier and interactive management of the exchange processes probably represents the most important advantage of the Internet, which, by fostering connectivity among the distribution channels, also paves the way for the implementation of a multi-channel distribution strategy.

2.5 Conclusion

This chapter has illustrated the relevance of the subject of research from the point of view of the financial services industry. The following conclusions can be drawn:

- The **distribution landscape for financial services** becomes increasingly competitive as new players enter the markets and/or existing intermediaries are replaced. Established players, e.g. the tied agent channels, are under extreme pressure, while bancassurance and IFAs channels appear to gain market share due to their emphasis on providing independent financial advice.
- **Consumption Behaviour:** Consumers are better informed and decide just how, when and where they purchase personalised product solutions. Since their behaviour is characterised by dynamic and unpredictable actions, customers can no longer be assigned to any particular distribution channel.

---

[156] Booz, Allen & Hamilton Inc., 1998.

- **Internet**: The Internet has three impacts on the distribution of financial services. Firstly, it facilitates the exchange processes and, thanks to its connectivity, enables the design of truly connected multi-channel distribution systems. Secondly, it creates new distribution formats which are more efficient and can offer competitive prices thereby increasing the pressure to optimise the distribution system. Thirdly, the Internet empowers the consumers by providing an unforeseen transparency in a traditionally opaque financial market.
- **Distribution dilemma**: Financial services providers need to respond to these changes by intensifying customer relationships and reducing distribution costs at the same time. This calls for the combination of different distribution channels so that expensive distribution channels can focus on value-adding services, whereby low-margin business and administrative transactions need to be shifted towards low-cost distribution channels.
- **Multi-Channel distribution capabilities** not only reduce the environmental uncertainties for the company as to the future evolution of the distribution landscape, but they also allow the financial services provider to develop a new business model in order to escape - at least to some extent - the efficiency trap.
- **Internal stability of the distribution system:** The more distribution channels are added or even integrated into the existing distribution channels, the more important it is to manage internal power relationships and potential conflicts in order to ensure the socio-political stability of the entire distribution system.

Some authors believe that distribution channels have become a major strategic battle ground: "Failure to establish a profitable distribution channel must lead, in the long term to a company's decline, no matter how good its investment performance, product range or administration".[157] This may also be the reason why top decision makers consider distribution as the key strategic priority, as confirmed by various surveys among CEOs and senior managers of financial services companies.[158] McKinsey concludes that, given the competitive landscape within the personal financial services industry, focusing on distribution channels and developing a deep understanding of consumer behaviour are the ways to accomplish this difficult task.[159]

The following chapter will now analyse how such a distribution system can be configured and co-ordinated given the specific internal and external dimensions which need to be taken into account when setting up a multi-channel strategy.

---

157 Easingwood, C. and Storey, C. 1996, p. 225.
158 Herzog, M. and Panzer, J. 2003, p. 49; Maynard, P. 2001, pp. 63-4.
159 Flur, D., Mendonca, L. and Nakache, P. 1997, p. 117.

II. Framework for the Design of Multi-Channel Distribution Systems

The second part develops the theoretical basis for the analysis of multi-channel distribution systems both from the perspective of the company (internal perspective) as well as from the market (external perspective). Chapter 3 conceives a framework for the analysis of distribution systems on the basis of a thorough analysis of economic and behavioural distribution theories. Chapter 4 then complements this analysis by the specific properties of services, the service delivery process as well as the specificity of financial services. Combining the two chapters allows one to develop a sound understanding of the company specific structures and processes of distribution systems. The following chapter then explores the extent to which the distribution strategy is also determined by the overall financial, strategic and marketing objectives of the corporation. These objectives - together with the internal dimensions of multi-channel distribution systems - represent the overall theoretical framework for the analysis of a multi-channel distribution system. This framework will then be applied to the study of two structurally opposing types of multi-channel distribution systems.

3. Major Analytical Dimensions of Distribution Systems

Although it is more or less agreed that distribution falls within the general arena of marketing, there is no generally accepted definition of the exact nature, objectives and tasks of the distribution function.[160] Cespedes qualifies distribution as the 'neglected side of marketing' which has only received increased attention from the late 1980s onwards.[161] In addition, most of today's literature on distribution deals with the distribution of physical goods, rather than with the delivery of services.[162]

The design and management of effective and efficient distribution channels offer significant, frequently untapped opportunities for firms to create unique, long-term strategic advantages.[163] Weitz and Jap conclude that "channel activities are a major source of value-added benefits to end users – greater than the value added by other marketing activities. Due to this substantial added value potential, firms can develop a competitive advantage by reducing the costs of performing these activities or using distribution activities to differentiate their offering."[164]

---

160 Rimpler, G. 1995, p. 31.
161 Cespedes, F. 1998, p. 98; Louis, W. and Weitz, B. 1997, p. 824.
162 Järvinen, R. 1998, p. 15; Popp, S. 1990, p. 47.
163 Louis, W. and Weitz, B. 1997, p. 823.
164 Weitz, B. and Jap, S. 1995, p. 308.

The objective of this chapter is to develop a general framework for the analysis of distribution systems. It is therefore necessary first of all to define the nature and function of distribution. Subsequently, in order to develop a more thorough understanding of the properties of distribution systems, both transaction cost analysis as well as social exchange theory will be studied. These theories are finally summed up in the Political Economy Paradigm, which constitutes the fundamental theoretical foundation for the analytical framework, used in this dissertation for the analysis of distribution systems.

3.1 Nature, Objectives and Tasks of Distribution

3.1.1 Nature and Objectives of Distribution

From a macro-economic perspective, distribution includes all measures necessary to overcome the restrictions in terms of time and place associated with the production and consumption of goods and services. On the micro-economic (i.e., company) level, distribution refers to specific marketing activities and is often defined with reference to the overall concept of the marketing mix.[165] In this perspective, distribution is defined as the "definition and co-ordination of all corporate activities aimed at transferring goods and services from their point of production to the place of consumption while overcoming restrictions in terms of time and place".[166] Similarly, Meffert sums up under the term 'distribution' (as part of the marketing mix) all decisions and activities which occur on the way from production to the end customer.[167]

This understanding of distribution is predicated on the classical microeconomic paradigm with its assumptions of perfect and complete markets and efficient market-based resource allocation mechanisms. Therefore, the research focus is placed on questions of cost efficiency, organisational arrangements, distribution logistics, physical attributes and channel design.[168] Distribution has been considered as part of the value chain with a strong emphasis on the question of how to (physically) transfer goods from the point of production to the point of consumption. Value chain analysis, which was popularised by Porter[169], involves an examination of the economic impact of each step in the extraction, production and distribution processes.

---

165 Schögel, M. 1997, p. 15; Specht, G. 1992, p. 25.

166 Nieschlag, R., Dichtl, E. and Hörschgen, H. 1997D, p. 263.

167 Meffert, H. 1996, p. 421.

168 Louis, W. and Weitz, B. 1997, p. 824; Robicheaux, R. and Coleman, J. 1994, p. 38; Stern, L. and Reve, T. 1980, p. 53.

169 Porter, M. 1985.

However, this traditional microeconomic framework, where distribution is restricted to the tasks of an efficient transfer of goods and services, has been considered to be too limiting. The **system theory** is one possibility to open up the perspective on distribution. Järvinen considers the channel system as a combination of three sub-systems: the economic (revenues, costs, equilibrium), social (formal and informal communication and behaviour) and political (bargain, control, power and conflict) system.[170] This perspective significantly expands the view on distribution, since both economic and behavioural aspects are integrated into the analytical framework.

Stern, El-Ansary and Coughlan also consider distribution channels as a system with particular emphasis on exchange processes. A distribution channel is considered to be an inter-organisational system comprised of a set of interdependent institutions and agencies involved in the task of moving anything of value from its point of conception, extraction, or production to the points of consumption.[171] This processual perspective on distribution channels is particularly suitable for services, since services, per se, can be interpreted as a 'service delivery process'.[172]

Apart from understanding distribution channels as a system, the emphasis on the **exchange process** represents a marked paradigmatic shift. Stern et al. point out that the fundamental objective of distribution is to manage the exchange process between the service provider and the customer.[173] This two-party relationship is referred to as channel dyad - a channel dyad is explained as any form of direct, goal-oriented social interactions occurring between actors in a channel.[174] For Arndt, the essence of marketing and distribution is to structure and organise the exchange process between (and within) marketing institutions.[175] Appropriate structures have to be designed to facilitate and effectively manage this exchange process. Distribution plays a pivotal role because a distribution "channel is the essence of the way customers and a business interact ... It is a business' route to its customers and a business' ongoing relationship with its customers".[176]

Stern further expands on this understanding of distribution by introducing the term **'marketing flow'**. Marketing flows which are understood as a set of functions performed in sequence by channel members can be separated into forward flows, i.e., flows from the producer to the end customer (e.g. physical possession, ownership, promotion), directional flows (e.g. nego-

---

170 Järvinen, R. 1998, pp. 57-8.
171 Stern, L. W., El-Ansary, A. and Coughlan, A. 1996, p. 8.
172 Järvinen, R. 1998, p. 59.
173 Stern, L. W., El-Ansary, A. and Coughlan, A. 1996, pp. 11-2.
174 Achrol, R., Reve, T. and Stern, L. 1983, p. 58.
175 Arndt, J. 1993, p. 44.
176 Wheeler, S. and Hirsh, E. 1999, p. xxii.

tiation, financing) and backward flows (e.g. risking, ordering and payment). In a similar framework, three fundamental roles have been identified for distribution channels: information flow, logistics to deliver products and services to the end consumer and value-added services that augment the product or service.[177] All of these marketing flows in the distribution channel are indispensable - at least one institution or agency within the system must assume responsibility for each of them if the channel is to operate properly. However, based on an efficiency rationale, certain channel members specialise in the fulfilment of specific marketing flows.

In the following, distribution is understood to deal with exchange processes, while distribution channels represent a system of interdependent agents.

3.1.2 Distribution Tasks

Channel management research[178] has identified two fundamental tasks for distribution: **configuration** as well as **co-ordination** (and control) of distribution channel(s). Configuration refers to the definition of the structure of the distribution system, whereby both the internal fit (i.e., within the distribution system) as well as the external fit (i.e., consistency with exchange environment) have to be assured. The second dimension refers to the mechanisms used to control and co-ordinate the channel activities and the channel context. Some authors argue that it is the nature of these specific control mechanisms, rather than channel types per se, that represent the ability to manage ongoing customer relationships.[179]

Distribution structures are normally classified based on three dimensions: use of proprietary vs. non-proprietary distribution channels, centralised vs. decentralised planning of distribution activities as well as direct vs. indirect distribution.[180] "Understanding the factors that give rise to differences in channel structure among countries and the forces that may induce or hinder channel evolution is considered to be among the fundamental tasks of channel research".[181]

Defining the channel structure also requires one to determine the number of channel members involved (so-called 'channel length') and the allocation of functions among channel members.[182] Channel length is an important and influential characteristic of channel structure as it

---

[177] Wheeler, S. and Hirsh, E., p. 2.
[178] For example: Nevin, J. 1995 or Schögel, M. 1997.
[179] Nevin, J. 1995, p. 328.
[180] Gutenberg, E. 1979, p. 104.
[181] Sharma, A. and Dominguez, L. 1992, p. 2.
[182] Sharma, A. and Dominguez, L. 1992, p. 2.

determines distribution costs and profitability. Shorter channels occur when channel members feel that they can increase the efficiency of or control over channel functions by circumventing other channel members. Longer channels are often justified by wider market coverage as well as by the degree of specialisation by distribution intermediaries. From a strategic point of view, global companies tend to reduce channel length in order to have closer linkages with final customers, which enable a swifter introduction of successful brands to other countries.[183]

Analysing the reasons for differences in channel length, Sharma and Dominguez conclude that greater product complexity and more severe competition increase the need to exercise control over all facets of the marketing mix in order to avoid quality debasement externalities.[184] Independent channels increase the costs of channel governance and monitoring.[185] In order to determine the 'appropriate' (contractual) structure of distribution systems, research has strongly recurred to transaction cost theory. The transaction cost theory helps to define the optimal level of channel structure and, more specifically, of channel length.

The second fundamental task for distribution is to **co-ordinate and control**[186] the different distribution activities across the various distribution channels, especially when distribution channels may be specialised in delivering specific marketing flows. This requires information sharing among channel members, as information exchange across distribution channels is crucial for the co-ordination of these different marketing flows.[187] Weitz and Jap believe that the co-ordination of channel functions is the fundamental decision variable for managing distribution channels.[188] Channel research has proposed various frameworks for the control of distribution exchanges, ranging from authoritative, contractual and normative control mechanisms[189] to control regimes based on markets, bureaucracies and clans.[190] Others focus more on authority and power as the basis for the co-ordination of distribution channels. It should be noted that exchange processes in distribution channels are rarely governed exclusively by markets, hierarchy or trust, but these mechanisms serve as the key complementary building blocks for co-ordinating the complex exchanges in distribution channels.[191]

To conclude, the fundamental objective of distribution is the management of exchange processes in dyadic channel relationships which are marked by economic, political and behav-

---

183 Sharma, A. and Dominguez, L. 1992, p. 3.
184 Quality debasement externalities arise with branded products that are expensive and complex, requiring specialised service, installation and technical expertise.
185 Sharma, A. and Dominguez, L. 1992, p. 7.
186 Weitz, B. and Jap, S. 1995, pp. 305-320.
187 Diepen, T. 2000, p. 38; Stern, L. W., El Ansary, A. I. and Coughlan, A. 1996, pp. 11-2.
188 Weitz, B. and Jap, S. 1995, pp. 305-9.
189 Weitz, B. and Jap, S. 1995.
190 Nevin, J. 1995, p. 329.
191 Nevin, J. 1995, p. 329.

ioural dimensions. Distribution channels are understood as a system of interdependent agencies and institutions, involved in the task of moving 'value-added' within the dyadic relationship. System theory permits one to analyse the distribution system both in terms of its internal functioning as well as with respect to its external fit with the exchange environments. In order to ensure efficient management of the exchange processes, distribution has to set up appropriate structures and processes (configuration) and to ensure an efficient co-ordination and control of marketing flows across channels (co-ordination and control). Now that the nature, objective and tasks of distribution have been defined, it is important to analyse the 'exchange process' in more detail in order to come up with a comprehensive framework, identifying the major dimensions of the exchange process. Therefore, the following sections review fundamental theories, which are appropriate for the analysis of dyadic relationships. Both economic as well as 'non-economic' theories will be studied and ultimately merged within the Political Economy Paradigm.

3.2 Theoretical Basis for the Analysis of Exchange Processes

3.2.1 Economic Theories: Transaction Cost Analysis

Institutional economics, and transaction cost analysis in particular, is a theoretical field that can be used for the analysis of relationships, although it was not originally developed for this purpose.[192] Transaction Cost Analysis (TCA) deals with the optimal (i.e., cost efficient) form of facilitating exchange relationships. The aim is to reduce the cost of performing transactions or to economise on transaction costs by implementing the most suitable and, therefore, efficient governance structure for administering a certain type of transaction. A transaction is defined as any transfer of goods and services between two distinct units. Companies organise their exchange relationships to minimise transaction costs which arise when it is difficult to value the goods or services exchanged.

This theoretical approach was first established by Coase who classified transactions according to organisational forms based on whether they occurred within a company or across markets. Using this basic dichotomy, Williamson distinguished the market-based co-ordination mechanisms, where competitive prices accurately reflect the value of goods and services, from hierarchy-based organisations, where agreed-upon rules are used to equitably divide the rewards of joint activities. Complementing this classification of corporate governance structures, Ouchi introduced the notion of goal compatibility to further distinguish hierarchy-based

---

[192] Hougaard, S. and Bjerre, M. 2002, p. 47.

transactions into bureaucracies and clans. Clan governance, where values are voluntarily shared among the parties involved, is preferred, since transaction costs are normally lower due to the ex-ante goal compatibility.[193]

TCA indicates that organisational performance is enhanced (i.e., transaction costs are lower), when the governance structure of the transaction is congruent with the underlying dimensions of the exchange. Williamson identified three fundamental dimensions:

- Asset Specificity: Degree to which transactions are supported by transaction-specific investments,
- frequency of transactions and
- uncertainty surrounding the exchange.

When applying the transaction cost analysis to multi-channel distribution systems, one can say that the distribution systems have to be configured and co-ordinated in such a way as to minimise transaction costs based on the consumer behaviour and the properties of the specific product. Parallel distribution channels therefore exist because, depending on the specific product purchase, the consumer will choose those distribution channels which involve the lowest transaction costs and risks in a given situation.[194] As will be shown later on, insurance services are characterised by a high degree of uncertainty, so personalised, long-lasting relationships between the agent, as the insurer's representative, and the customer constitute one possibility to efficiently deal with this uncertainty surrounding the exchange.

In a later work,[195] Williamson expanded the fundamental dichotomy of market- vs. hierarchy based organisation forms to recognise intermediate forms of facilitating exchange relationships, e.g. relational contracting. In this perspective, the **theory of relational exchange**[196] offers a logical complement to Williamson's approach. Relational exchange defines the concept of contract more broadly. In Macneil's sense, a contract refers to any relationship between two or more parties who expect to sustain that relationship into the future. Thus defined, the perception of contracts as relations facilitates the ordering of contractual relationships along a continuum from discrete[197] to relational transactions rather than from markets to hierarchies.[198]

A discrete transaction is a one-off, non-recurrent exchange of services, i.e., there is no correlation between the individual transactions. This notion perfectly corresponds to the assump-

---

[193] Ouchi, W. 1980, pp. 129-141.
[194] Böhler, J. 1992, pp. 30-1; Schramm-Klein, H. 2003, pp. 28-9.
[195] Williamson, 1985.
[196] MacNeil, I. 1980; Dwyer, F., Schurr, P. and Oh. S. 1987, p. 124.
[197] A discrete transaction may be A one-time cash purchase of unbranded petrol out of town at an independent station. Dwyer, F., Schurr, P. and Oh. S. 1987, p. 12; MacNeil, I. 1980, p. 10 and p. 60.
[198] To the extent possible 'discrete' and market-based as well as 'relational' and 'rules-based' are synonyms.

tions of the neo-classical paradigm, where in perfect and complete markets the price includes all information relevant to the co-ordination of transactions. On the other end of the continuum, individual transactions can no longer be separated form each other and the price as the only co-ordination mechanism is replaced by the definition of relations ('relational exchange').[199]

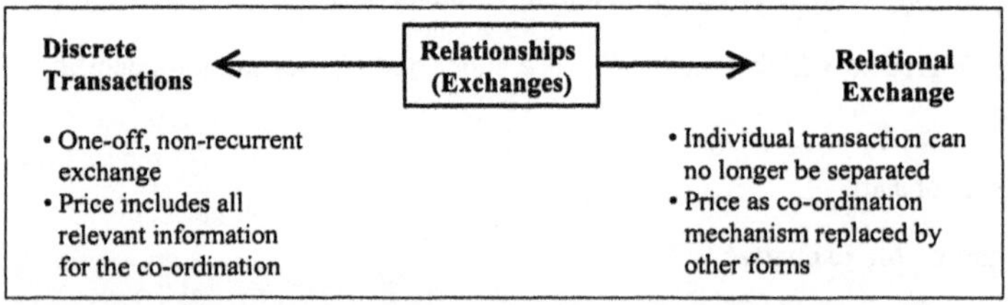

Figure 13: Dichotomy between Discrete Transactions and Relational Exchange[200]

Shifting from the notion of governance structures to the concept of 'relational exchanges' renders it possible to study antecedent conditions and processes for buyer-seller relationships.[201] In this context, both economic as well as non-economic (i.e., behavioural, social, political) variables can be analysed. Some authors have come up with indicators of non-discrete (i.e., relational) transactions, e.g. expectation of a long-time relationship, sharing of benefits and burden, mutual trust among transaction partners and planning for future transactions. From the point of view of transaction cost analysis, criteria, such as high asset specificity, high transaction frequency and high uncertainty within the channel, are also indicative of transactions, which are normally best governed by relational exchange concepts.

3.2.2 Behaviour-oriented Theories

The gradual move from transaction cost analysis to the theory of relational exchange as well as the shift from a 'channel structure' to a 'channel systems view' illustrate that channel research, focussing purely on economic variables, does not capture the entirety of the research problems in distribution. The fact that distribution channels are increasingly viewed as a complex economic, social and political system, gave rise at the end of the 1960s to the emergence of behaviour-oriented channel research streams, viewing distribution channels as social systems and focusing on the explanation of social phenomena such as power, dependency, con-

---

199 Dwyer, F., Schurr, P. and Oh. S. 1987, pp. 11-15; MacNeil, I. 1980, p. 60; Robichaeux, R. and Coleman, J. 1994, p. 40.

200 Own illustration taken from the theory of relational exchange.

201 Dwyer, F., Schurr, P. and Oh. S. 1987, p. 11.

flict and satisfaction.[202] The behavioural research approach constitutes a clear countervailing force to the micro-economic based transaction cost analysis, which is primarily driven by efficiency criteria. This research stream is founded on the Social Exchange Theory as well as the Resource Dependency Theory.

The **Social Exchange Theory**[203] deals with the analysis of mutual exchange activities between at least two actors. The theory is based on three assumptions: first, social behaviour can be explained by rewards; secondly, individuals try to maximise the difference between rewards and costs, whereby costs include both financial and non-financial variables, and, thirdly, social exchange occurs, as some individuals control certain resources and can, therefore, give rewards to other individuals for exchange transactions.

Power plays an integral part in the Social Exchange Theory. Although power is one of the central notions in social science, there is no clear and consistent theoretical foundation for defining and especially for operationalising the abstract term 'power'.[204] Despite the diversity in the definitions of the concept 'power', power is generally defined as a relational term, i.e., with reference to the ability to control or influence another institution or agent. A classical definition of power is provided by Emerson: "The power of A over actor B is the amount of resistance on the part of B which can be potentially overcome by A".[205] Emerson explains the power of A by the degree to which B is dependent on A and elaborates on some mechanisms, how B can reduce his dependency on A by for example reducing his motivational investment vis-à-vis A or by developing alternative relationships to other actors. The base (or source) of this power is determined by resources,[206] which A can use (e.g. opportunities, acts, objects.) to influence the behaviour of B.[207]

The idea of power-dependency relations was later adopted by marketing and channel research. El-Ansary and Stern define the power of a channel member as "his ability to control the decision variables in the marketing strategy of another member in a given channel at a different level of distribution".[208] In current channel research, power is defined as a 'potential for influence' and no longer as a basis to exert power or coercion. This potential for influence is tied

202 Blommen, D. 1997, p. 6.
203 Thibaut, J. and Kelley, H. 1959.
204 Blommen, D. 1997, p. 6.
205 Emerson, R. 1962, p. 32.
206 In the relevant literature, the base of power may be classified in the following categories: rewards, punishments, specific knowledge, identification as well as legitimacy. Blommen, D. 1997, pp. 10-11.
207 Blommen, D. 1997, p. 10.
208 Stern, L.W., El Ansary, A.I. and Coughlan, A., 1996, p. 287.

to the other firm's dependence or need to maintain the channel relationship to achieve the desired goals. When each firm possesses a high level of dependence in a dyadic channel relationship, interdependence is high in magnitude and symmetric. High joint power is likely to promote trust, commitment and relational behaviour because of the common interests, attention, and support found in such channel relationships.[209]

The perceived power-dependence patterns not only determine the dominance of specific distribution channels (e.g. unilateral vs. multi-lateral power system), but also characterise the dominant sentiments and behaviour characterising the interactions between channel members. Generally speaking, exchange processes can be influenced by either conflicts or co-operation existing between channel members.

Social Exchange Theory has also been used to explain the concept of customer loyalty. It is assumed that customers evaluate a business relationship against two benchmarks: the comparison level and the comparison level given alternatives. Customer loyalty is explained by the fact that the customer compares the perceived outcome of a service (outcome, OC) with his comparison level (CL). If OC exceeds CL, the customer is satisfied. But the customer only stays with the company, if the perceived outcome is higher than the comparison level given alternatives. In the model, the two notions 'attractiveness of a business relationship' and 'dependence on a business relationship' are explained. If OC is higher than CL, the business relationship is attractive, but if CL is below OC, but CL_{alt} (given alternatives) is also below CL, then the relationship is unattractive, but the customer is dependent.

The Social Exchange Theory has been complemented by the **Resource Dependency Theory** which focuses on the explanation of social constructs, such as dependency, power and control. This theoretical approach is used to analyse power and dependency relations in distribution channels. In addition, it is assumed that organisations are open systems, and the organisation therefore has to interact with its environment to acquire the necessary resources and, thus, to ensure its existence. The exchange of resources between the organisation and the external partners and the resulting dependency relations explain the level of uncertainty as well as the distribution of power between the various internal and external actors. Hence, dependencies, particularly on external providers of necessary resources, give rise to uncertainty. Therefore, it is the fundamental tasks of management to pursue appropriate strategies to influence these power-dependency relations to the advantage of the company.[210]

---

[209] Frazier, G. 1999, p. 227.
[210] Blommen, D. 1997, p. 6.

3.3 Political Economy Paradigm

Stern and Reve were among the first, to start to acknowledge that neither the economic nor the behavioural perspective on distribution captures the entirety of the research problem and that they should therefore be viewed as complementary research streams. Consequently, they are the first and most prominent proponents of viewing distribution channels as a set of interdependent and interrelated socio-economic factors.[211] The Political Economy, dealing with the analysis of the interactions between the economic and socio-political world, is an appropriate research paradigm to integrate these different dimensions.[212] Similarly, Arndt concludes that "the political economy paradigm integrates important concepts from traditions such as social exchange, the behavioral theory of the firm and transaction costs economics by synthesising them into one world view".[213]

Stern and Reve applied the **Political Economy** to the analysis of distribution systems and developed a framework for distribution channel analysis in two important journal articles.[214] The Political Economy Paradigm views a social system "as comprising interacting sets of major economic and sociopolitical forces which affect collective behaviour and performance".[215] The outcome of the exchange depends on structural arrangements, bargaining, negotiations, power, conflict and the shared affect or cognitive images existing between the parties.[216]

3.3.1 The Internal Economy and Polity of the Distribution System

For the analysis of channel dyads, Stern and Reve identified two important dimensions: Economy vs. Polity as well as structure vs. processes of distribution systems.[217] The 'economy' refers to the classical distribution functions as well as to the allocation of scarce economic resources to particular channels. This dimension can be divided further into the two components of structure and processes. The **economic structure** comprises all decisions regarding the vertical economic arrangements or transactional form in the channel, which, in the terminology of the transaction cost analysis, would be called 'governance structure'. These arrangements range from independently owned units, co-ordinated by market prices, to completely integrated units governed by contractual (i.e., rule-based) arrangements. Each economic

[211] Stern, L. and Reve, R. 1980; Achrol, R., Reve, T. and Stern, L. 1983.
[212] Arndt, J. 1984, pp. 47-8; Blommen, D. 1997, p. 31.
[213] Arndt, J. 1984, p. 51.
[214] Stern, L. and Reve, T. 1980; Achrol, R., Reve, T. and Stern, L. 1983.
[215] Stern, L. W. and Reve, T. 1980, p. 53.
[216] Achrol, R. S., Torger, R. and Stern, L. W. 1983, p. 58.
[217] They also distinguished between the internal and external dimension of the distribution system. The external dimension will be dealt with in the following sub-section.

structure of a channel also requires specific internal **economic processes** (decision mechanisms), referring to the way marketing functions are divided among channel members and resources are allocated and controlled across distribution channels.[218] The resource allocation mechanism can range from central planning (rule-based) to price-mediated (market-based) mechanisms. In this context, the monitoring and rewarding of financial performance represents an important control dimension.[219]

The second important dimension relates to the **polity of distribution channels**, which refers to the allocation and use of authority and power (i.e., potential for influence) as well as to the decision-making mechanisms within the distribution system. The **socio-political structure** is defined by the power-dependence relations between the organisation, running along a continuum with atomised, minimal power at the one end and maximal, centralised power at the other end. Due to the numerous interdependencies between channel members, power is normally evenly distributed, as separate channel members exercise control over different marketing flows. The opposite to such a mixed power system is a unilateral power system, where one single organisation is the undisputed channel administrator (unilateral power system). The concept of power is most relevant to the insurance industry. It is widely understood that the primary challenge for insurers is to ensure the organisational acceptance of the tied agent channel to build up alternative distribution channels. Situations marked by mutual dependency and potential for reciprocal influence between the insurer and its proprietary distribution channels may be the best basis to promote trust, commitment and relational behaviour. For example, the introduction of the Internet channel alongside the tied agent or branch distribution channel represents a tightrope walk, since these new direct channels are often viewed as a threat, rather than as a cross-selling opportunity.[220]

These power-dependence relationships may also determine the interactions (i.e., **socio-political processes**) between channel members. Although these interactions are multi-dimensional constructs, they can be categorised in a relationship of co-operation or conflict – based on the degree of compatibility of goals, aims and values. Channel management has to fulfil its control role in the sense of minimising the divergence of preferences among channel members. In this context, Robicheaux and Colemann distinguish between clan-like and bureaucracy-like channel relations. Clan-like channel relations are characterised by perfect compatibility of goals among channel members and shared values. The following figure shows that the concept of discrete vs. relational exchange needs to be complemented by a secondary dimension of clan-like vs. bureaucracy-like decision-making processes.

---

[218] Schögel, M. 1997, pp. 160-4.
[219] Nevin, J. 1995, p. 328.
[220] Herzog, M. and Panzer, J. 2003, p. 49.

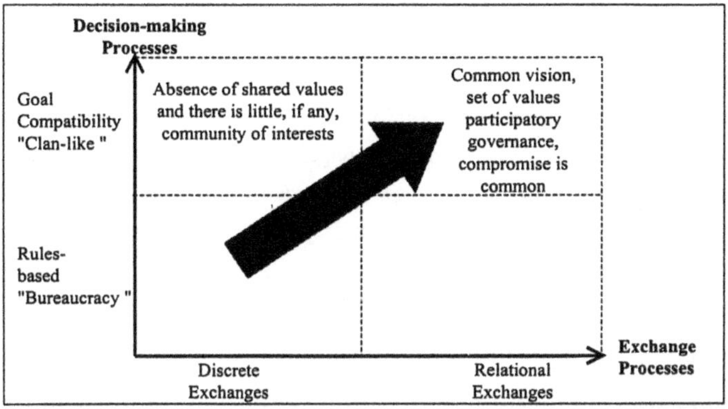

Figure 14: Discrete vs. Relational Exchanges and Clan- vs. Bureaucracy-like Decision-Making Processes[221]

In a clan-like scenario, decision-making is decentralised and informal communications are common. Members are most likely to subordinate their short-term interests to those of the system, and through participatory governance, compromise is common. In bureaucratic relationships, there is an absence of shared values and there is little, if any, community of interests.[222] Indeed, companies endeavour to create a vision and a set of common values and principles in order to move into the direction towards stronger compatibility of goals and shared interests, since bureaucratic regimes are too static, rigid and less able to respond to a dynamic market environment. Nevertheless, it should be born in mind that a complete lack of conflict may not necessarily produce maximal joint efforts, but rather passivity and complacency.

Stern and Reve proceed to point out that there are various interdependencies between the economy and polity of a distribution system. For example, in a system, where market transactions dominate, a relative power advantage is often used to centralise at least certain channel activities (e.g. promotion activities) and, thus, account for the inherent disadvantages (e.g. opportunistic behaviour) of market co-ordination mechanisms. Hence, it can be concluded that distribution needs to reconcile the economic objectives with the polity of the distribution system.

In addition to the analysis of the internal economy and polity of the internal channel environment, distribution also has to evaluate to what extent the management of channel dyads is impacted by the external relevant task environments, most notably by the end customer.

[221] Own illustration based on Robichaeux, R. and Coleman, J. 1994, pp. 46-7.
[222] Robichaeux, R. and Coleman, J. 1994, pp. 46-7.

3.3.2 The Task Environments of the Distribution System

The PEP framework emphasises that the distribution system, as the unit of analysis, is connected through economic and socio-political relationships variables with the exchange environment. From the point of view of a customer-centric management approach it is most evident that the requirements of the exchange environments, the distribution system interacts with and/or is exposed to, certainly has a clear impact on the configuration and on the co-ordination of the distribution system itself.

Stern et. al. identify three important task environments, which have an impact on the focal dyadic distribution relationship.

1. The **Exchange Environment** comprises the immediate suppliers and customers of the dyad. Hence, this includes the product providers on the one side, who, in an open product architecture, could be proprietary and non-proprietary product providers, and the end customers on the other side.
2. The **Non-exchange Environment** comprises all groups with no immediate direct contact to the exchange dyad, e.g. competitors (actual and potential competitors), consumers (in general), regulators or interest aggregators.
3. The **Macro Environment,** which includes general social, economic, political, and technological forces, also influence the configuration of a distribution system.[223] Changes in the macroeconomic environment will be analysed only to the extent that they have an impact on the qualitative dimension of the non-exchange or exchange environment.

Above all, the **targeted end customer** has the most direct impact on the configuration of the distribution system. In fact, customer preferences determine the ultimate boundaries of any distribution system. It is important to map the customer's key buying criteria with the specific distribution channel, as distribution channels generally differ in their ability to satisfy various buying criteria. Friedman and Furey conclude that customer-channel alignment is the foundation of a successful channel strategy. In order to design new innovative distribution systems, it may be necessary not only to analyse actual buying behaviour, but also buying criteria.[224] **Product suppliers** can also determine the structure of a distribution system. It has to be made sure that the product offering is consistent with the channel characteristics, e.g. in terms of product complexity and service levels.[225]

---

[223] Achrol, R., Reve, T. and Stern, L. 1983, pp. 57-8; Stern, L., El-Ansary, A. and Coughlan, A. 1996, pp. 14-5.

[224] Friedman, L. and Furey, T. 1999, pp. 42-3.

[225] With respect to the insurance industry, this refers to a constellation where independent distribution companies, e.g. AWD or MLP, source in their products from third-party insurers. Here, the distribution requirements have to be aligned with the requirements of the product providers.

Whereas the impact of the exchange environment on the configuration of the distribution system is clear and can be reduced to the two most prominent groups, product provider and end customers, the number of relevant non-exchange environmental items is infinite and their impact on the channel dyad may only be valid in a specific situation and/or time period. Therefore, Achrol, Reve and Stern use the concept of '**environmental uncertainty**'. The idea that uncertainty of the exchange environment determine – among other factors (e.g. asset specificity and frequency of transaction) - the governance structure of a transaction and thus also of a distribution system is taken from the theory of transaction cost analysis.[226]

Achrol, Reve and Stern propose the following environmental framework to explain the emergence of environmental uncertainty:[227]

- **Environmental Capacity (rich/lean)**: the relative abundance or scarcity of input and output resources available to an organisation within its domain of operation.
- **Environmental Homogeneity and Heterogeneity (Simplicity or Complexity)**: this relates to the complexity of decision making. The more numerous and heterogeneous the informational inputs, the more complex the environment.
- **Environmental Stability and Instability:** the rate of variability in elements of the environment (pace of change).
- **Environmental Concentration and Dispersion** of relevant input and output resources. This variable is also related to geographic concentration.
- **Environmental Turbulence** refers to the degree of interconnectedness between the various players in the environment.

Based on this environmental framework, it can now be argued that the more the task environments move away from being rich, homogenous, stable, dispersed, and placid (as opposed to turbulent), the more environmental uncertainty will affect the distribution system. More specifically, the financial services industry is especially characterised by increasing environmental complexity, instability and turbulence in terms of the end consumer markets. Consumers more often switch distribution channels, banks and insurers move closer together (if not merge) and thus generate interconnectedness. Consequently, the task environments for financial services are changing drastically. Hence, financial services companies have to deal with a high degree of uncertainty when they actually design and implement viable distribution systems.

---

226 Williamson, O. 1985.

227 Achrol, R., Reve, T. and Stern, L. 1983, p. 61. See also Arndt, J. 1983, pp. 48-9; Hougaard, S. and Bjerre, M. 2002, pp. 63-66.

Environmental uncertainty influences the functioning and structuring of marketing channel dyads. Companies may react to this environmental uncertainty by trying to change the power balance of the distribution system or decision-making arrangements in such a way that they are more in command of the distribution system. In terms of its internal economic structure, a dyad may move – in the medium term - from market mediation to some level of vertical integration.[228]

Generally speaking, since environments of corporations are, per se, characterised by some kind of uncertainty, it is the important task of distribution management to find the appropriate structures and processes (i.e., the external fit) to effectively cope with and survive in uncertain environments. Changes in the socio-political structures and processes are one way of compensating for increasing environmental uncertainty. Higher environmental uncertainty could be met by better planning, more co-ordinated actions, and by a stronger focus on each other's competitive strengths. Furthermore, power shifts towards the unit, which is better able to cope with and therefore absorb the sources of uncertainty. Achrol, Reve and Stern[229] acknowledge that increasing uncertainty leads to more centralised planning, co-ordination, and decision processes.[230]

If uncertainty continues for longer periods of time and high levels of conflict thwart any effective formation of co-ordinating mechanisms, then producers will begin to employ or build up separate distribution channels to diversify environmental uncertainty.[231] This is certainly one important justification for the emergence of multi-channel distribution systems in the financial services sector, where companies invest in multiple distribution channels in order to ensure their survival in a market environment, where strong uncertainty as to the future distribution landscape prevails.

---

[228] The merger of the Allianz and Dresdner Bank might be interpreted as a response by Allianz to an uncertain distribution environment, where it is uncertain which distribution channels will survive in the future and whether majority shareholding of Allianz in Dresdner will be enough to safeguard this distribution channel from competitors.

[229] Achrol, R., Reve, T. and Stern, L. 1983, p. 64.

[230] With the advent of the Internet, insurers invested huge amounts in this new technology. This was one way to cope with possible changes induced by the technological innovation. As a consequence, tied agents become more dependent on the insurer as to the question of whether tied agents will benefit from these investments or not.

[231] Achrol, R., Reve, T. and Stern, L. 1983, p. 64.

3.4 Conclusion

In this chapter, the nature of distribution as well as the fundamental dimensions of distribution systems have been discussed and can be summed up with the following key insights:

- **Nature of distribution**: the fundamental objective of distribution is the management of exchange processes in dyadic channel relationships, which are marked by economic, political and behavioural dimensions. Distribution channels are understood as a system of interdependent agencies and institutions involved in the task of managing exchange processes.
- **Tasks of distribution**: distribution has two fundamental tasks: configuration and co-ordination of the distribution channels in order to ensure the internal as well as external fit of the entire distribution system. For this purpose, it is necessary to understand the fundamental properties of a distribution system. Both economic as well as behavioural theories have therefore been analysed.
- **Theoretical dimensions of distribution systems**: Transaction cost analysis classify 'exchange transactions' into market-based vs. hierarchy-based co-ordination systems. This structure was later refined by the theory of relational exchange, where dyadic channel relationships were distinguished into discrete and relational exchanges. However, this economic view on distribution systems needs to be complemented by behavioural theories. The Social Exchange Theory, as a behavioural distribution theory, underlines the importance of socio-economic variables, e.g. power-dependence relationships for the understanding of distribution systems. Therefore, both economic and behavioural theories have to to be combined to analyse distribution systems. The Political Economy Paradigm has achieved this combination.

The **Political Economy Paradigm** analyses both the internal and external economy and polity of the distribution systems as well as their respective interactions. While the economy refers to the economic integration and management of the channel system, the polity relates to the decision-making mechanisms, which could range from a fully decentralised, informal, participatory style to highly bureaucratic rules with no shared values and a dominance of power-based decision structures.[232] In other words, distribution deals with the allocation of scarce economic resources and assignment of power/authority to different channel members. In this perspective, both structural and processual variables are taken into account. In addition, the external exchange environments impact the channel dyads and thereby the overall distribution system. It has to be seen to what extent the distribution system is able to cope

232 Robichaeux, R. and Coleman, J. 1994, pp. 45-7.

with environmental changes ('shocks') and external environmental uncertainty. Increasing levels of environmental uncertainty tend to lead to more centralised decision-making and governance structures, with less allowance for decentralised planning.

The following figure sums up the major dimensions, which are used in the following to analyse the functioning of different multi-channel distribution systems.

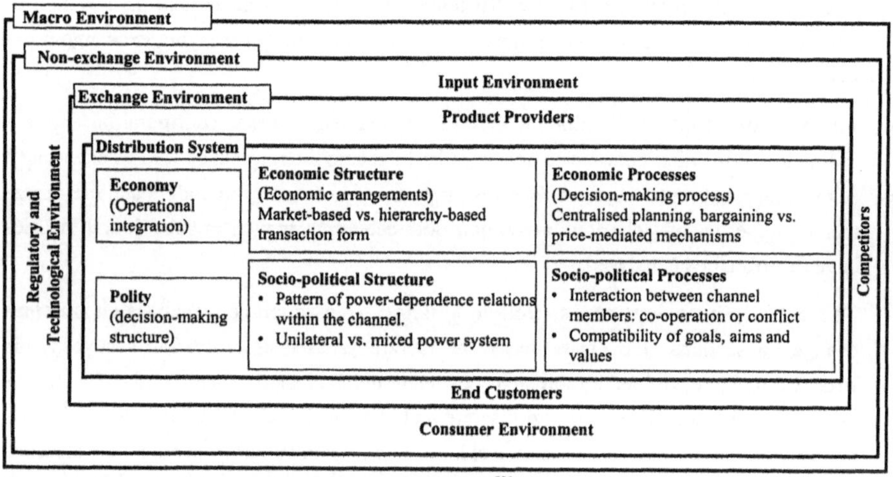

Figure 15: The Analytical Dimensions of Distribution Systems[233]

To conclude, in this dissertation distribution systems are analysed based on the Political Economy Paradigm – both the Polity and the Economy dimension of distribution systems are to be taken into account, while each of these two dimensions can be broken down further into structure and process related aspects.

[233] Own illustration based on Stern, L. and Reve, R. 1980; Achrol, R., Reve, T. and Stern, L. 1983.

4. Particularities in the Distribution of Retail Financial Services

While the analytical dimensions for the study of distribution systems have been defined in the previous chapter, it is now important to apply this framework more specifically to services. The objective of this chapter is to understand and analyse the specific characteristics of and challenges in the distribution of services and subsequently of financial services. In fact, the specific characteristics of services, such as intangibility, inseparability, heterogeneity and process orientation, have clear impacts on the purchase decision-making process and thus on the way financial services are distributed.[234] At the end of the chapter, the consequences of the specific properties of (financial) services for the management of the company are reviewed. The concepts of service management help to define an overall framework and two generic service strategies are derived from the analysis of the actual properties of services.

4.1 The Constituent Elements of Services

In the literature on services, a lot of efforts have been undertaken in vain to provide a terminological and theoretical basis for a coherent definition of services. Due to the extreme **heterogeneity of services** today, a large number of different uni- and pluri-dimensional classification structures co-exist.[235] Some authors therefore recommend to refrain from any classification of services. Irrespective of this ongoing discussion within the scientific community, the resource-, process- and result-based view will be used hereafter to specify the properties of services in this dissertation.

The **resource-based view** on services focuses on the ability and readiness of a provider to deliver a certain service. It will be analysed how certain internal resources need to be combined and kept available, so that the actual process of service delivery can take place.[236] This view on services particularly reveals the **intangible**[237] character of services. Given this intangibility, Meffert, for example, defines services with reference to the input factors necessary for the subsequent service delivery process.[238] Potential customers will predominantly assess these input factors (e.g. professional and credible positioning in the market, well designed and appealing product brochures) in order to anticipate the actual service quality. Thus, all tangible factors (e.g. buildings, service personnel, letters, interior design) play an important role in

---

[234] McKechnie, S. and Harrison, T. 1995, p. 36.
[235] Bezold, T. 1996, pp. 26-29; Corsten, H. 1997, pp. 21-30; Meffert, H. and Bruhn, M. 2000, pp. 22-40.
[236] Hentschel, B. 1992, p. 19; Meffert, H. and Bruhn, M. 2000, p. 28.
[237] Intangibility means that services cannot physically be grasped, stored, transported or inventoried. Zeithaml, V. and Bitner, M. 1996, p. 19.
[238] Hentschel, B. 1992, p. 20.

service provision and may be classified in three categories: ambient factors (e.g. background conditions), design factors (architecture) as well as social factors (e.g. behaviour of service provider).[239] Lehmann argues that, while services are more and more intangible, metaphors, allegories and symbols become increasingly important for signalling the actual service quality to the customer.[240]

The **process-based view** emphasises the actual service delivery process, when internal and external resources are combined to deliver a specific service.[241] In this perspective, the interactive nature of service delivery is emphasised, since production and consumption are **inseparable** or, in other words, take place at the same time (so-called **uno-actu principle**).[242] Grönroos points out that, for services, the value-generating process and the process of service production and delivery take place to a large extent simultaneously.[243] In fact, services are processes and consumption of a service is 'process consumption' rather than 'outcome consumption'[244], where the consumer perceives the service production process as part of service consumption and not only the outcome of that process as is the case in traditional consumer packaged goods marketing. The problem of place and time availability of services is particularly stressed by the fact that service delivery requires the integration of the external factor (customer, customer's data input etc.) into the process. The integration of the external factor is necessary due to production constraints (e.g. hairdressing), as a result of the nature of service (e.g. concerts, lectures) or due to information needs (e.g. insurance).[245]

This **integration of the customer into the service delivery process** implies that the consumer is both producer and consumer, so that the term 'prosumer' or 'servunction' (service and production) is sometimes used.[246] The quality and productivity of service is not only determined by internal processes, but also by the consumer's interaction. The consumer himself will, in fact, influence the actual quality of service delivery.[247] Therefore, the inter-active, inter-personal and emotional aspects of service delivery are of fundamental importance.[248] Standardising all essential processes and providing service tools can mitigate the problem of

---

239 Berry, L. and Parasuraman, A. 1991, pp. 95-98.
240 Lehmann, A. 1993, p. 24.
241 Meffert, H. and Bruhn, M. 2000, pp. 27-30.
242 Zeithaml, V. and Bitner, M. 1996, p. 19.
243 Grönroos, C. 2000, p. 3.
244 Grönroos, C. 1998a; Grönroos, C. 2000, p. 286.
245 Lehmann, A. 1998, p. 26.
246 Lehmann, A. 1998, pp. 26-7.
247 Meyer, A. and Mattmüller, R. 1987, pp. 192-193.
248 Ehrler, B. 1999, p. 66.

varying service quality. The service provider can also leverage the interactivity of service delivery by transferring some elements of service delivery to the end customer.[249]

In the **result-based view,** services are defined as the immaterial result ('outcome') of a certain activity. Lehmann and Meyer define services as the change or maintenance of a certain, desired state of the external factor (people or objects of those), which is not under the entire control of the service provider.[250] To solve the problem of intangibility at least to some extent, some tangible support objects (e.g. disk, certificates) will be provided and can be considered as the result and point of reference for a service delivery.[251]

These three fundamental views on services are summed up in the following figure, illustrating that the service delivery process can also be sub-divided into three distinct phases: pre-contact, contact and post-contact phase.

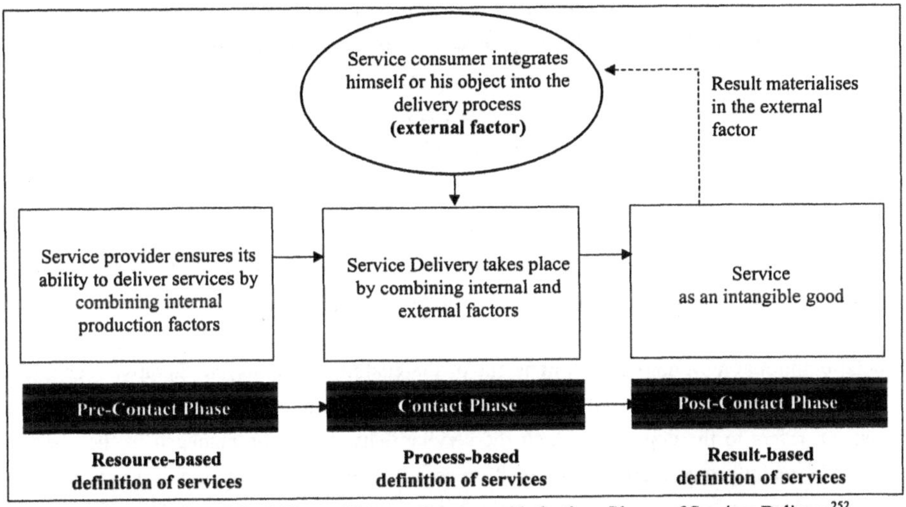

Figure 16: Reconciliation of the Different Views on Services with the three Phases of Services Delivery[252]

Hentschel has shown that these three phases can be harmonised with the resource-, process- and result-based view on services (so-called **implicit phase view**).[253] The process of service delivery can hence be described by a three-phase concept, while in each phase different constituent elements of services are dominant, as explained by the resource-, process- and result-

249 Lehmann, A. 1998, pp. 28-9.
250 Lehmann, A. 1989, p. 80; Meyer, A. 1991, p. 198.
251 Hentschel, B. 1992, p. 24.
252 Corsten, H. 1997, p. 26; Hentschel, B. 1992, p. 21.
253 Hentschel, B. 1992, p. 21.

based view. Certain internal resources have to be kept available (resource-based view), which will be combined with external resources to deliver a specific service (process-based view). This process of service delivery will be beneficial in some form to the end customer (result-based view).[254]

The view of the inevitable **inseparability of production and consumption** has been questioned by some authors. Palmer and Cole, for example, classify services as to the extent a direct contact between producer and consumer is necessary. In this direct - non-direct dichotomy, certain services exhibit some flexibility in production and/or consumption. Service providers can reduce the inseparability of services by designing services that have the advantages of centralised production and flexible consumption.[255] As an example, any IT advancements can change the service delivery processes, since new communication methods (e.g. Internet) may reduce the usually strong interaction between the service provider and customer to such an extent that the customer will primarily only appreciate the result without getting involved anymore in the actual service delivery process (e.g. online quoting and ordering of insurance services).[256] Alternatively, Internet technology itself manages the interaction process, so physical interference no longer becomes necessary. For example, the consumer can purchase insurance services via Internet at the time and place of his choice, whereas underwriting and processing can be managed at a central location.

Lehmann distinguishes services along two dimensions – the **intensity of interpersonal interactions** as well as the possibility of **mass-production and standardisation**. The intensity of personal interactions refers to the degree to which service delivery requires a strong personal involvement of the customer as well as to the fact that the service itself rather appeals to the social-emotional, psychological dimensions of the customer (e.g. psychotherapy, coaching) - as opposed to a more fact-based service delivery (e.g. software development). The second dimension refers to the degree to which the service delivery can be managed in the classical form of a manufacturing-oriented production process (i.e., input-throughput-output model) or requires more personalised interaction with the customer. Combining these two dimensions, Lehmann classifies services into three classes: purely production-oriented services, mixed problem-oriented services as well as personal, interaction-oriented services.[257]

The intangibility of services as well as the integration of the external factor also cause problems of **information asymmetry** between the service provider and the customer. In fact, customers can generally evaluate the service quality only at the moment of service delivery

[254] Meffert, H. and Bruhn, M. 2000, p. 30.
[255] Berman, B. 1996, p. 593.
[256] Järvinen, R. 1998, pp. 61-2.
[257] Lehmann, W. 1994, pp. 28-34.

and some services can never be examined by the end customer himself.[258] Therefore, information economics classifies services according to the predominance of search, experience and credence qualities. Search qualities refer to those elements which can only be examined during the pre-contact and evaluation phase, while experience qualities can only be verified during or after the use of certain services. Some of the quality characteristics of services, the so-called credence qualities, can never be checked by the consumer, who, in this case, has to entirely trust the service provider. These three qualities of services give rise to a certain information asymmetry and to uncertainty between the producer and consumer of services.[259] Therefore, the fundamental task of service marketing is to reduce the high degree of uncertainty as well as information asymmetries. Companies may use signalling and screening methods. While signalling refers to the transmittance of credible information to the market partner, screening methods include the active search for additional information in order to close any information deficit. Companies may, on the one hand, use their communication policy (e.g. commercials, sponsoring, branding) to signal their service quality to the market or, on the other hand, analyse data (e.g. market research data, complaints data) to acquire information on customer expectations and satisfaction ('screening'). In this context, the brand plays an important role, as it provides orientation and confidence to the customer ('signalling').[260]

The following figure provides a framework for the analysis of services and their delivery process. The three major dimensions of services as well as the three phases of the service delivery process are combined with the information properties of services as well as with the classification approach by Lehmann, where services are classified by their degree of interaction and the possibility of mass production. This framework provides a more concrete basis for designing the external fit between the service provider and the customer.

---

258 Meffert, H. and Bruhn, M. 2000, pp. 62-65.
259 Meffert, H. and Bruhn, M. 2000, pp. 65-67.
260 Meffert, H. and Schleusener, M. 2001, p. 137.

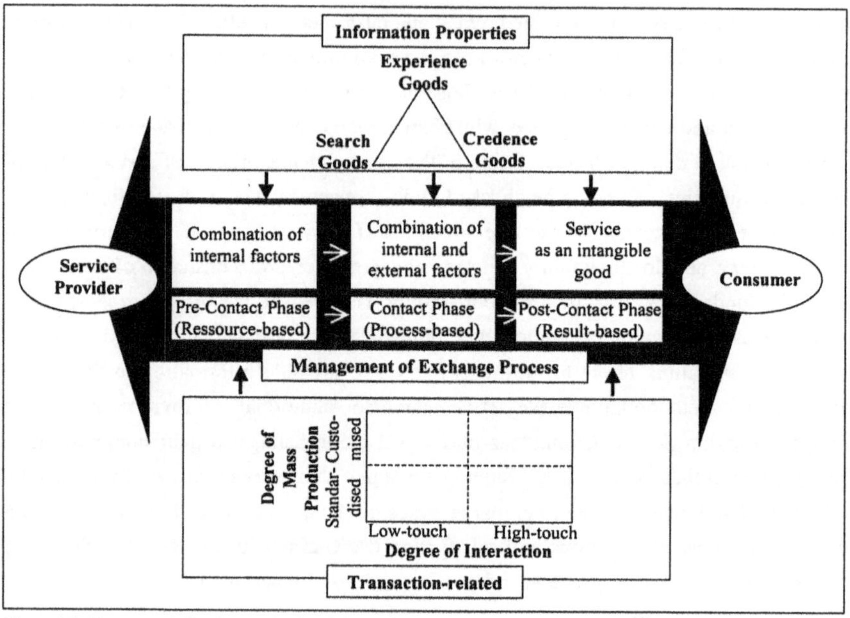

Figure 17: Framework for the Analysis of the Different Dimensions of Services[261]

Services are characterised by a high degree of interactivity, process-orientation and a certain involvement of the customer in the service delivery process. Compared to goods, customers generally incur higher search and information costs due to the intangible character and information properties of services. The ultimate objective is to manage the exchange process between the service provider and the customer across the different phases of the service delivery process. This exchange process is further influenced by the information properties of the service as well as by the degree of desired interaction and the possibility of mass production. The last two aspects are determined by the specific service strategy of the company, as will be shown at the end of this chapter. This overall conclusion underlines the close link of service management to the fundamental objective of distribution, as defined by the notion of marketing flows or by the theory of relational exchange.

Now that the specific properties of services including the implications for the service delivery process have been defined, the following section analyses the extent to which financial services constitute additional constraints, to be taken into account when designing multi-channel distribution strategies for financial services.

---

[261] Illustration based on Meffert, H. and Bruhn, M. 2000, pp. 65-67.

4.2 The Specific Properties of Retail Financial Services

Retail financial services, as defined in the Chapter 2.1[262], are part of the overall group of services, so the major characteristics of services also apply to financial services.[263] Retail financial services are generally characterised by a high degree of experience and credence qualities, as the consumer lacks the necessary competence to clearly evaluate the financial services product. In addition, the consumer generally needs to be integrated very strongly into the delivery process for financial services. For example, Lehmann stresses the particular interactive and co-operative character of insurance services.[264] Gronover underlines the importance to align the customer relationship with the underlying business process given the particularly interactive nature of retail financial services.[265]

The intangible and abstract nature of financial services combined with a certain product complexity give rise to information deficiency as well as to consumer uncertainty, primarily regarding the question of, whether one can trust and rely on a financial advisor or insurance agent. Therefore, trust in the distributor and in the financial company is important.[266] The establishment of trust can also bring about a degree of inertia in buyer-seller relationships. Due to the fact that an irreversible amount of time and effort is required by an individual to gain the necessary experience and information on which to assess an institution's reliability, it is usually the case that once a consumer is satisfied, he is more likely to remain with that institution than incur the costs of searching for alternative suppliers.[267]

A large number of surveys on the analysis of consumer purchasing behaviour in financial services show that the consumer is more interested in the functional quality dimension (i.e., <u>how</u> the service is delivered), rather than in the technical quality dimension (i.e., <u>what</u> is actually received as the outcome of the production process).[268] This finding clearly underlines the importance of the distribution function for financial services, since distribution is responsible for the management of the exchange process with the customer.

Devlin[269] identified three elements, which influence the consumer's position and activity in the entire interaction process: complexity of the product, financial maturity of the consumer as well as the interest and participation of the consumer in the process. Consumers are more willing to become involved in a search process for simple financial products, which tend to be

---

262 See Chapter 2.1, pp. 15-6.
263 Delisle, E. 1993, pp. 6-7; McKechnie, S. and Harrison, T. 1995, p. 38; Salmen, S.-M. 2002, p. 88.
264 Lehmann, A. 1989, p. 34.
265 Gronover, S. 2003, p. 24.
266 Heinsen, A. 2001, p. 18.
267 McKechnie, S. and Harrison, T. 1995, p. 38.
268 McKechnie, S. and Harrison, T. 1995, p. 44.
269 Devlin, J. 2001, pp. 645. See also Salmen, S.-M. 2002, pp. 91-2.

straightforward and accessible. In the case of more complex financial products, there may be a lack of voluntary need recognition by consumers, which means that such services need to be sold rather than bought and other elements outside the core product become more important.[270] Financial maturity refers to the aspect whether the consumer is more concerned with short-term financial protection needs or long-term investment and financing activities.

The lack of voluntary need recognition is certainly true for the classical insurance products, since the customer considers insurance products as a low-interest, emotionless product.[271] As a result, the consumer does not sufficiently identify his specific needs for risk coverage and often underestimates his risks, since these risks (e.g. accidents, death) evoke clearly negative, perturbing associations, so that the individual rather prefers not to deal with insurance issues at all. Therefore, the initial distribution challenge for insurance products is to overcome the customer's resistance and to win his attention and trust.

Financial services can, furthermore, be differentiated to the degree that the customer gets involved in the service delivery process. In the case of simple investment products, the customer only gets involved to support the process (so-called supportive-interactive services), whereby in the case of a loan agreement, the customer exchanges an amount of data and thus the interaction process represents a crucial part of the entire product (so-called product-oriented, interactive services). In the last group of services (so-called personal-interactive services), the interaction between the service provider and the customer represents the core of the service, since the actual service has a strong impact on the customer's intellectual and emotional side, e.g. financial planning services fall under this category.[272]

On the basis of the attributes of financial services, Haller has developed a comprehensive product and marketing concept for financial services. Based on the (ongoing) analysis of customer needs, the insurer has to identify product functions (e.g. financial protection, convenience), which allow the consumer to fulfil his needs. Products in the sense of 'solution concepts' will then be designed to respond to these functions and customer needs. Insurers will try to optimally and continuously respond to these needs in their interactions with the customer. This function-oriented marketing understanding marks a clear shift from a 'goods-producing' to a 'customer-satisfying' distribution process.[273]

Haller points out that such a wide product understanding is inherent in the intangible and interactive (i.e., process-oriented) nature of insurance services, and it is therefore necessary to widen the understanding of the limits of an insurance product. With his three-level concept,

---

270 Ehrler, B. 1999, pp. 64-82; Haller, M. 1986, pp. 1097-1124.
271 Kühlmann, U. et al. 2000, pp. 1-5.; Kurtenbach, W., Kühlmann, K., Käßer-Pawelka, G. 1995, pp. 18-22.
272 Salmen, S.-M. 2002, p. 93.
273 Levitt, T. 1960, p. 55.

Haller illustrates that beyond the core product of risk protection on the first level, other convenience and after-sales services (e.g. efficient claims handling) complement the actual core product on the second level. On the third level, the product will even be extended further to incorporate other, insurance-related services (e.g. risk management services, bancassurance services) in a constant effort to optimally fulfil customer's needs.[274] Similarly, Belz has developed the concept of performance and customer systems, where customer problems are solved in a comprehensive manner by integrating different perspectives into the definition and expansion of the core product, e.g. relationship marketing represents a crucial aspect of the performance system.[275]

Grönroos has also taken up this product understanding and uses the term "bundle of different services and service elements" which, together, form a service package. He defines the basic service package as consisting of the core service as well as facilitating and supporting services; but he even goes beyond this product understanding. In fact, the Augmented Service Offering Concept requires not only the definition of the service via the three elements of the core, facilitating and supporting services, but it also needs to respond to the following three questions: how the basic package is made accessible, how interactions are developed, and how customers are prepared to participate in the process.[276] The following figure illustrates this concept of the augmented service offering.

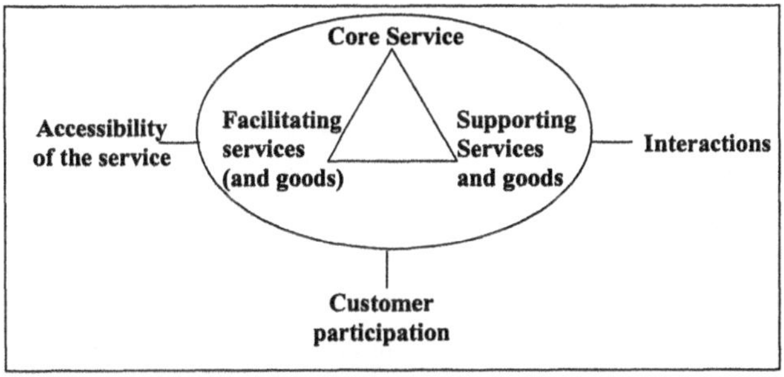

Figure 18: The Augmented Service Offering[277]

The first element of **accessibility[278] of the service** refers to the resources provided by the service provider (e.g. offices or information technology), enabling the customer to gain access to the service provider and the service process. Grönroos deliberately uses the term 'accessi-

[274] Ehrler, B. 1999, pp. 68-82; Haller, M. 1986, pp. 1097-1124.
[275] Belz, C. 1998a, pp. 32-33; Belz, C. 2001, pp. 65-6.
[276] Grönroos, C. 2000, p. 170.
[277] Grönroos, C. 2000, p. 168.
[278] Accessibility may further be sub-divided into four components: Site accessibility, customer ease of use of the physical resources, frontline personnel's contribution to accessibility and ease of customer participation.

bility' instead of distribution in order to emphasise the wide spectrum of tasks, distribution has to take care of. In such a perspective, multi-channel distribution should rather be considered as a 'multi-access' strategy. Research on the consumer choice of distribution channels has shown that the accessibility of a channel (i.e., the ease with which it can be accessed) is probably the most basic determinant for the set of distribution channels considered by the customer.[279] **Interaction with the service organisation** refers to interactions with physical or technical resources, IT systems or with other departments of the corporation. Thirdly, **customer participation** means that the customer has an impact on the service he perceives, i.e., the customer's involvement due to the inseparability of production and consumption of services determine the service quality.

In such a wide product understanding, the service delivery process or accessibility of the services becomes an integral part of the financial services product. In other words, the management of the interaction process with the customer, which, by definition, defines the distribution function, represents the fundamental element of the financial services product itself. In fact, convenient communication, simplicity, speed and availability of services are of increasing importance, the more the actual core service (e.g. risk protection) becomes interchangeable among the different service providers.[280]

It can therefore be concluded that customer value is not only derived from the transactional elements of the financial services itself, but also from the ongoing relationship with the organisation over a series of two-way exchanges with the financial services provider.[281] Consumers often do not approach the purchase of financial services as a series of discrete transactions, but act out of a feeling of commitment to a particular service provider. Commitment is recognised as the key element in the conceptualisation of 'relationship', representing an additional value of the service offering. Service delivery will thus become a continuous process, in which all members of the service provider try to satisfy customer needs along all phases of service delivery.[282] Distribution of financial services, therefore, evolves towards the **permanent management of a long-term customer relationship**. In the course of this relationship, the customer will experience multiple moments of truth,[283] which will determine the sustainability of the relationship to the company. The management of this **exchange process of truths** will be the fundamental distribution task for the financial services provider, i.e., this requires the development of a responsive relationship management.[284]

---

279 Black, N., Lockett, A., Ennew, C., Winkelhofer, H. and McKechnie, S. 2002, p. 168.
280 Lehmann, A. 1995, p. 57.
281 McKechnie, S. and Harrison, T. 1995, p. 39.
282 Devlin, J. 2001, p. 650; McKechnie, S. and Harrison, T. 1995, pp. 44-5.
283 Carlzon, J. 1989, p. 19.
284 McKechnie, S. and Harrison, T. 1995, pp. 44-5.

To conclude, financial services are characterised by a high degree of experience and credence qualities as well as by a strong interactivity between the customer and the financial services provider, so mutual trust needs to be established. The customer's degree of involvement in the service delivery process depends on the complexity of the individual financial services product as well as the customer's financial maturity and overall interest in financial services. Financial services need to be defined over and above their core product and include other support and facilitating services. Therefore, distribution, responsible for the management of the customer's interaction process, becomes an integral part of the product.

Most of the financial services tend not to be one-off purchases, but ones which are required on a recurring basis instead, so that the customer extracts additional value from the relationship process, which has been established with the financial services provider. However, the management of this exchange process, which is certainly not required for all financial services and customer groups, represents a particular challenge for the management of financial services companies. It is therefore important to analyse the managerial and specific distribution consequences, which result from such a product understanding. In the next section, the perspective will change from the consumer to the company and their responses to an effective management and distribution of (financial) services.

4.3 Service Management: Distribution of Retail Financial Services

From the classical, goods-producing management perspective, emphasis is on economies of scale and on the intention to decrease the costs of production and administration, in order to minimise the unit cost of the products. In the classical profit equation, as the differential of revenues and costs, the internal efficiency of a company is primarily guided by cost considerations, while marketing is given the responsibility for the successful positioning of the company in the market place (i.e., external efficiency). Consequently, strategic decisions concerning internal and external efficiency are separated. However, due to the constituent properties of services, e.g. customer interaction, uno-actu principle, process-orientation, this rigid split between an external and internal perspective is not possible, as cost optimisation efforts always have a direct impact on the service delivery process, especially on service quality. Given these interrelationships between revenue-generating and cost-optimising measures, Grönroos concludes that strategic decisions on services should be governed by their impact on buyer/seller interactions, whereas the cost implications of such decisions are to be viewed as constraints to achieving better customer relations.[285] These ideas have given rise to the crea-

[285] Grönroos, C. 1991, pp. 50-63.

tion of the term 'Service Management', which has particularly been developed by university scholars in Europe since the beginning of the 1980s.[286]

Service Management is a clearly customer-driven, holistic management style, emphasising the importance of intra-organisational, cross-functions collaboration. Attention is given to the external efficiency of the firm (i.e., maximisation of the long-term customer profitability) and the customer's perception of the service quality. Lehmann concludes that, in service companies, organisations should not be predicated on internal processes and corporate functions (e.g. sales, production), but rather centred around the sequence of customer interactions (so-called 'moments of truth').[287] Creating the optimal **context** for customer interactions constitutes the primary management challenge in service companies.[288] Distribution plays a fundamental role in creating the right context and in managing the multiple interfaces with the customer. In the following figure, Lehmann graphically summarises the managerial implication of such a constant management of the 'process of truth'-relationship. All corporate activities and capabilities have to be (re)directed towards this fundamental service task.

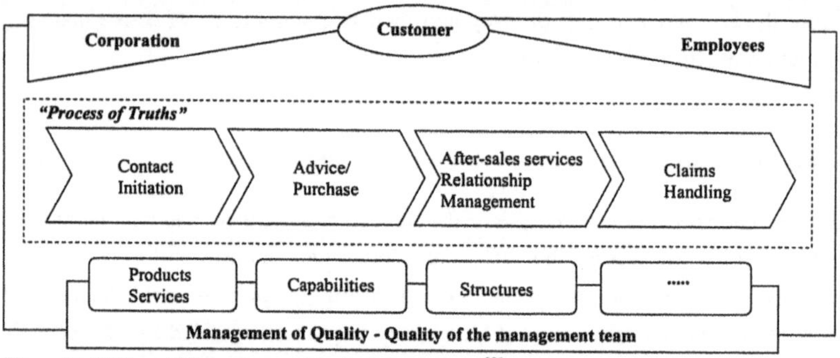

Figure 19: Different Dimensions of Service Management[289]

This constant management of 'moments of truth' can best be structured around the customer buying cycle, classifying the interaction process with the customer into four phases: Purchase Initiation; Evaluation, Purchase and After-Sales.[290] In the figure above, the buying cycle has been adapted to the specific aspects of insurance or financial services. During the first phase, the initial contact between the service provider and the customer is established. In the case of new customers, the service provider needs to gradually gather information on the customer to

---

286 Grönroos, C. 1994, pp. 5-20.
287 Lehmann, A. 1995, pp. 46-7.
288 Lehmann, A. 1995, p. 50.
289 Lehmann, A. 1995, p. 58.
290 Devlin, J. 2001, pp. 641-2; McKechnie, S. and Harrison, T. 1995, p. 39; Muther, A. 1999, p. 15; Schramm-Klein, H. 2003, pp. 48-52.

tailor the service offering to the specific needs of the customer. It is thus the objective of this first phase to identify the customer needs, raise interest and react by proposing a specific service offering.[291] In the subsequent evaluation phase (pre-sales phase), the customer clearly identifies his needs and solicits advice, and, in case of satisfaction with the offering, the customer accepts the offering in the following 'purchase phase'. Given the generally long time span between the purchase of an insurance contract and the occurrence of an insurance incident (i.e., claims handling), the company needs to increase customer loyalty through a pro-active management of the customer relationship. Constant management of the customer exchange process throughout the buying cycle requires the use of different distribution and communication channels.[292]

In the first section of this chapter, a comprehensive framework for the analysis of services[293] was developed. It was stated that the service delivery process also depends on the information properties, the degree of customer interaction as well as on the desired level of process standardisation or process customisation. Therefore, the actual nature and intensity with which the exchange process is to be managed, certainly varies for different kinds of services. Services with a high degree of standardisation, low customer involvement, a dominance of the result-based dimension and only low levels of information asymmetry certainly require less interactivity and weaker customer relationships than services with a strong integration of the external factor, a clear dominance of the process dimension and strong information asymmetries or information complexities. Therefore, even strong advocates of an entirely customer-centric service management view acknowledge that economies of scale based on a production-line approach may be possible to realise if the service outcome and the production and delivery processes can be highly standardised.[294]

From the point of view of a top-down management perspective, Lehmann has derived two generic service strategies from classifying services into four fields based on the two dimensions of product and information complexity and the desired nature and intensity of customer interactions.[295] The actual positioning in one of these four fields is then determined by customer requirements as well as the strategic considerations of the company.

---

[291] See www.wirtschaftsinformatik.de/wi/wiprofessionals/pdf/9802_02.pdf [Muther and Österle].
[292] Eschke, S., Bölscher, J. and Schulenburg, J. - M. Graf v. d. 2001, p. 20.
[293] See Chapter 4.1, p. 64.
[294] Grönroos, C. 1994, pp. 5-20.
[295] Lehmann, A. 1998, pp. 128-138.

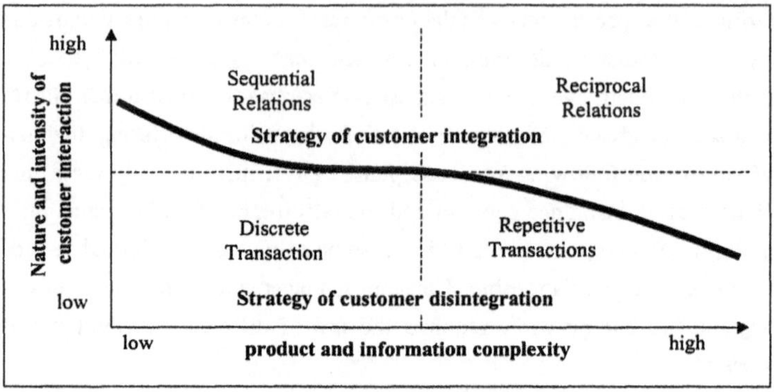

Figure 20: Description of two Generic Service Strategies[296]

In order to describe the four strategic fields, Lehmann borrows the terminology from the theory of relational exchange.[297] **Discrete services** are marked by clear, formalised and standardised processes and low product complexity, where customer interactions can be reduced to the minimum level. Services in the area of **sequential relations** can no longer be considered as low-touch interactions. Although the core product is similar to discrete transactions in the sense that the customer only incurs low search and information costs to evaluate the service product, the service provider deliberately maintains the customer relationship, as value creation does not only stem from the delivery of the core product, but is also generated by other service components (e.g. delivery and processing time, availability of services, etc.). This idea of tailoring products to the individual needs of the customer is also at the heart of customised marketing.[298]

In the field of **reciprocal relations**, establishing and maintaining confidence and reliability is particularly important for services with a high degree of both product complexity and relationship dynamics. The customer is particularly involved in the process of service delivery and hence the social relationship plays an important role. Transaction costs for both parties involved can only be reduced at sustainable levels by clearly integrating the customer into the process. However, this process cannot be governed by clear formal rules, but only by an intuitive understanding of mutual dependencies and by mutually shared values, norms and convictions (see clan-like decision-making mechanisms[299]).[300] Value is derived from an ongoing relationship with a particular organisation and the customer shows clear commitment to this

---

296 Lehmann, A. 1998, pp. 128-38.
297 See Chapter 3.2.1, pp. 47-8; Dwyer, F., Schurr, P. and Sejo, O. 1987, pp. 11-15; Macneil, I. 1980, pp. 60; Robichaeux, R. and Coleman, J. 1994, p. 40.
298 Salmen, S.-M. 2002, pp. 66-70.
299 See Chapter 3.3.1, pp. 52-3.
300 Lehmann, A. 1998, p. 132.

organisation. The tight integration of the customer into the service delivery process as well as the special focus on managing the customer interaction process with the intent to build up and maintain a sustainable customer relationship then paves the way for the emergence of the concept of individualised marketing. This marketing approach combines both the adaptation of the product bundle to the individual needs of the customers as well as the build-up of a relationship process with the customer. This individualised marketing approach seems to be very appropriate for financial services given their very interactive, intangible, process-oriented properties with a high dominance of credence and experience qualities.[301]

Repetitive transactions are characterised by clear and stable input-output relations, where customer integration and interactions only depend on the (technical) product properties. The customer generally has a sound knowledge of the financial products and a specific interest in financial affairs. From the customer point of view, the service provider is interchangeable and does not provide any added value beyond the core product itself.[302]

Lehmann derives two generic service strategies of customer integration vs. customer disintegration from this four-field classification. The **strategy of customer integration** tries to fully integrate the customer into all phases of service delivery and to strengthen the customer relationship. Services with a high degree of uncertainty (i.e., dominance of experience and credence qualities) are particularly appropriate for strong customer integration in order to reduce uncertainty by regular inter-personal interactions and shared resources. For the customer, value is derived from the value of the relationship process based on a product understanding, whereby the product is defined far beyond its core product. In return, the company can generate far more financial value, as the customer's cross-selling potential can be fully leveraged over time. This strategy could be pursued in those instances when the mutual creation of value during the different phases of service delivery is emphasised.[303]

Conversely, the **strategy of customer disintegration** tries to reduce the uncertainty factor of service interaction to its minimum. Emphasis is placed on the efficiency of service delivery and business processes are protected from unpredictable customer interventions. Services with a low level of complexity and a transparent offering can best be co-ordinated by price and market mechanisms.[304] Hence, the cost-efficient delivery of services (i.e., execution of the transaction) is considered to be more important than an active involvement of the end customer. The total value proposition focuses on establishing an attractive price to quality relationship, so cost efficient processes are crucial.

---

[301] Salmen, S.-M. 2002, p. 70.
[302] Lehmann, A. 2001, p. 98.
[303] Lehmann, A. 1998, p. 134.
[304] Lehmann, A. 2001, p. 96.

The framework by Lehmann on the appropriate classification of service strategies can be illustrated by the example of Deutsche Bank, which illustrates the actual use and validity of Lehmann's framework in the professional world.

The following figure shows how **Deutsche Bank** has adapted its service and distribution strategy towards the three identified customer groups.

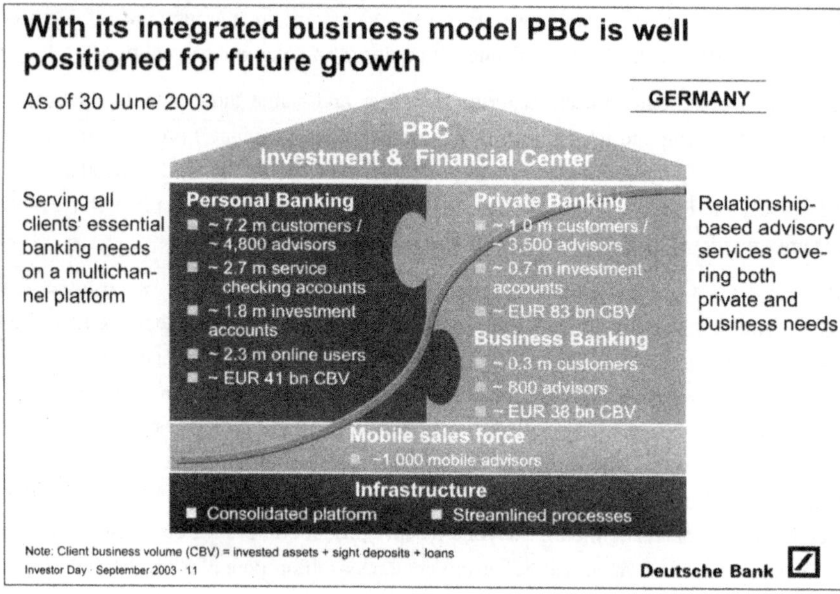

Figure 21: Sales Approach for Different Customer Segments at Deutsche Bank[305]

While in classical retail banking ("Personal Banking"), customers are served on a multi-channel framework, the degree of relationship orientation increases in the case of private and business banking. In these segments, mobile sales forces or dedicated sales teams are employed to offer advisory services. The curve across all segments shows that, in the case of Private Banking, the degree of relationship orientation (i.e., customer integration in the sales process) increases.[306]

To conclude, distribution needs to take the intangible and particularly interactive properties of financial services into account. While for some products and customer groups, a clear relationship oriented distribution approach with a constant management of the exchange processes is appropriate, this may not hold true for other constellations of products and customers.

[305] Neske, R. 2003, p. 11.
[306] Neske, R. 2003, p. 11.

4.4 Conclusion

This chapter has derived overall service strategies from a thorough analysis of the properties of retail financial services. The following conclusions can be drawn:

- Services can be characterised by **three distinct views** (resource-, process- and result-based view) with a strong dominance of the process view and the inseparability of production and consumption (uno-actu principle). In addition, services can be divided into **three phases**: pre-contact, contact and post-contact phase, whereby each phase corresponds to a specific view **(implicit phase view).**
- Services are intangible and exhibit a high level of experience- and credence qualities, which give rise to **information asymmetries** between the service provider and the customer and thus to uncertainties.
- Service delivery depends on the actual degree of **customer interaction** and the desired **degree of service standardisation.**
- Given the intangible and interactive properties, **retail financial services,** including all products fulfilling the financial needs of the private mass market, have to be defined over and above their core product and thus include other support and facilitating services in the value proposition. The accessibility of services, the interaction with the service organisation and customer participation are also important elements of retail financial services. Service delivery will become a continuous process, whereby exchange processes with the customer are to be constantly managed. In this perspective, distribution becomes an important element of the product 'retail financial services'.
- This product understanding has clear **managerial implications**. Distribution shifts from a 'mere product providing function' to a customer relationship function as it provides multi-access points to the customer and therefore the basis for an ongoing process of truth management. All corporate activities and capabilities have to be (re)directed towards this fundamental service task, whereby this **constant management of "moments of truth"** can best be structured around the customer buying cycle.

From a corporate perspective, it has to be reviewed whether such a comprehensive strategy of customer integration is possible, justified and necessary in all instances. For this purpose, Lehmann has developed two distinct **service strategies** of customer integration and customer disintegration based on the criteria of product and information complexity as well as on the desired intensity of customer interaction.

It is now time to combine the conceptual results of the third and fourth chapter in **one comprehensive framework**. The following figure illustrates this framework.

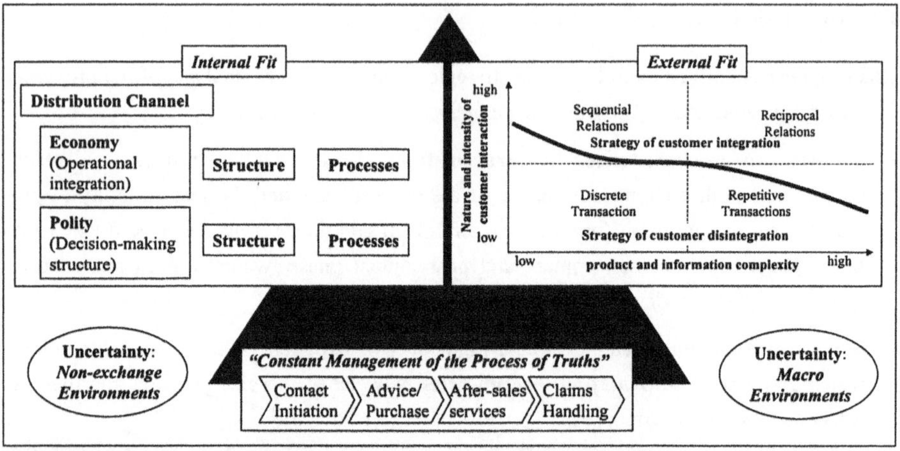

Figure 22: Comprehensive Framework for the Analysis of Distribution Systems[307]

Distribution has the overall task of the configuration and co-ordination of the distribution system to ensure the internal as well as external fit of the entire distribution system.[308] The **internal fit** refers to the 'internal functioning' of the distribution system. Here, the PEP framework clearly identifies two important dimensions: the internal economic integration of the distribution channels (economy) as well as the decision-making mechanisms (polity). In the case of financial services, most notably insurance services, particular attention needs to be paid to the management of internal conflicts (socio-economic processes) as well as to the distribution of power (socio-economic structures). The **external fit** refers, above all, to the appropriate fit between the service provider and the customer. Lehmann's framework for the development of the two generic service strategies of customer integration and disintegration provides a more concrete basis for the concept of the 'external customer fit'.

Furthermore, the internal and external fit ultimately need to relate to the **management of the exchange processes** with the customer during the different phases of the customer buying cycle. The more the customer is integrated into the different phases of the buying cycle, the more the internal functioning of the distribution system is also influenced by the customer interaction process. Therefore, the buying cycle needs to be recognised as a distinct dimension of a multi-channel distribution system. Creating the optimal context for customer interactions represents a real distribution and service challenge. All corporate activities and capabilities have to be directed to this fundamental service task and centred around this sequence of customer interactions.

---

[307] Own Illustration.

[308] Regarding the internal and external fit of distribution systems see Schögel, M. 1996, p. 147.

In addition, the PEP framework clearly points out that uncertainty, arising from the **non-exchange and macro exchange environment**, also impacts the distribution system. The more uncertain the environment is, the more likely the financial service provider will try to integrate the distribution channels as tightly as possible, leading to more centralised planning, co-ordination and decision processes.

This comprehensive framework can now be used not only for the analysis, but also for the management of multi-channel distribution systems, as all major internal and external dimensions have clearly been identified. However, as stated before, distribution is part of general management and the management of the distribution system therefore needs to be embedded in the overall strategy of the company. While the integration of the distribution function into the overall strategic and marketing management context will be discussed in the next chapter, chapter 6 will actually use the comprehensive framework of this chapter in order to analyse two distinct structures of multi-channel distribution strategies.

5. Impact of the Corporate Positioning on the Distribution Strategy

Since the nature, objectives and tasks of the distribution function have been defined and the managerial consequences for the delivery of retail financial services have been analysed, this chapter will embed distribution management in the overall strategic and marketing framework of the company. The extent to which the configuration of the distribution system also depends on the strategic and marketing objectives of the company will be analysed hereunder.

5.1 The Nature and Positioning of Distribution Management

It is discussed both in theory and practice, whether distribution management is part of the marketing mix and only has an instrumental character, or whether it is an integral part of general management. Cespedes posits that distribution management is general management due to the multitude of implications distribution has for the company and its organisation.[309] In a similar manner, Stern states that "of all marketing decisions, the ones regarding distribution are the most far-reaching. A company can easily change its prices or its advertising. It can hire or fire a market research agency, revamp its sales promotion programme, even modify its product line. But once a company sets up its distribution channels, it will generally find changing them to be difficult".[310] Porter also acknowledges that access-based strategies (i.e., strategies defining the way to reach the customer best) represent one out of three sources of strategic positioning.[311] Järvinen similarly concludes that "channel decisions are always a matter of company strategy".[312] In fact, the key source of competitive value has shifted from product-based differentiation to a more systematic management of the customer relationship: "Differences that can't be copied are differences in service and support – in relationship with the customer – and those differences are all features of the channel".[313] This may also be the reason, why top decision makers consider distribution as the key strategic priority, as confirmed by various surveys among CEOs and senior managers of financial services companies.[314]

Channel Management deals with the management of inter-organisation relationships in distribution channels with the overall objective to enhance customer relationships and minimise

---

[309] Cespedes, F. 1988, p. 99. See similarly Sherden, W. A. 1992, p. 28: "Distribution effectiveness is a major driver of success in insurance because it is the source of new business, involves most of the critical processes of the operation and is a major determinant of the quality and value delivered to the customer."
[310] Stern, L. and Sturdivant, F. 1987, p. 34.
[311] Porter, M. 1996, p. 67.
[312] Järvinen, R. 1998, pp. 25-30.
[313] Wheeler, S. and Hirsh, E. 1999, p. xxiii.
[314] Herzog, M. and Panzer, J. 2003, p. 49; Maynard, P. 2001, pp. 63-4.

delivery costs. Channel management is necessary, as distribution channels do not operate successfully without any co-ordination, controlling and motivation of the channel members."[315] Wheeler and Hirsh provide a very pragmatic and customer-oriented definition of channel management: "Channel Management is a systematic means of reaching and taking care of your customers, wherever they are and however they like to be reached".[316] Specht defines channel management (also known as distribution management) as a sub-function of general management, dealing with the systematic organisation, management, planning and controlling of the distribution system. If one changes the point of view from the company to the customer's perspective, channel management can also be interpreted as a "systematic means of reaching and taking care of your customers wherever they are and however they like to be reached".[317]

Hereafter, distribution management, understood as an alternative terminology for channel management, is considered to be an integral part of general management and its core task is to provide multiple access points to the customer. Above all this task requires the systematic organisation, management, planning and controlling of the distribution system. Therefore, successful distribution management first of all requires the development of an overall concept for the strategic and marketing positioning of the company.[318] As illustrated in the following figure, the objectives of distribution are derived from the overall financial, strategic and marketing objectives of the company. It is therefore important to understand first the overall strategic and marketing position before a concrete (multi-)channel distribution strategy can be developed.[319] As shown later, multi-channel distribution systems can be set up differently, depending on the actual strategic and marketing objectives.

[315] Stern, L., El-Ansary, A. and Coughlan, A. 1996, pp. 324-5.
[316] Wheeler, S. and Hirsh, E. 1999, p. xxiii.
[317] Wheeler, S. and Hirsh, E. 1999, p. xxiii.
[318] Fischer, K. 1999, pp. 1627-31.
[319] Bergmann, G. 1988, pp. 113-118; Popp, S. 1990, p. 138; Schögel, M. 1997, p. 113; Specht, G. 1992, p. 45.

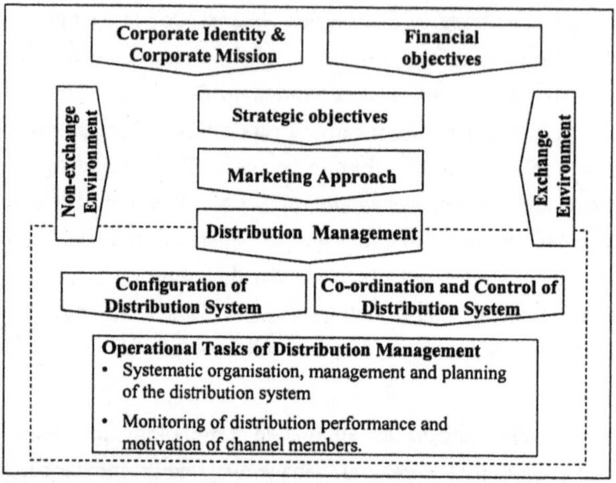

Figure 23: Management Context for Distribution Management[320]

Distribution Management can be broken down into the two fundamental tasks of the configuration (set-up) as well as co-ordination and control of the distribution system. Once the distribution system is in place, distribution management operationally deals with the systematic organisation, management, planning and financial steering of the entire distribution system. How the formal positioning of the company, the corporate strategy as well as the marketing approach determine the distribution strategy will be described in more detail in the following section.

5.2 Objectives of Distribution Management

5.2.1 Overall Corporate Orientation and Financial Objectives

The objectives of distribution management ultimately relate to the basic set of values (corporate identity) as well as to the corporate mission of the company.[321] It has already been illustrated in the context of the internal decision-making processes that clan-like decision processes are more effective and require, above all, a common sharing of the corporate values and vision.[322] The **Corporate Identity** particularly defines how a company intends to position itself in the market and to differentiate itself from the market environment. Therefore, decisions on the selection of distribution channels have to be seen in connection with the actual or in-

---

320 Own illustration based on Specht, G. 1992, p. 45.
321 Bergmann, G. 1988, p. 114; Popp, S. 1990, pp. 138-151.
322 See Chapter 3.3.1, pp. 52-3.

tended image of the corporation. For example, it might be entirely inconsistent with the corporate image of a bank to co-operate with a pyramid sales force organisation (multi-level marketing organisation). The high-profile image of a bank could collide with the reputation of the pyramid sales force organisation.[323]

The **Corporate mission** also sets the direction for the distribution system. A Corporate Mission is generally defined as a long-term vision of what the business is or is striving to become. The basic issue is: what is our business and what should it be?[324] The answer to these questions is particularly relevant to the definition of the distribution strategy in the financial services industry, since this industry is characterised by a deconstruction of the traditionally integrated value chain as well as by the emergence of new business models.[325] For example, more product-focussed, manufacturer-type companies will have to establish a wholesale distribution system, while consumer-oriented companies will have to focus, in particular, on the configuration of their retail distribution system. The example of the corporate mission of TSB Retail Banking and Insurance (UK) illustrates how the corporate mission defines the overall guidelines for the distribution strategy.

> Mission Statement of **TSB Retail Banking and Insurance**: "To be the UK's leading financial retailer through understanding and meeting customer needs by being more professional and innovative than our competitors".

The Corporate Mission of TSB Retail Banking and Insurance clearly requires a distribution strategy, which is based on a relationship market approach ("to understand and meet customers") as well as to be sufficiently flexible and innovative in order to react to any changes in the market.

Since corporations can be interpreted as purposeful socio-economic systems, the **set of formal, i.e., financial, targets** constitutes the normative guidelines for any decision on the distribution system.[326] Whereas the classical theory of business administration still assumes a clear hierarchy of corporate objectives, modern management theory now tends to accept the existence of parallel objectives, over and above the 'classical' objectives of profitability, liquidity and security. While in the past, emphasis has been placed on market share and growth targets (i.e., volume targets), a gradual shift towards profitability measures could be noticed in the 1980s; at the end of the 90s profit and value creation became the predominant financial target, at least for capital market oriented financial services companies. The following figure

---

323 Süchting, J. 1984, p. 319.
324 Ennew, C. 1995, p. 63; Kollat, D., Blackwell, R. and Robeson, J. 1972, p. 14.
325 Ackermann, W. 2001, pp. 70-81.
326 Bergmann, G. 1988, pp. 122-135.

illustrates that different financial targets may require significantly different distribution strategies:

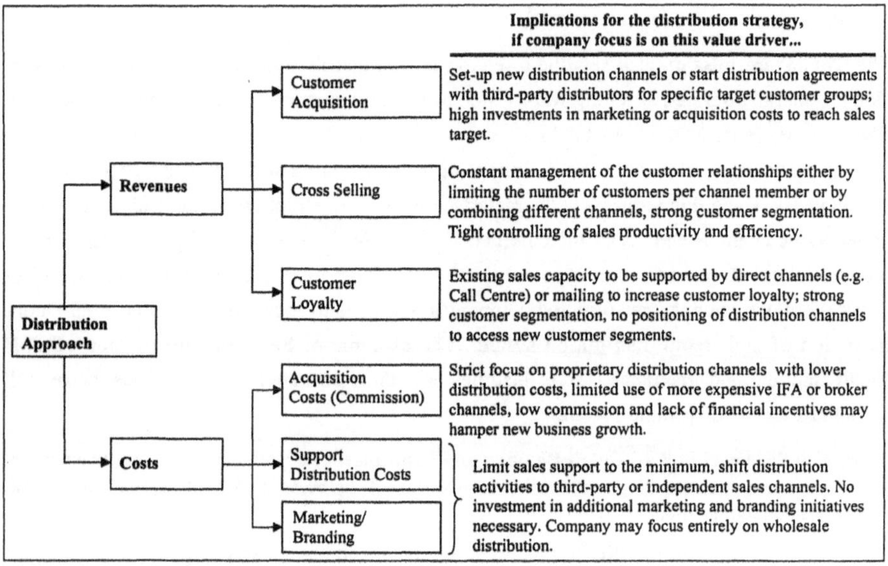

Figure 24: Implications of Different Financial Targets for the Distribution Strategy[327]

As can be inferred from the above figure, a company, which defines a clear priority for growth measured by the amount of new customers, will opt for a distribution strategy, which will either open up new proprietary distribution channels or enter into additional sales agreement with third party providers. Conversely, if the lowering of cancellation rates (customer loyalty) is what the company chooses to focus on, existing distribution channels may be supported by Call Centres or other CRM-based marketing campaigns to actively manage customer relationships, especially those customers, who are likely to cancel their contracts. In addition, different distribution concepts will be designed for individual customer segments. Furthermore, a company which has the clear objective of improving its profitability irrespective of growth targets will either focus almost exclusively on its own sales force and/or cut all additional distribution and marketing expenses. The distribution system is not likely to expand in terms of customer growth or to be characterised by extremely new sales approaches.

[327] Own Illustration.

5.2.2 Strategic Objectives

While the corporate mission provides overall guidance for a business and financial targets define the primary quantitative targets to be achieved, clear business strategies explain how to achieve the defined financial targets and, thus, define the concrete guidelines for any marketing and distribution strategy.[328] The primary objective of strategic management is to develop and expand the company's competitive advantages to maintain long-term company performance – as measured by growth, profits and company value.[329] It is important to understand that competitive advantages result from clear advantages, as they are perceived by the customers themselves.[330] The essence of strategic positioning is to choose activities that are different from rivals and to make explicit trade-off decisions in choosing what not to do. In addition, strategic fit among activities is fundamental not only to competitive advantages, but also to the sustainability of an advantage. Positions built on systems of activities are far more sustainable than those built on individual activities.[331] The following example illustrates the importance of aligning the strategic objectives with the underlying operational elements to ensure an utmost consistency between the corporate strategy and the distribution approach.

> The example of a **US bank**, which expanded into retail banking by setting up Call Centres, showed the consequence of a misfit between the strategic positioning and the operational implementation: Although management had espoused a strategy of customer excellence, this had been inadequately interpreted, articulated and communicated throughout the organisation. Without clear objectives and priorities, people end up working towards contradictory goals. Some elements are designed to produce service excellence, some to promote sales performance, some to engender an efficiency focus. In combination, they produce a sub-optimal result.[332]

As there is a large amount of literature on strategic management describing how strategies can be developed, the following paragraphs are only meant to give an overview of selected and the most well-known concepts for the development of strategies, which also represent the basis for the development of a corresponding marketing and distribution strategy hereafter.

Ansoff[333], one of the most well-known strategic thinkers, has used a **product/market opportunity matrix** to develop four generic strategies, as illustrated in the following figure. It can be seen from the description of the four generic strategies below that the distribution approach is most distinctly linked to the strategic positioning of a company, as distribution provides the interface between the customer markets and the product. First, the market penetration strategy tries either to penetrate the existing customer basis by leveraging the existing product offering

---

328 Bergmann, G. 1988, pp. 126-169.
329 Ehrler, B. 1999, p. 21; Tomczak, T. and Reinecke, S. 1999, p. 297.
330 Belz, C. 2001, p. 63.
331 Porter, M. 1996, p. 73.
332 Frenkel, S. and Donoghue, L. 1996, p. 25.
333 Ansoff, H. 1965.

more effectively or to acquire customers from competitors. In this strategy, the cross-selling ratio as well as the extension of the customer lifetime (e.g. reduction of defection rates) are two important value drivers. A second strategy places the strategic focus on the continuous expansion of the product offering in the existing customer markets. Thirdly, market development strategies are characterised by the transfer of an existing product offering to new customer segments – either by regional expansion or by access to completely new customer groups (e.g. by opening up a new distribution channel). Diversification strategies then finally intend to sell new products to new customer groups, which undoubtedly involve the highest entrepreneurial risk.

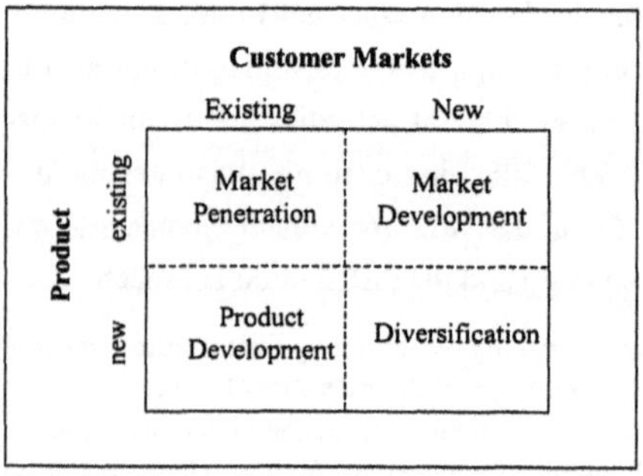

Figure 25: Product / Market Opportunity Matrix[334]

Ansoff's strategic directions only provide general strategic guidance. A competitive advantage can, however, only exist in relation to the market and more specifically in relation to the strategic positioning of the company's competitors. **Porter** is probably the most prominent representative of **industry analysis,** which is based on the Structure-Conduct-Performance paradigm, stating that the structure and attractiveness of the industry directly determines the profitability of a company.[335] The industry is defined as "the group of firms producing products that are close substitutes for each other".[336] For the industry (i.e., structural) analysis, Porter proposes the well-known five-forces model, emphasising the importance of analysing the company's positioning within its industry. These forces include the analysis of suppliers, customers, entry barriers, substitute products as well as the competitive dynamism of the industry (rivalry between firms).

Porter identified two important dimensions of a company's positioning: **price vs. quality** as well as **niche vs. total market coverage**. Based on these two dimensions Porter has devel-

---

334 Ansoff, H. 1965.
335 Haertsch, P. 2000, p. 61.
336 Porter, M. 1998, p. 5.

oped three generic strategies: overall cost leadership, differentiation strategy as well as focus on niche markets.[337] Regarding the strategy of cost leadership, there is increasing scepticism whether, particularly in the digital economy, a company succeeds in developing competitive advantages by focusing entirely on a cost leadership strategy.[338] Porter then proposes the **concept of the value chain**, breaking the firm down into its strategically relevant activities, in order to understand the behaviour of costs and the existing and potential sources of differentiation. The value chain analysis helps to identify the key building blocks for the total value proposition. The concept of value chains can also be transferred to distribution channels, so-called channel value chains.[339] The more the strategic positioning is built on a system of interrelated activities and not on individual activities, the more sustainable the competitive advantage is.[340] This also explains why multi-channel distribution strategies, regrouping a number of channel activities in a complex and interrelated framework, represent a very valuable and sustainable competitive advantage. Porter explicitly states that access-based strategies represent one source of strategic positioning.[341]

Treacy and Wiersema further developed Porter's concept of generic strategies. Their strategic alternatives (**customer intimacy**[342], **operational excellence**[343] and **product innovation**) each imply quite different relationships with the customer and, consequently, require different approaches to customer service and thus a fundamentally different configuration of the distribution system.[344]

A strategy of customer intimacy needs to be supported by a highly responsive service capability, whereby the quality of the customer relationship over the long term takes precedence over short-term cost reduction initiatives. In fact, customers particularly ask for a more customised service promise, especially at times when all financial services providers transfer an increasing amount of customer processes to fully automated distribution channels.[345] In contrast to a strategy of customer intimacy, operational excellence requires a pre-determined, uni-

---

337 Porter, M. 1998.
338 Haertsch, P. 2000, pp. 133-4.
339 Stern, L.W., El Ansary, A.I. and Coughlan, A. 1996, p. 28.
340 Porter, M. 1996, p. 73.
341 Porter, M. 1996, p. 67.
342 The strategy of customer intimacy is also known under the term 'customer service excellence'.
343 Porter argues that operational excellence, which he calls operational effectiveness, is not a source of long-term competitive advantage. Operational effectiveness means performing similar activities *better* than rivals perform them. However, differences in operational effectiveness among companies are pervasive. In fact, competition in operational effectiveness shifts the productivity frontier outward, thereby leading to absolute improvements, but no to a change in the relative operational effectiveness of the company compared to the market. See Porter, M. 1996, pp. 62-3.
344 Description of the strategic framework of Treacy and Wiersema taken from Frenkel, S. and Donoghue, L. 1996.
345 Layr, W. and Dahlem, C. 2001, pp. 55-7.

form service offering to be delivered reliably and efficiently. Product innovation requires a strong focus on research and development in order to support a stream of product or service innovations.

In the 1990s, Porter's market-based view with its assumption of an almost direct correlation between industry structure and a company's profitability was challenged by Prahalad, Hamel and others. They argue that the specific set of internal capabilities is also relevant to determining a company's position in the market. While the **market-based view** defines competitive advantages based on the analysis of specific product-markets (outside-in perspective), the **resource-based view** believes that competitive advantages can also be derived from intelligent leveraging or development of internal capabilities and resources (inside-out perspective). The **competence-based management approach** combines both perspectives, arguing that strategic management has to identify, develop and enhance both internal and external potentials to secure the company's long-term performance and economic viability.[346]

Similarly, Tomczak and Reinecke focus both on the internal and external perspectives and have identified the acquisition of new customers and the penetration of existing customer segments as well as product maintenance and product innovation as the four fundamental value drivers, which have to be developed by strategic management.[347]

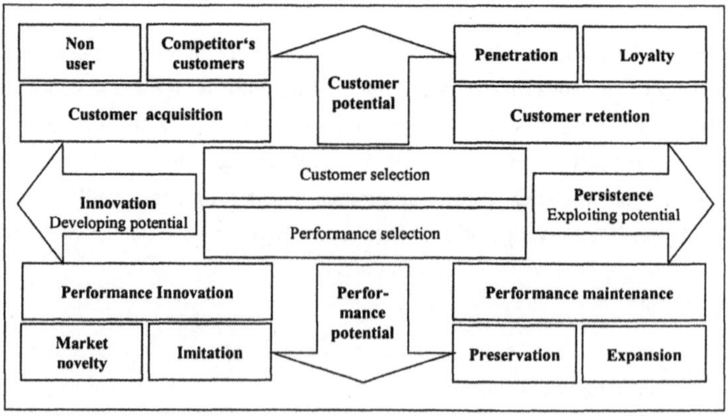

Figure 26: Task-oriented Management Approach by Tomczak and Reinecke[348]

In their framework of the **task-oriented approach,** Tomczak and Reinecke distinguish between internal (capabilities) and external (customer) resources, while further differentiating

[346] Ackermann, W. 2001, p. 76; Ehrler, B. 1999, pp. 48-9.
[347] Tomczak, T. and Reinecke, S. 1999, pp. 294-5.
[348] Tomczak, T. and Reinecke, S. 1999, pp. 294-5.

between a strategy of innovation or persistency. While an innovation strategy means that new potentials should be developed more quickly or more cost-effective than those of competitors, persistency orientation refers to a quicker and more cost-effective leveraging of existing potentials. Tomczak and Reinecke combine these four basic strategies with the four marketing tasks of customer acquisition, customer retention, product maintenance and product innovation.[349]

Based on these contributions to strategic management, it can be concluded that the process of developing a corporate strategy can be subdivided into the following three phases.

1
- **Analysis of the Industry** and the positioning of the company in this industry
- **Analysis of the internal resources and capabilities** of the company

Company Positioning (outside-in)
- Analysis of suppliers,
- Customers,
- Entry barriers,
- Substitute products
- Competitive dynamism of the industry (rivalry between firms).

Internal Resources, capabilities (inside-out)
- Products and product development
- Effectiveness of processes
- Resources: financial, infrastructure, skills
- Distribution
- Customer relationships
- Brand strength

2
- **Development of a clear corporate strategy**

Porter
- Overall cost leadership
- Differentiation strategy
- Focus on niche markets

Ansoff
- Market Pentetration
- Market Development
- Product Development
- Diversification

Treacy and Wiersema
- Customer intimacy
- Operational excellence
- Product innovation

Tomczak and Reinecke
- Acquisition of new customers
- Penetration of existing customer segments
- Product maintenance
- Product innovation

3
- **Detailing corporate strategy** by identifying fundamental business processes

Value Chain (Porter)
- Primary activities (based on customer's buying cycle)
- Support activities (IT, HR, administration, etc.)

Figure 27: Phases for Defining the Strategic Positioning of a Company[350]

In the first phase, it is important to analyse both the company's competitive position with respect to its major competitors. This outside-in analysis needs to be complemented by the analysis of internal resources and capabilities, which the company can leverage in order to perform different activities compared to rivals or to perform similar activities in different ways. In the subsequent phase, the concrete corporate strategy can then be developed based on the results of this first phase. Various authors have provided some guidance as to the iden-

---

[349] Tomczak, T. and Reinecke, S. 1999, pp. 304-8.
[350] Own Illustration.

tification of the major drivers, which can be used to develop a corporate strategy. The impact of purely product-based differentiation declines as a result of an increasing number of global competitors, rapid technological evolution as well as the increasing emulation of product innovations. So, in addition to product differentiation, differentiation in terms of services and products - vis-à-vis the customer - becomes a strategic necessity. In the third phase, it is then important to identify the most relevant and value-generating processes from the customer's point of view. Porter's concept of the value chain then helps to structure this process to identify a system of interdependent activities to create sustainable and long-lasting competitive advantages.

To conclude, strategic management identifies the fundamental value drivers, the company should focus on; hereby both internal and external capabilities are taken into account. The decision about the corporate strategy has clear implications for the configuration of the multi-channel distribution strategy. In case of a cost leadership strategy, the service provider will certainly try to reduce customer integration to the bare minimum in order to focus more on standardisation and mass delivery processes. On the contrary, in a quality strategy, an active management of the customer interaction process is more important. While the corporate strategy provides clear orientation for the overall direction of the company's development, this strategy then needs to be developed further for actual implementation via the concrete definition of the marketing and distribution strategy.

5.2.3 Marketing Objectives: Relationship vs. Transaction Marketing

The marketing strategy provides answers to the concrete implementation of a corporate strategy regarding the interaction with the customer. As illustrated in the previous chapter, the marketing of services represents a particular managerial challenge. In fact, services per se have to be good enough to provide a competitive advantage, but what creates a sustainable competitive advantage is the development of every element of the customer relationship.[351]

The question of whether services can be interpreted as a one-off interaction with the customer or as a constant exchange of information, whereby a long-lasting relationship is established, has important implications for the underlying marketing philosophy. These two different views on the delivery process have given rise to the two distinct marketing concepts of transaction vs. relationship marketing. The major difference can be explained by the way the exchange process between the customer and the service provider takes place. Based on the the-

---

[351] Grönroos, C. 2000, p. 6; Morgan, R. and Hunt, S. 1994, p. 22; Nevin, J. 1995, pp. 327-8.

ory of relational exchange, one can recur to the distinction between discrete transactions and relational exchanges, as explained in chapter 3.2.1.[352]

While simple, mass products (e.g. car insurance) are governed rather by discrete transactions, where the price is sufficient enough to co-ordinate the exchange process, more complex products with a higher level of perceived risks and high switching costs are more suitable for a relationship marketing approach. In fact, customers will be more likely to engage in relational behaviour when they perceive risk (financial risks, performance risks, social risks, physical risk, etc.) and incur high switching costs, defined as the one-time costs that the buyer encounters in switching from one supplier's product to another's.[353] The classification of services proposed by Lehman has actually been derived from the same theoretical basis: while a strategy of customer disintegration is more appropriate for discrete transactions, relational exchanges are suitable for a strategy of customer integration.

Relationship marketing reflects a strategy integrating customers, suppliers, and other partners in the interaction process with the company. While transaction marketing is characterised by clear product orientation as well as by a focus on short-term goals and on a standardised, non-recurrent exchange of services, relationship marketing argues that one has to establish, maintain and enhance the customer relationship far beyond the point of the individual transaction.[354] Grönroos extended this definition stating that "marketing is to establish, maintain, enhance and commercialise customer relationships [...] by a mutual exchange and fulfilment of promises".[355] In addition to the emphasis on the management of the customer interaction process, the concept of promise is particularly accentuated.[356]

Relationship marketing is a dynamic concept, focussing on the customer relationship over the entire customer's lifetime. Dwyer, Schurr, and Oh distinguish five general phases: awareness (customer becomes aware of the provider), exploration (customer makes trial purchases), expansion (continuation of purchases results in an increase in benefits received), commitment (a commitment to the service provider develops due to the benefits received) and dissolution (customer's withdrawal from the relationship).[357] Similarly, Diller uses lifecycle theory to model the dynamics of relationship marketing.[358] This process moves from identifying potential customers to establishing a relationship with them, and then to maintaining the relationship that has been established and to enhance it so that more business as well as good refer-

---

352 See Chaper 3.2.1, pp. 50-1.
353 Bhattachary, C. and Bolton, R. 2000, p. 335.
354 Berry, L. 1983, p. 25; Grönroos, C. 1995, p. 253.
355 Grönroos, C. 1990, p. 5.
356 Berry, L . 1995, p. 239; Grönroos, C. 1993, p. 12.
357 Dwyer, F., Schurr, P. and Oh, S. 1987, pp. 15-20.
358 Diller, H. 1995.

ences and favourable word of mouth are generated. Finally, if necessary, relationships which are, for example, not profitable in the long run should be terminated. Similar concepts have been developed by other authors and represent the basis for the management of customer relationships (e.g. sales cycle).[359] The example of Deutsche Bank illustrates that these concepts are used in practice to design a distribution strategy.

Deutsche Bank believes that consistent management of the customer interaction process represents a very crucial element in the execution of a distribution strategy.

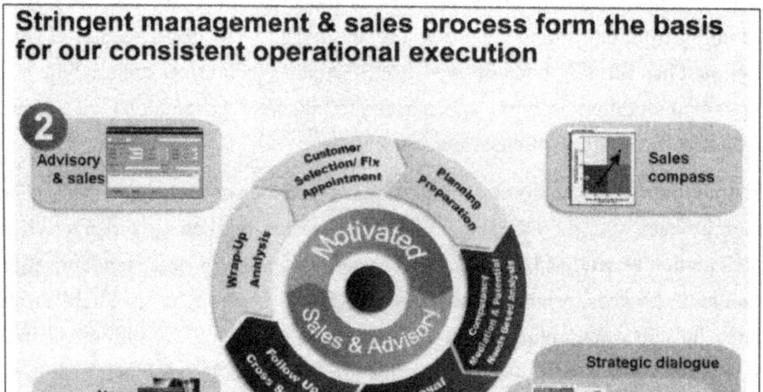

Figure 28: Management and Monitoring of the Sales Cycle at the Deutsche Bank[360]

The figure above shows that, based on a clear understanding of customer needs, the customer interaction process is managed consistently and sales success is clearly monitored.[361]

The **process of creating value** for customers is different between a relationship-oriented perspective and a transaction-oriented perspective. From the traditional, transaction-oriented perspective, value is separately created by a company and embedded in a product, which is distributed to customers. Marketing is concerned with the distribution of this value in a mass market, where the individual consumer is anonymous. Conversely, in relationship marketing, the focus is on value creation rather than on value distribution and on facilitating and supporting a value-creating process. Hereby, the emphasis shifts from a perspective of competition to co-operation between the service provider and the customer. In other words, where in-

---

[359] Belz, C. 1998a, p. 37 and p. 40.
[360] Neske, R. 2003, p. 16.
[361] Neske, R. 2003, p. 16.

teractions and co-operation exist at some level, the customer and the supplier or service provider are not totally isolated from each other and consumption decisions therefore depend, to some extent, on mutual influences in the interactions.

Relationship and Transaction Marketing intend to leverage **different value drivers** within the company. Transaction Marketing is more concerned with attracting new customers (i.e., customer acquisition), while trying to improve their internal operations to render the transaction processes as efficient as possible. Thus, transaction marketing identifies customer acquisition combined with operational efficiency as the primary value drivers. On the other hand, Relationship Marketing – from the outset – is concerned with customer retention, i.e., customer loyalty and increasing of cross-selling ratios. These companies pursue a more service and quality-oriented service strategy and have identified the 'increase of profitability of existing customers' as well as 'extension of customer lifetime' as important value drivers. Stronger growth in sales results from increased cross-selling ratios, positive word of mouth by loyal customers and the willingness of loyal customers to pay a price premium.[362]

Studies have shown that the acquisition of new customers is five times more expensive than the management of existing customer relationships.[363] While the benefits of relationship marketing refer to the economics of customer retention and to the insulation from competition, the benefits for the customers include customisation as well as lower search costs and risk reduction (e.g. financial risks).[364] Dwyer, Schurr and Oh clearly develop criteria to decide under which conditions a relationship or transaction-oriented marketing approach should be pursued. Generally speaking, relationship marketing strategies should only be pursued, if the benefits exceed the costs associated with establishing or maintaining the relationship approach. Using social exchange theory, benefits and costs[365] include both financial as well as non-financial (e.g. convenience) dimensions.[366]

Berry and Parasuraman[367] have identified three elements of customer relationship building: trust supposing fair play, access to service based on two-way communication, and those extras (part of the service offering), that are valued by customers. Others consider customisation, customer intimacy and two-way interactions as the necessary conditions for relationship marketing.[368] In order to establish customer relations, companies need to gather information about

---

362 Henning-Thura, T. and Hansen, U. 2000, p. 7.
363 Berry, L. 1995, p. 237-9; Grönroos, C. 1993, p. 10; Reichheld, F. and Sasser, W. 1990, pp. 105-111.
364 Berry, L. 1995, p. 237-8; Bhattachary, C. and Bolton, R. 2000, p. 329.
365 While benefits refer to any kind of resource, aimed at satisfying one's needs (e.g. love, status, information, money, goods), costs equally go far beyond its economic definition, including also for example negative sentiments.
366 Dwyer, F., Schurr, P. and Oh, S. 1987, pp. 14-5.
367 Berry, L. and Parasuraman, A. 1991, pp. 144-47.
368 Bhattachary, C. and Bolton, R. 2000, pp. 329-31.

their customers and their preferences. For this purpose, a large array of different instruments has to be put in place, e.g. Frequent-Flyer programmes, Lead-user co-operations, customer clubs, customer magazines, service hotlines, database- and direct marketing. In recent years, the Internet has become an additional, important instrument to establish and maintain customer relationships.[369] Some companies have issued standards on customer interaction and periodically measure the extent to which these standards are complied with.[370]

Since distribution, by definition, deals with the management of the exchange process, the pursuit of a transaction vs. relationship-oriented marketing strategy have clear implications for the distribution strategy. While distribution strategies influenced by transaction marketing place emphasis on efficient and optimal service delivery with only limited customer interactions, relationship marketing uses the distribution system to build up the desired customer relationships. From the latter perspective, customer contact is considered to be an ongoing process over the entire buying cycle as well as via different distribution and communication channels.[371] In this perspective, distribution management includes all measures of managing the contact with the customer. The process of developing and enhancing relationships has traditionally been undertaken through face-to-face interaction between the customer and the personnel of a service provider. However, the information revolution - as shown by the example of Nordea hereafter - has created opportunities and/or alternative ways of creating and maintaining relationships.[372]

> **Nordea's** multi-channel distribution strategy is to ensure its customers ubiquitous accessibility to, convenience and simplicity of its services. In a next move, Nordea intends to strengthen its relationship with the customer even further by providing personalised and customised services. Nordea argues that information overflow creates intense competition for customer attention. Therefore, in its financial portal, customers will have the opportunity to enter additional personal information, thereby enabling Nordea to tailor its service offering even more to the individual customer. Thus, Nordea's multi-channel distribution strategy ultimately results in a one-to-one relationship marketing approach.[373]

It is fundamental to understand that relationship marketing is not a purely marketing concept, which can be implemented irrespective of the overall normative, strategic and organisational context. The corporate strategy, in particular, has to be closely aligned with the relationship concept and, in addition, an appropriate organisation structure, a powerful HR policy, incorporating adequate incentive and reward systems for company employees, and a corresponding

[369] Bauer, H., Leach, M. and Grether, M. 1998, p. 2, Belz, C. 1998a, pp. 69-70.
[370] Belz, C. 1998a, p. 70.
[371] Bauer, H., Leach, M. and Grether, M. 1998, p. 6.
[372] Lang, B. and Colgate, M. 2003, p. 29.
[373] TECTEM 2002, p. 87.

management control system have to be created. The following figure provides a summary of the major differences between a relationship and transaction-oriented marketing approach.

	Relationship Marketing	Transaction Marketing
Objective	Establish, maintain, enhance and commercialise customer relationships via a mutual exchange and fulfilment of promises.	Management of the single transaction, instruments of the marketing mix are used to opitmise the transaction.
Paradigm	Individual transactions can no longer be separated, price not sufficient to govern exchange process	Transaction considered as one-off, non-recurring exchange, governed by the price mechanism in efficient markets.
Economic Equation	Cost optimisation always has an impact on service delivery, therefore it is not possible to optimise cost and revenues separately.	Marketing focuses on revenues and internal departments focus on cost efficiency (separate optimisation of revenues and cost)
Source of Value Creation	Value created by the process - facilitate and support a value creating process (process consumption)	Value created by products, which are distributed to customers (outcome consumption)
Marketing Approach	Customer contacts seen as a continuous process, two-way exchange process. High degree of customer integration.	Focus on products, "end of pipe" philosophy; Low degree of customer integration.
Time Horizon	Long-term orientation	Short-Term Orientation
Value Drivers	Increase customer retention and improve cross-selling	Acquisitions of new customer, operational efficiency

Figure 29: Comparison of Relationship and Transaction Marketing[374]

It is important to bear in mind that a company can simultaneously pursue a relationship as well as transaction-oriented marketing strategy depending on the profitability of each customer segment.[375]

[374] Own Illustration.
[375] Berry, L. 1995, p. 239. See also Chapter 4.3, p. 79.

5.3 Conclusion

This chapter has positioned distribution management within the overall context of strategic and marketing management. The following conclusions can be derived from from this chapter:

- **Distribution management** is considered to be as part of general management and is responsible for the planning, organisation, management and controlling of the distribution systems. The objectives and overall orientation of distribution management are derived from the financial and strategic positioning of the company. The following figure illustrates that financial and strategic targets of a company ultimately define the cornerstones of the distribution strategy.

Financial Targets	• Growth (Market Share) vs. Profitability targets
Strategic Positioning	• Step 1: Internal and external analysis of the company • Step 2: Development of a corporate strategy based on clearly identified value drivers • Step 3: Detailing of corporate strategy: identification of most relevant business processes.
Marketing Approach	• Transaction Marketing vs. Relationship Marketing
Distribution	• **Task**: configuration and co-ordination of distribution systems • **Internal Fit**: economy and polity as well as structure and processes • **External Fit**: degree of customer integration and disintegration • **Exchange Environment**: customer's expectation and behaviour • **Nonexchange Environment**: level of uncertainty

Figure 30: Impact of the Financial, Strategic and Marketing Targets on the Distribution System[376]

- While the corporate mission provides overall guidelines for the distribution strategy, the priority of **financial targets,** with a basic distinction between growth vs. value orientation, has clear implications for the distribution strategy.

- **Strategic management** has to define the set of activities which allow the company to differentiate itself from rivals on a sustainable basis. There are generally four important value drivers, which can be addressed by a corporate strategy: customer acquisition and

376 Own Illustration.

customer retention as well as product maintenance and product development. Access-based strategies represent one important source of strategic positioning.

- The **marketing approach** designs customer interaction in the service delivery process more specifically. This interaction process can either be seen as an ongoing management of an exchange process or as a one-off transaction. These two different views on market transactions lead to entirely different marketing concepts. While transaction-oriented marketing focuses on optimising the individual exchange by limiting the degree of customer involvement to a minimum, relationship marketing considers that the customer extracts additional value from the on-going exchange processes itself.

The fundamental basis for the understanding of multi-channel distribution systems has now been established. A comprehensive framework for the analysis of distribution systems has been developed in Chapters three and four. Distribution management can use this framework, where all relevant dimensions of distribution systems are outlined, to fulfil its two fundamental tasks of the configuration and co-ordination of the distribution system. In this chapter, the extent to which the distribution system is determined by the overall management context of the company has also been explained.

This comprehensive framework for the analysis of distribution systems will now be applied to the classification and analysis of different structural types of multi-channel distribution systems.

6. Classification of Multi-Channel Distribution Systems

In this chapter, two fundamentally opposing types of multi-channel distribution systems will be presented and analysed. The relevant analytical dimensions to describe these two different types of multi-channel distribution systems have been derived from the comprehensive framework[377], as developed in Chapters three and four, as well as from the positioning of distribution management within the overall management context of the financial, strategic and marketing objectives.

6.1 Nature, Characteristics and Objectives of Multi-Channel Distribution Systems

Although there is no generally accepted definition of multi-channel distribution systems, it can at least be said that multi-channel distribution refers to the parallel use of multiple distribution channels[378], which do not necessarily need to be conceptually different in terms of product offering, interaction mode, etc..[379] Multi-channel distribution is also known under the term 'multi-channel-marketing', multiple distribution, poly distribution, multi-access system or hypbrid marketing systems.[380] There is no general academic consensus whether multi-channel distribution has to fulfil certain criteria regarding the combination of different distribution channels, i.e., product and pricing policy, communication and marketing of distribution channels, integration of customer-related and internal processes and functions across channels as well as the organisational and legal integration of distribution channels.[381] While some authors emphasise the leveraging of financial synergies resulting from combining internal functions across channels, others evaluate the multi-channel distribution system to the extent the end customer can use different distribution channels during the buying cycle.[382]

In this dissertation, multi-channel distribution systems are defined by the fact that more than one distribution channel exists and these multi-channel distribution systems are actively managed in order to ensure both the internal and external fit of the distribution system within the context of the respective market environment. In addition, the multi-channel distribution system is purposefully set up and co-ordinated in terms of the most important constituent

---

377 See Chapter 4.4, p. 76.
378 Schramm-Klein, H. 2003, p. 16.
379 Schögel, M. 1997, p. 22.
380 Hurth, J. 2001, pp. 463-9; Moriatry, M. and Moran, U. 1990, pp. 146-155; Schögel, M. 1997, p. 22; Schramm-Klein, H. 2003, pp. 16-17; Weinhold-Stünzi, H. 1994, pp. 2-8.
381 Schramm-Klein, H. 2003, p. 17.
382 Friedman, L. and Furey, T. 1999, p. 182; Schramm-Klein, H. 2003, p. 20.

elements of the multiple-channel distribution system, e.g. product and pricing, communication and branding as well as the organisational set-up and processes, remuneration and financial steering. This active and purposeful management of a system of more than one distribution channel represents a clear change from the mere existence of multiple channels, where new channels are merely added to the existing distribution channels[383]. This latter strategy is also known as a multiple channel strategy, where multiple channels are simply made available.[384]

A major criterion for producers in choosing the number of channels is the sales potential delivered by one channel. The decision of whether to use single or multiple channels depends upon the spectrum of target customers, the deliverable sales potential per channel, the bargaining power of the producers and an assessment of the conflict that will be generated between producers and intermediaries.[385] Winkelmann identifies three reasons for having multiple distribution channels: increase in revenues, increase in sales productivity and stronger proximity to customers.[386] McKinsey adds that the degree of channel substitutability (the degree to which customer can switch channels to do their business) also forces financial services companies to provide multiple channels to safeguard their existence in the marketplace.[387] It can thus be concluded, also based on the experience of the benchmarking project, that multichannel distribution systems generally pursue one, two or all of the following three fundamental objectives:

- **Increase in revenues** either through the acquisition of new customers and/or through improved quality and higher interactivity of customer contacts to increase product density per customer (cross-selling).[388]
- **Reduction of distribution costs**, e.g. by shifting low-margin business to more efficient, less labour intensive distribution channels.[389]
- **Safeguarding the financial existence and stability** of the distribution system in an environment of high uncertainty regarding future consumer behaviour by offering a larger number of distribution channels (minimisation of risk by having a diversified portfolio of

---

383 Macchi, M. 2002, p. 118.
384 McKinsey 2000, p. 4.
385 Hardy, K. and Magrath, A. 1988, p. 14; Järvinen, R. 1998, p. 37.
386 Winkelmann, P. 2000, p. 353.
387 McKinsey 2000, p. 4.
388 Gronover, S. 2003, p. 48; Ladwig, F. 2002, p. 32-5; Macchi, M. 2002, p. 118; Stone, M., Hobbs, M. and Khaleeli, M. 2002, pp. 39-52.
389 Studies by Siebel and Forrester have approximated the average cost per customer contact. The external sales organisation has average costs per customer contact of €500 compared to €65 in a Call Center and less than €5 Euro in the Internet. Lammenett, E. and Meister, G. 2003, p. 102. See also Ambros, H. 2001, p. 194; Gronover, S. 2003, p. 48.

distribution channels)[390] With accelerating product life cycles, proliferation of products and fragmentation of customers, multi-channel approaches are often the only way to provide market coverage. Different customers with different market behaviour will seek channels that best serve their needs.[391] The frequency of customer contact as well as the degree of channel substitutability (i.e., the degree to which one channel can easily be replaced by a different channel) are clear indicators for a multi-channel distribution strategy. The more frequent the customer is in contact with the service provider and the higher the degree of channel substitutability, the more important it is to combine multiple distribution channels.[392]

The question as to what extent these fundamental objectives will be addressed depends on the actual structure of the distribution system. Holmsen, Palter, Simon and Weberg[393] distinguish between three forms of multi-channel distribution strategies: co-ordinated channels model, managed competition and competing channel models. Some research has been undertaken on the analysis of the appropriate co-ordination mechanisms for different structural types of multi-channel distribution systems: one can fundamentally distinguish between market-based vs. rule-based co-ordination mechanisms.[394]

Hereafter, multi-channel distribution systems are therefore classified based on the criteria of whether each distribution channel is focussed on a separate customer group or whether all distribution channels actively work together to serve the same customer group. Given these criteria, multi-channel distribution systems can best be described by a continuum, defined by the two extreme points of a focussed vs. co-ordinated multi-channel distribution strategy.[395] The following figure illustrates the analytical grid, which is used to classify multi-channel distribution systems.

---

[390] Easingwood, C. and Coelho, F. 2003, pp. 40-4.
[391] Anderson, E., Day, G. and Rangan, K. 1997, p. 64.
[392] Gronover, S. 2003, p. 27.
[393] Holmsen, C., Palter, R., Simon, P. and Weberg, P. 1998, pp. 83-92.
[394] Cespedes, F. V. and Corey, R. E. 1990, pp. 72-4; Schierenbeck, H. 1999, pp. 44-5; Schögel, M. 1997, pp. 148-157; Schögel, M. and Tomczak, T. 1999, pp. 28-30; Specht, G. 1992, p. 44.
[395] Cespedes, F. V. and Corey, R. E. 1990, pp. 72-4; Gulati, R. and Garino, J. 2000, p. 110; Schierenbeck, H. 1999, pp. 44-5; Schögel, M. 1997, pp. 148-157; Schögel, M. and Tomczak, T. 1999, pp. 28-30; Späth, P. 2000, p. 158-162; Specht, G. 1992, p. 44.

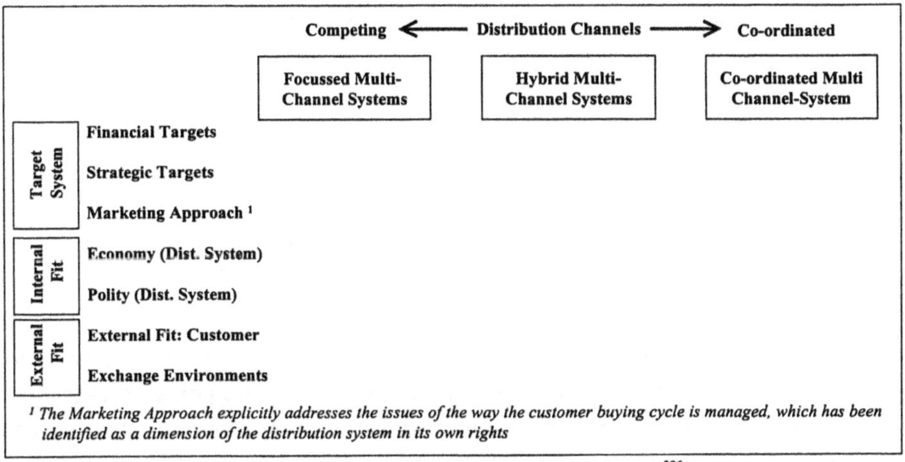

Figure 31: Analytical Grid for the Analysis of Multi-Channel Distribution Systems[396]

This analytical grid has been derived from the comprehensive framework for the analysis of multi-channel distribution systems (internal and external fit) as well as from the overall management context of financial, strategic and marketing objectives (target system). While in focussed distribution systems each distribution system is entirely separate and the distribution system is co-ordinated by market mechanisms, in a co-ordinated multi-channel environment all distribution channels work together closely and rule-based co-ordination mechanisms are applied. A number of variants can be identified between those two extreme points. In reality, hybrid multi-channel distribution systems are far more common than those 'pure' extreme forms. It is more advisable to clearly examine which elements of a distribution system can be shared across channels and which elements need to be separated.[397] Even in a focussed distribution system, at least back-office processes and systems, e.g. IT system, are normally shared across distribution channels due to increasing cost pressure.[398] In addition, in co-ordinated distribution systems the instruments of the marketing mix are used in such a way as to at least partially differentiate the product offering across channels to reduce the risk of cross-channel cannibalisation.

In the first phase of the benchmarking project (survey based on 38 returned questionnaires), more than 80% of the companies indicated that they pursue a co-ordinated multi-channel approach. Most of the companies pursue the strategic objective of strengthening the customer

396 Own Illustration.
397 Gulati, R. and Garino, J. 2000, p. 108.
398 Deutsche Bank has three separate customer segments: Personal Banking, Private Banking and Business Banking. Nevertheless, all three customer segments share the same infrastructure (consolidated platform) and have the same streamlined processes. See Neske, R. 2003, p. 11.

relationship, while the acquisition of customers represents a subordinated priority due to high customer acquisition costs. This prioritisation of strategic objectives was also validated by the telephone interviews.[399]

The following sections describe these two fundamentally opposing structural types of multi-channel distribution system in more detail, based on the analytical dimensions as shown on the previous page.

6.2 Focussed Multi-Channel Distribution System

Focussed Multi-Channel Distribution Systems are generally used to explore new growth opportunities in new markets and/or new customer segments. One of the primary strategic reasons for pursuing a focussed multi-channel strategy is the existence of relatively large, homogenous, clear-cut and different customer segments, which can be targeted by specific and separate distribution channels. Each distribution channel is closely aligned with the respective customer group. It is specialised to service a specific buying pattern and, therefore, requires its own corporate and marketing strategy.[400] Companies can address different target groups with their product offering and react in a flexible manner to market changes. New distribution channels can be added to address new customer segments[401], while the established distribution channels focus on the penetration of the existing customer groups. This distribution system is consistent with a clear, innovation-led strategy, where new innovative distribution concepts can be explored in a separate company and do not destabilise the existing distribution system. For example, regarding the integration or separation of the Internet channel, some companies "believe that the very nature of traditional business - its protectiveness of current customers, its fear of cannibalisation, its general myopia - will smother any Internet initiative"[402]. In fact, the higher entrepreneurial freedom of a focussed distribution strategy can best be illustrated by the establishment of First Direct, a telephone-banking subsidiary of HSBC Bank.

> The management of **First Direct** believed that developing a new operation was simpler and less costly than introducing quality programmes into branches and coming up against existing attitudes, systems and cultures.[403] Within four years, it had acquired 400,000 customers and managed to achieve a cost/income ratio 10 percentage points below the typical average ratios of most tradi-

---

[399] TECTEM 2001, p. 3.
[400] Anderson, E., Day, G. and Rangan, K. 1997, p. 65; Späth, P. 2000, p. 163.
[401] Easingwood, C. and Storey, C. 1996, p. 224.
[402] Gulati, R. and Garino, J. 2000, p. 108. See also Cramer, J. E. 1998, p. 20; McDonald, L. 1999, pp. 88-99.
[403] Hughes, T. 2001, pp. 222-231.

tional banks.[404] Their value proposition is based on four fundamental beliefs: speed, convenience, value for money and quality of service.[405]

Nevertheless, the positive returns from a differentiated product and pricing strategy have to be compared with the additional costs for duplicating certain marketing and distribution functions as well as back-office functions. In other words, the optimal positioning vis-à-vis different customer segments has to be offset against the criterion of cost efficiency.[406] This particularly refers to the duplication of investments in IT systems as well as spending on multiple brands and brand promotion (i.e., communication and marketing), often seen as the major drawback of a focussed multi-channel distribution strategy.[407] These higher costs may seriously question the entire economic rationale of this distribution approach.[408] Therefore, in practice focussed distribution systems share at least the back-office IT systems and support functions.[409]

The following example of the Generali Group in Germany illustrates the implementation of a typically focussed multi-channel distribution strategy. This strategy is primarily justified by the existence of distinctly different market segments.

The **Generali Group in Germany (AMB Group)** pursues a focussed multi-channel distribution strategy. The several tied agents organisations (AM Versicherung, Thuringia, Volksfürsorge) are considered to be the core or pivotal distribution channel. The segment of customers with a high need for advice and demand for an ongoing relationship is serviced by the DVAG, the biggest independent financial distribution company in Germany. More than 25,000 independent financial consultants give advice to their customers and account for 70 % of new business at AM Lebensversicherung. In the broker market, AMB has around 17,500 broker relationships – in future Generali Lloyd will focus particularly on this distribution channel, especially in the life segment. COSMOS, as a direct insurer, is market leader among the pure direct insurers in Germany. Additional growth opportunities will emerge from the co-operation with Otto Versand (a mail-order company) as well as Volkswagen Bank.

The AMB Group in Germany also pursues a bancassurance strategy, as Commerzbank and AMB group can mutually exploit each other's customer basis, which is estimated to amount to 13.5 million (AMB group) vs. 3.6 million (Commerzbank). A separate, joint distribution company was established to promote the business idea of bancassurance. The AMB group pursues aggressive growth targets: by 2005 about 1.5 bn. in life production is to be distributed via the banking channel. Currently, a separate distribution unit is operating and 500 bancassurance centres will be established at Commerzbank branches. Conversely, Commerzbank will open up 250 Banking-Centres at AMB locations to support the distribution of banking products via the insurance network.

---

404 Leichtfuss, R. and Mattern, F. 1996, p. 48.
405 Wheeler, S. and Hirsh, E. 1999, p. 166.
406 Belz, C. 1995, pp. 7-8; Schögel, M. 1997, pp. 40-1.
407 Holmsen, C. Palter, R., Simon, P. and Weberg, P. 1998, p. 91; Schüller, S. and Riedl, M. 2000, p. 831; Stone, M., Hobbs, M. and Khaleeli, M. 2002, p. 48.
408 Wings, H. 1999, p. 234.
409 Krings, M. 2002, pp. 419-20.

Although the AMB Group is a typical example of a focussed multi-channel distribution strategy, this does not apply to the back-end system. In order to ensure operational efficiency, all distribution channels operate on the same IT platform, thus leveraging IT synergies via standardisation. In the distribution strategy, emphasis is placed on a 'product-distribution-customer' fit and, hence, each distribution channel targets a specific customer group – with a clear-cut distinction between purely transaction-oriented channels (e.g. Cosmos) vs. heavily advice-driven, relationship-based distribution channels (e.g. DVAG). The overall emphasis for AMB in its distribution strategy seems to lie on the growth target via customer acquisition. In 2000, the AMB group grew in terms of premium volume by 10.9%, while the market only grew by 3.1%.

It is difficult to generally state whether a company can still pursue a relationship marketing approach in a focussed multi-channel distribution system. Due to constraints in distribution capacity, it is hardly possible for a single distribution channel to actually come up to the marketing postulate to continuously manage the relational exchange with the end customer. Companies, which recognise these capacity constraints, may move from a purely focussed system to a hybrid distribution approach, where the individual distribution channel is supported – at least in specific cases - by a direct Call Centre.[410] Another way of pursuing a relationship marketing approach would also be to limit the number of clients for each channel member, so that active management of this 'relational exchange' is actually possible.[411]

The following example of Allstate shows that one can also combine different structural types of multi-channel distribution strategies. On the corporate level, Allstate pursues a focussed distribution approach, while, on the retail side, Allstate has set up probably one of the most well-known, co-ordinated multi-channel distribution systems in the insurance industry.

On the corporate level, **Allstate** pursues a clearly focussed multi-channel distribution system and distributes its life and P&C products via a multitude of distribution channels ranging from brokers, banks, brokerage house, financial planners, independent agents to its own tied agent sales force. The strategic rationale for this channel policy is the constant quest for growth or expansion of market share in profitable customer segments: "*Reach out to more consumers through a multi-channel, multi-brand, multi-product approach*".

The following figure provides an overview of this distribution approach:

410 In 1998 AXA in Germany began to set up a Call Centre to support its tied agents sales force in a clear effort to reduce cancellation rates.

411 MLP, which traditionally only has one distribution channel of personal advisors, limits the customer basis per advisor to 200 in order to ensure a personal relationship between the advisor and the client.

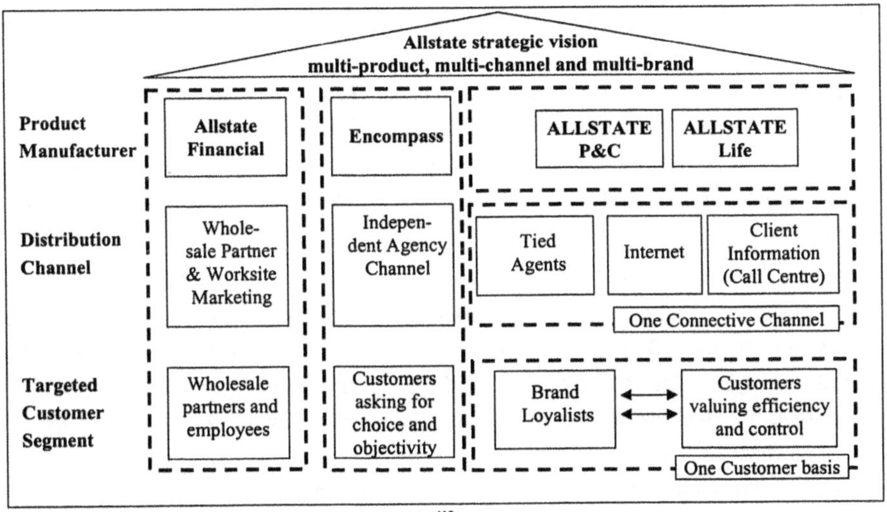

Figure 32: Distribution System of Allstate Inc. (USA)[412]

On a corporate level, the company maintains three separate distribution channels. First, Allstate Financial is used as a platform for distribution of proprietary products via different wholesale partners, e.g. brokers, banks, etc. In the field of worksite marketing, Allstate pursues a joint distribution channel approach. Allstate tied agents identify prospects, may make a first call and then transfer the agent to benefit specialists, who have the status of independent agents. Secondly, Allstate gained access via an acquisition of an independent agency channel and is now the leading provider of motor and homeowner insurance in the USA. This distribution channel has its own brand 'Encompass Insurance' and is managed separately in terms of product offering, branding and positioning vis-à-vis the clients. Allstate knows that via this distribution channel they can get access to customers, asking for choice and objectivity (independent advice), since their proprietary distribution channels could not access these customers. It was thus necessary to set up a different distribution channel for this customer segment. Thirdly, Allstate distributes its own proprietary products under the Allstate brand via a strictly co-ordinated multi-channel approach ('Allstate Good Hands Network'). This distribution is centred around its 12,900 agents in the US and Canada. The tied agents, the Call Centre and the Internet operation work together to leverage channel synergies and cross-selling opportunities. [413]

As illustrated by the previous examples, regarding the **economic structure** of the distribution system, individual distribution channels are either organised as profit centres or as separate distribution companies. Brokers or independent financial advisors fall into this category, as only the insurer has limited control over these distribution channels and, hence, any direct control over this distribution or effort to align this channel with the distribution policy more closely, is, per se, not possible.

---

[412] Own illustration based on TECTEM 2002, pp. 35-6.
[413] TECTEM 2002, pp. 35-6.

This structure increases economic transparency and, thus, accountability for the distribution activities per channel. A focussed multi-channel distribution system is normally characterised by a high degree of system differentiation, e.g. companies may combine direct and indirect channels.[414] Since the management of such a system requires a large range of different managerial skills, it is advisable to manage these distribution channels in different legal entities in order to have clear economic transparency and accountability of the management of each channel.

Regarding the **economic processes**, co-ordination or centralisation of marketing and distribution tasks does not take place – each distribution channel assumes responsibility for its own marketing activities. Overall guidelines or top-down objectives for the management of the distribution system are centrally defined and then given to each distribution channel as financial targets.[415] Co-ordination is limited to the efficient allocation of capital to the different distribution channels. The overall steering of the distribution systems is undertaken via the definition of budget and profitability targets. [416] Based on the control framework developed by Weitz and Jap[417], authoritative (to the extent possible) or contractual control modes are used to manage channel activities.

Given that the distribution channels are entirely separate and independent, the **polity of the distribution system** is marked by an equal distribution of power across the different distribution channels. However, this might change if one distribution channel is particularly successful and, as a result, has easier access to capital, which is necessary for any expansion of the channel. Although power may be evenly distributed across the distribution channels, the relationship between the distribution channels is more characterised by conflicts. Each distribution channel will defend its own position and shelter its customer basis from any cannibalisation attempts.[418] Strong channel conflicts can be limited through clear product-based demarcations, separate branding strategies, as well as clearly defined and separate customer segments.[419] Despite these efforts, there is always some level of perceivable tension among the different distribution channels due to the fear of cannibalisation. However, the experience gained from German online banking clearly shows that the feared cannibalisation effects amount to maximum 10 % and, are, thus, far lower than predicted by the critics.[420]

---

414 Schögel, M. 1997, p. 133.
415 Schögel, M. 1997, p. 162.
416 Schierenbeck, H. 1999, p. 45.
417 Weitz, B. and Jap, S. 1995, p. 307.
418 Frazier, G. 1999, pp. 232-3.
419 Berman, B. 1996, p. 486; Wheeler, S. and Hirsh, E. 1999, p. 149.
420 Wings, H. 1999, p. 233.

The objective of distribution management is to find the optimal 'conflict level', which ensures the highest efficiency of the distribution system.[421] Schögel identifies three reasons for intra-channel conflicts: lack of a clearly perceivable, differentiated product offering across competing distribution channels, unclear split of distribution and marketing tasks among channel members and insufficient evaluation of the persistency of conflicts over time.[422] Intra-channel conflicts (e.g. cannibalisation) constitute the key risk of insufficiently separated multi-channel strategies.[423] This can ultimately undermine the entire distribution system.

In a 'high-velocity' market environment marked by a higher degree of environmental uncertainty and high competition, market-based co-ordination of distribution channels seems to be the best and most effective way.[424] The service provider can easily introduce ('test') new distribution channels in order to react to market changes without destabilising the entire distribution system.[425] However, the company needs to be in command of the entire distribution system with a clear focus on active management of the power relationships in the system. Focussed multi-channel systems, where each channel is clearly specialised in serving a specific buying pattern without much co-ordination, typically exist in fast-changing market environments. However, it is important that the company views these channels as alternative strategic options (rather than individual significant investments). As environments stabilise, the number of distribution channels should be reduced and distribution arrangements should become more substantial.[426]

6.3 Co-ordinated Multi-Channel Distribution Systems

Co-ordinated distribution approaches are often motivated by stricter management of the exchange processes with the customer across the entire lifetime of the relationship with the customer. Therefore, this distribution approach is very much consistent with a service strategy of customer integration or, more broadly, with the concept of relationship marketing. The idea of this distribution approach is to leverage the cross-selling potential of a customer more efficiently or extend the lifetime of the customer relationship.[427] The customer should interact

---

421 Schögel, M. 1997, pp. 92-3.
422 Schögel, M. 1997, pp. 93-5.
423 Schögel, M. 1999, pp. 28-9.
424 Frazier, G. and Antia, K. 1995, p. 323.
425 A good example to support the argument of increased flexibility in a focussed distribution system is First Direct, a telephone-banking subsidiary of HSBC Bank. Developing a new operation was simpler and less costly than introducing quality programmes into branches and coming up against existing attitudes, systems and cultures. See Hughes, T. 2001, pp. 222-3; Li, F. 2002, p. 147.
426 Anderson, E., Day, G. and Rangan, K. 1997, p. 65.
427 Holmsen, C., Palter, R., Simon, P. and Weberg, P. 1998, pp. 83-92.

with the service providers in ways that he has chosen in order to make the service encounter as easy and painless as possible. Locket and Littler provide evidence for the UK banking market that the introduction of direct banking services was not purely an efficiency drive through cost cutting. It also enabled the financial institution to build the kind of personal relationship with customers that too rarely is achieved through the branch and cannot be achieved through ATMs.[428]

In order to ensure a better leverage of customer potentials, distribution channels are combined at different stages of the customer buying cycle[429]. In fact, the key strengths of each distribution channel along the customer buying cycle[430] can be blended into a competitive value proposition for the end customer.[431] Experience from the USA confirms that these distribution strategies actually work in reality.

> In the US, **retail banking** has, for a long time now, combined the traditional cost-intensive branch network with the automated cash terminals not only to reduce distribution costs, but also to strengthen customer relationships. When undertaking standardised banking transactions at the cash machine, the customer receives customised information about his bank accounts, customised advice about investment opportunities and can arrange follow-up meetings with specialised dedicated advisory teams inside the branch or at the call centre. The customer uses the cash machine on average three times a month and the bank intends to leverage this customer frequency for cross-selling purposes. It is believed that the trend of combining automated and personalised distribution channels will continue in the future.[432]

In addition to leveraging the customer basis, resources will be used efficiently in a co-ordinated distribution approach, since marketing resources (e.g. brand, product offering, more targeted customer mailings), customer data, IT infrastructure, and support functions can be shared across distribution channels.[433] This particularly refers to the lead generation programmes. It is often the case that direct channels (e.g. Call Centre or Direct) generate customer leads, which are then followed up by face-to-face channels. Given the increased competition in the financial services industry, it is imperative that face-to-face channels are provided with more customer leads. For example, for US life producers the overall conversion

---

428 Lockett, A. and Littler, D. 1997, p. 792.

429 According to Dwyer, Schurr and Oh relationships evolve through five general phases identified as (1) awareness, (2) exploration, (3) expansion, (4) commitment, and (5) dissolution. Dwyer, R., Schurr, P. and Oh, S. 1987, p. 15. See also Devlin, J. 2001, pp. 641-2.

430 Ladwig points out that the primary objective of multi-channel commerce is to support all phases of the buying cycle via multimedia. Ladwig, F. 2002, p. 18.

431 Cespedes, F. V. and Corey, R. E., 1990, p. 76; Heinrich, D. 2002, p. 113; Rasch, S. Lintner, A. and Mogelvang, S. 2003, p. 116; Tsay, A. and Agrawal, N. 2002, p. 44; Wings, H. 1999, p. 230.

432 Ladwig, F. 2002, pp. 27-.8; Roesler, S. and Dettenbach, J. 2003, pp. 36-38.

433 Easingwood, C. and Storey, C. 1996, p. 224; Wirtz, B. 2002, p. 49; Sohler, M. 2003, pp. 670-1.

rates have dropped dramatically over the past 50 years, now requiring 50% more sales calls to close the same number of sales.[434]

The efficient use of resources also refers to the question of how advisory or sales related (i.e., value creating) activities and administrative tasks are spread across the distribution channels. In fact, surveys explain why German retail banks need to focus more rigorously on efficient customer servicing as well as on strictly profit-oriented customer relationship management. Internal studies have shown that banks spend up to 50% of their time on back-office related activities (i.e non-sales activities). In addition, there is no profit-oriented sales approach: banks spend approximately the same amount of time on high- and low-margin customers, although – as illustrated in the following figure - high-margin customers account for 60% of bank profits.[435]

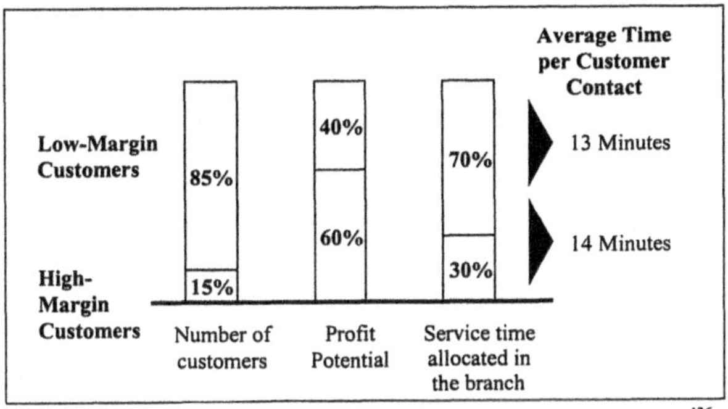

Figure 33: Split of Profit and Service Time in German Retail Banking[436]

Other studies sketch out an even more critical future for German retail banks: If one takes the overall amount of time of all bank staff assigned to advisory services into account, only 5% of the entire working time of bank staff is available to give advice to customers. The example of the Savings Banking in Munich shows that about three quarters of the entire bank staff deals with administrative activities.[437] Therefore, it is not surprising that in retail banking, only 1.3% of all customer contacts are taken up by the retail branch to advise customers.[438] A coordinated multi-channel distribution system could help to shift low-margin business or administrative business to less expensive distribution channels.

---

[434] Insurance Advisory Board, 2003.
[435] Riedl, M. and Schüller, S. 2000, p. 829. See also Pauluhn, B. 1999, p. 135.
[436] McKinsey & Company, taken from Schüller, S. and Riedl, M. 2000, p. 829.
[437] Brunner, W. and Lutz, S. 2001, p. 257.
[438] Ambros, H. 2001, p. 183.

Results recorded by the consulting firm Accenture also confirm that co-ordinated multi-channel distribution in retail banking can increase average customer profitability by 20 to 22%. Thereof, 8 to 10% can be explained by the fact that additional customer information can be used to undertake more targeted cross- and up-selling activities. 10 to 12% of the profitability increase results from a reduction in distribution costs, especially by transferring low-margin transactions to more efficient distribution channels.[439]

The following examples of the Benchmarking Study confirm that financial services providers combine two strategic objectives in their co-ordinated multi-channel distribution strategy: stronger leveraging of the existing customer base (i.e., achieve higher product density per customer), while reducing distribution costs by combining certain resources across all distribution channels.

Allstate[440], a US P&C insurer in the retail market, pursues a co-ordinated multi-access distribution strategy, where customers have equal access to the Internet, the agency as well as the Call Centre. However, the agents still represent the lead channel. Allstate has identified the following value drivers for its multi-access distribution strategy:

- **Growth**: Allstate can access a new market segment, so-called self-directed pragmatists. Compared to its organic growth of 3 to 4 % the new strategy has defined an annual growth target of 8 to 10 %. Thereby, Allstate expects that the new multi-distribution strategy will significantly increase the market shares in motor and homeowners insurance beyond its current market share of 12 %. Furthermore, by 2004, the Internet will contribute 7 to 10 % of total insurance revenues.
- **Cross-Selling Ratio**: The combination of different distribution channels increases product density per customer by higher and more focussed cross-selling activities.
- **Increase Sales Agents Productivity** (increases in agent's time available for sale): Administrative and non-commission generating tasks can be moved away from the agent to the call centre, so that the agents can concentrate on their sales activities.
- **Reduction of commission expenses**: Midterm, Allstate will adjust the commission system of its agents to adjust for the transfer of work from the agents to Allstate.
- **Reduction of operating costs** due to field operations alignment and workforce reduction. Allstate expects to save around 600 million US$ mainly due to realignment of different agency programs (54%), concentration of field support activities (29%) as well as the elimination of outside professional services (17%).

The **Citibank Privatkunden AG** in Germany also pursues a co-ordinated multi-channel strategy in retail banking by offering the following channels to its customers: 300 branches in Germany, mobile customer advisors (to be increased to 120 advisors until year-end 2003), Call Centre, the multifunctional Citibank Express Terminals as well as the Internet. Recently they expanded their distribution channels even further. In May 2002, they opened up their first investment centre for customers requiring special advice; another 13 investment centres were planned to have been opened up in 13 major German cities by the year-end 2003. In February 2003, Citibank also opened up a

---

[439] Macchi, M. 2002, p. 133.
[440] TECTEM, 2002, pp. 42-3.

TV-based channel: Citibank Finance Shop is an advice and sales service, which operates ten times a month in RTL Shop. Citibank believes in a virtuous circle of cost reduction and income generation via a multi-channel strategy:

- **Cost Reduction**: transfer of all non-sales activities to the Call Centre or the Express Terminals. It is the core objective to reduce customer acquisition and follow-up costs to a minimum. For example, between 1998 and 2002 money transfers increased by 75%, while the number of money transfers processed by branch offices halved.
- **Income Generation**: Increase existing customer's profitability as well as extension of customer lifetime value by raising permanently service and advisory standards as well as the level of targeted customer campaigns. Most importantly, the branches have been freed up from all transactional tasks. For example, customer appointments have been transferred from the branches to the Call Centre, so that sales agents can concentrate on their core activity of selling. As a result of a clear transfer of administrative tasks to the Call Centre, advisors in the bank offices spend more than half of their time on advisory services, compared to a market average of around 20%.

Citibank has set up 'bank factories', where the entire administrative tasks for all of the 287 branches are undertaken. These bank factories comprise call centre facilities, interactive voice response services as well as large back- office services for the administrative tasks related to current accounts. An E-Workforce Management, entirely flexible working hours from 7 to 21 h as well as the employment of temporary staff enable the bank to manage their entirely standardised processes in a very efficient manner. Due to this split of tasks, productivity at their branches is about three times higher compared to other 'typical' German branches, as stated by Peter Blatter, member of the board of the German subsidiary of the Citibank Group.[441]

Nordea, a leading financial services group in the Nordic and Baltic Sea Region, also pursues a multi-channel strategy in its retail banking and insurance market: The value proposition is to provide customers with the freedom to decide when, where and how they handle their banking transactions, i.e., convenience and accessibility to the business are fundamental. Nordea management emphasises the importance of ubiquitous accessibility to its services, convenience and simplicity of services, enhancing the value for the customer. Thereby, the customer saves time and money. The Customer has access to a Call Centre, to an Internet-based electronic market base (so-called Solo Market) for undertaking both financial and commercial transactions as well as to a branch network, which represents the lead channel. Thereby, Nordea intends to achieve the following objectives:

- **Reduction of operating costs**[442] by continuous migration of recurring, easy-to-handle transactions to low-cost distribution channels (especially the Solo platform). Nordea has successfully used its pricing policy to migrate customers to less expensive channels. While, over the past three years (1999 to 2001), manual and thus cost-intensive transactions (at the branch offices as well as central booking centres) decreased by about CAGR 16.4% (in absolute terms this repre-

---

441 Buschbeck, P. 2003, pp. 472-476; Peitsmeier, H. 2003, p. 17; TECTEM 2002, pp. 48-9.

442 Nordea was exposed to a serious cost problem. For example, in Finland, while the number of branches fell from about 1,300 in 1990 to about 400 by the end of 2000, the number of transactions steadily increased, amounting to almost 400 million by year-end 2000. At the same time, the number of employees working for Merita Bank (part of the Nordea group) also decreased from about 23,000 in 1990 to below 10,000 in 2000. TECTEM 2002, pp. 84. A similar development is currently taking place in German retail banking. It is believed that by 2010 only 20-30% of transactions and 40-50% of advisory services will be undertaken by the newly designed and positioned bank branches. See Heinrich, D. 2002, p. 115.

sents a reduction by 19 million in three years), the amount of online based transactions (via the Solo platform) increased by about 23 %.

- **Opening up new revenue sources**: The Internet is not only an efficiency driver, but also represents a source of revenues in its own right.
- **Increase of income per customer** (i.e., share of wallet) by stronger cross- and up-selling activities across all distribution channels.

In Switzerland, the **retail banking arm of Credit Suisse**, also allows its clients to choose among four distribution channels: branches, contact centres (Call Centres), cash services and the Internet, while the branch represents the major distribution channel. Customers below CHF 25,000 have been allocated to five customer centres, where a group of customer advisors takes care of their financial needs. The focus of the Credit Suisse distribution strategy is on customer retention and efficient customer servicing. In fact, Credit Suisse deliberately decided against a focussed distribution strategy for the retail sector for three major reasons:

- They identified important **cross/up-selling potentials** (about 40,000 customers are transferred each year from the retail to the affluent sector)
- Realisation of **significant cost reduction potential** due to better use of IT systems and infrastructure (in fact, the operational costs in the retail sector could be cut by about 30%)
- They wanted to avoid socio-political issues of power play and fear of cannibalisation.[443]

On the basis of these best-practice examples, it can be concluded that a multi-channel strategy tries to actively manage the exchange process with the customer in order to optimally leverage the customer potential. The customer is tightly integrated into the service delivery process, where it is necessary and profitable, e.g. in the advisory process, while in other more repetitive tasks, the customer interaction process is limited to the minimum and transferred to direct, less-labour intensive distribution channels.

Despite the benefits of co-ordinated multi-channel distribution systems, these systems are also associated with high complexity and high co-ordination costs, which particularly applies to the necessary IT investments in a common platform as well as to the organisational process and structural re-arrangements to co-ordinate channel activities.[444] The costs of complexity and IT investments must be more than offset by higher cross-selling efficiency, lower customer acquisition costs, and better customer retention.[445] Therefore, only large companies with a substantial product range can finance these investments in the distribution system.[446] In addition, there is the risk of confused customers, who are exposed to conflicting product offerings (e.g. on price, service levels) in different distribution channels,[447] as well as the free-rider

[443] TECTEM 2002, p. 64.

[444] Diepen van, T. 2000, pp. 42-44. See also "The more complex the organisational structure, the more complex the co-ordination of the various processes and activities". Diepen, T. van 2000, p. 42.

[445] Holmsen, C., Palter, R., Simon, P. and Weberg, P. 1998, p. 88.

[446] Easingwood, C. and Coelho, F. 2003, p. 39.

[447] Schramm-Klein, H. 2003, p. 45.

issues, where customers contact high-service channels for advice and purchase their financial services in low-price channels. In all, costs may actually increase and not decrease due to the increased efforts in managing and monitoring the channel system.[448] As a result, in low-margin industries, a co-ordinated distribution system seems to work only for market leaders.[449]

Regarding the **economy of this distribution approach** , a co-ordinated distribution system is normally characterised by a lower degree of system differentiation – a more or less common platform is necessary to implement hierarchy-based co-ordination mechanisms. In order to effectively guarantee co-ordination of all customer activities, the economic processes of the multi-channel distribution systems are characterised by a high degree of centralisation. Normally, each distribution is given distinct sales targets for specific customer segments. A co-ordinated model has a clear hierarchy, defined channel roles and integrated capacity management. To succeed, this highly structured, centralised model requires a carefully designed governance structure and a responsive IT system.[450]

The **polity of the distribution system** is generally characterised by a certain centralisation of power, which generally lies within one distribution channel (so-called lead channel). The examples from Citibank, Nordea or Allstate clearly show that the 'face-to-face' distribution channel typically represents the lead channel. In order to effectively leverage the benefits of a co-ordinated distribution approach, the distribution system requires socio-political processes, which are characterised by co-operation, rather than conflict or opposition.[451] Conflicts among distribution channels need to be actively managed in order to minimise competition among different distribution channels.[452] The example of Allstate illustrates the risks, which result from an unstable socio-political environment.

> For **Allstate**, the unstable polity of the newly designed distribution system turned out to be the biggest execution risk[453], since Allstate obliged the agents to change their legal status from employees to independent agents who are contractually tied to Allstate. The agents remained sceptical about the amount and cross-selling potential of Internet-generated accounts or leads. Furthermore, they consider their new independent status incompatible with the requirement of selling only Allstate-branded products. In their view, the multi-channel distribution strategy should go hand in hand with allowing them to sell non-proprietary products (open architecture).[454] By February 2000, a group of dissident Allstate agents, backed by the National Association of Professional Allstate Agents (NA-PAA), publicly announced to file a federal class-action lawsuit accusing Allstate of unfair labour

---

448 Easingwood, C. and Storey, C. 1996, p. 224; Frazier, G. 1999, pp. 232-3; Macchi, M. 2002, p. 130.

449 Anderson, E., Day, G. and Rangan, K. 1997, p. 67.

450 Holmsen, C. Palter, R., Simon, P. and Weberg, P. 1998, p. 87.

451 Schögel, M. 1997, p. 168.

452 Wheeler, S. and Hirsh, E. 1999, p. 149.

453 Goldmann Sachs conclude in their equity report on Allstate: "the biggest execution risk Allstate faces is not in the development of an Internet and direct platform, but is the degree of organisational acceptance of its agents."

454 Crain's Chicago Business, February 28, 2000.

practices. They demand to be kept as Allstate employees, get paid for overtime and receive the same commissions paid to independent agents. Such a change would burden Allstate with additional expenses of 300 m. US$ per annum, so that the projected savings of 600 m. US$ could not have been met. However, by September 2000, Allstate has succeeded in shifting is entire agency force from a mixed contract system to a 100 % independent agent system. The company expects that the sales force will decrease by 30 % by the year-end 2001.[455]

Regarding the **exchange environment**, co-ordinated multi-channel systems partially absorb this uncertainty of changes in consumer preferences by providing multiple contact points and thereby leave the decision regarding channel choice to the customer. However, since co-ordinated multi-channel distribution systems need to be thoroughly planned and co-ordinated, the distribution system remains more in a steady-state than in a position of continuous adaptation to a changing environment. As a result, any changes in the distribution system can only be implemented in the form of a one-off, fundamental change ('revolutionary adaptation').[456] In this respect, co-ordinated distribution systems require some level of environmental stability.

6.4 Conclusion

Multi-channel distribution systems can be classified based on the two extremes of purely focussed vs. entirely co-ordinated multi-channel distribution systems. In practice, hybrid distribution systems are far more common, whereby each element of the distribution system will be reviewed as to the extent to which this element needs to be particularly maintained for one channel or can be shared across all channels.

Focussed distribution systems intend to pursue price- and product-differentiation across their different customer groups. This requires customer segments to be significantly large and to have very little overlap. The additional costs of maintaining separate distribution channels are justified by the possibility of realising higher margins in the different customer segments. The advantage is that new channels can be added easily without destabilising the remaining distribution system. In a highly uncertain market environment, a number of distribution can be maintained simultaneously to see how the market will develop.

Co-ordinated multi-channel distribution strategies try to leverage the potential of existing customers more strongly. The idea is that the primary sales channel should be freed from all administrative tasks to concentrate primarily on sales activities. In addition, other channels

455 Chicago Daily Herald, November 12, 1999.
456 Schögel, M. 1997, p. 171.

support sales activities throughout the entire buying cycle to ensure utmost customer integration, thereby strengthening the customer relationship even further. Furthermore, by shifting non-sales activities to less labour-intensive and thus more efficient sales channels, distribution costs can also be reduced. In order to ensure that all distribution channels work together effectively, strong, centralised management of all channel activities is necessary. The power relationship needs to be actively managed to ensure utmost co-operation among the channel members. Despite these benefits, this distribution strategy is also associated with a significant increase in complexity and co-ordination requirements, which inevitably causes higher costs (IT costs, management costs, etc.). Therefore, this distribution strategy may only be possible in high-margin industries or in companies of a sufficient size.

The following figure evaluates the two extreme types of multi-channel distribution systems based on an assessment of the primary and secondary value drivers of each distribution strategy.

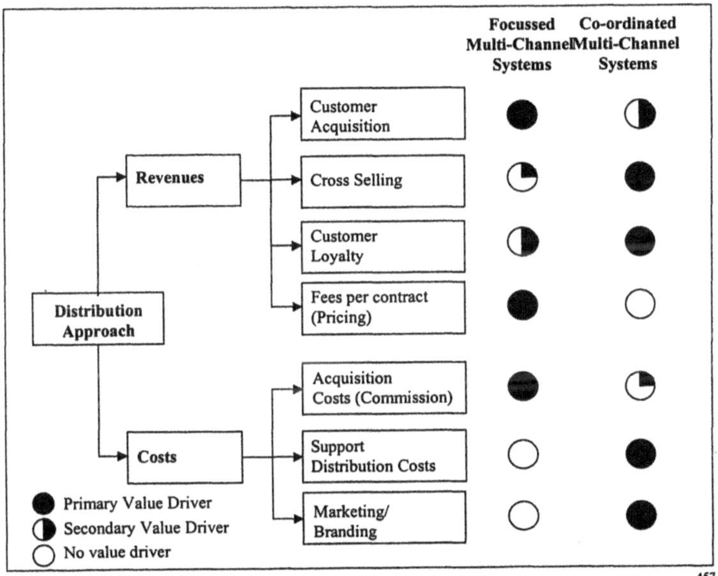

Figure 34: Major Value Drivers for Focussed and Co-ordinated Multi-Channel Systems[457]

Focussed multi-channel systems are normally used to acquire new customers via multiple channels and to generate additional revenues by ensuring an optimal fit between the channel, the product offering and the targeted customer segment. Regarding the cost structure, com-

457 Own Illustration.

mission rates can be aligned with the profitability of each distribution channel, while other marketing and support costs need to be duplicated for each channel. **Co-ordinated multi-channel systems** are focussed on stronger leveraging of existing customer relationships (cross-selling rates and customer loyalty) by an integration of the customer in all value-enhancing processes, whereby distribution costs can be reduced by optimal sharing of resources across channels and by shifting low-margin transactions to low-costs distribution channels. Nevertheless, these distribution systems also incur higher costs as a result of higher complexity and tighter co-ordination and control activities.

Two structurally different multi-channel distribution systems have been described based on an analytical grid, which has been derived from the major conclusions of the previous chapters. The third part of the dissertation will now deal with the description of the operational constituent elements of the two structural types of the distribution system, including the discussion of an effective steering ('control') framework for the day-to-day management of the distribution system.

III. Operational Implementation of Multi-Channel Distribution Strategies

In the second part, the fundamental dimensions of the distribution systems for services were identified and distribution management was embedded in the overall management process. At the end of the second part, this framework was applied to describe two different structural types of multi-channel distributions systems from a top-down perspective. In the third part, the major operational elements of multi-channel distribution systems will be described, as these operational elements represent the basis for the actual management and controlling of any multi-channel distribution system. The third part consists of three chapters. While chapter 7 identifies and analyses those operational elements which determine the external fit with the customer, chapter 8 focuses on the description of the operational elements of the internal fit. The final chapter then rounds off this part and focuses on the important elements regarding the financial steering of these multi-channel distribution systems.

7. External Fit of the Distribution System

First of all, the operational implementation of a multi-channel system needs to ensure the external customer fit. At the beginning of this chapter, the question of branding and communication, which can basically be managed across all channels or separately for each distribution channel, is discussed. Afterwards, the question of customer segmentation is addressed, since distribution channels are only effective if they can target well defined customer segments. The product and pricing decisions will be addressed in the following section as it is a very likely source of conflict. To conclude, particular emphasis will be placed on the change management processes which are necessary to transform the distribution system. Regarding the external fit, this question primarily refers to the issue of how customer behaviour can actually be changed in line with a new distribution strategy, as the entire success of any distribution system ultimately depends on its adoption by the customers.

7.1 Branding and Communication

Given the intangible character of financial services with the high dominance of credence and experience elements, the overall objective of communication policy is to convey trust, solidity and confidence to the consumer. Regular, open and two-way communication is crucial to build trust[458] as well as to reduce customer's uncertainty in the buying process.[459] In this context, brands play an important part in building a trust-based relationship with the consumer.

Branding is an important source of service differentiation and thus an option to increase customer value, since the brand refers to the image, reputation and credibility of the organisation.[460] Meffert defines the brand for services as "imagination of the service itself profoundly embedded within the consumer's psyche... the underlying service is offered to a maximum market over a longer period of time in a uniform design and at constant or improving quality levels".[461] The brand plays two important parts: identification of the origin of the service as well as clear differentiation from competitors. Similarly, Grönroos defines the brand "as an image in the minds of customers".[462]

In retail financial services, the brand is established at organisational level, rather than at product level. However, as a result of a general tendency to break- up the traditional value chain of financial products into product- and customer-oriented units, the question also needs to be answered as to whether products and distribution channels should be branded differently (similar to the retail consumer goods industry). Research has revealed that only progressive customers with vast experience in financial affairs attach specific benefits to the product brand, while all the other customer segments rather focus on the brand of the distribution channel.[463]

In line with the two extremes of multi-channel distribution systems, the branding of the individual distribution channels can also vary between a uniform appearance across all distribution channels and a clear-cut demarcation of each distribution channel:[464]

- **One corporate brand**: all distribution channels and business units are under one brand. The intention is to build up strong and often global brand equity.
- **Umbrella brand**: There is a relatively strong overall brand, which is used to support the individual brands focussing on products or distribution channels. Within this category, the umbrella brand represents a kind of master brand, while a number of sub-brands exists concurrently. These sub-brands are positioned based on the attributes of the master brand, whereby the sub-brand adds new brand attributes to the master brand in return. It is im-

---

[458] Berry, L. 1995, pp. 242-3.
[459] Duncan, T. and Moriarty, S. 1998, p. 5.
[460] Devlin, J. 2001, p. 649; Ennew, C. 1995a, p. 105.
[461] Meffert, H. 2000, p. 312.
[462] Grönroos, C. 2000, p. 287.
[463] Bäte, O., Esser, M. and Esser, M. 2002.
[464] Meffert, H. 2001, p. 141.

portant that the master brand and the sub-brands have complementary and not conflicting brand attributes.[465]

- **Individual brands with no link across all brands**: Focus is on setting up individual brands based on products or distribution channels. This approach is used for the separate branding of distribution channels in the case of focussed multi-channel distribution systems. Another variant of this approach is furtive branding, in which a separate identity is created for a product or distribution channel in order to deliberately disguise the corporate relationships.[466]

In the first phase of the benchmarking project (survey based on 38 returned questionnaires), about 80% of the companies surveyed indicated that they do not differentiate their brand across distribution channels. In the telephone interviews, companies justified this uniform branding policy by the extremely high costs of developing and maintaining separate brands. Despite the absence of different brands across distribution channels, about half of the companies indicated that they do, however, differentiate their communication policy across distribution channels.[467] Similarly, in a survey among 41 Germany companies, especially insurance, banks and retail companies, almost all companies have confirmed that they pursue a single brand strategy across all distribution channels, as customers show a high degree of brand loyalty, but a low degree of loyalty to one specific distribution channel. Nevertheless, about 80% of the companies in the survey differentiate their advertising and communication policy across the distribution channels.[468] These results indicate, that for reasons of marketing efficiencies, companies opt for a uniform brand strategy, while the communication and service policy is adapted to the specific properties of each distribution channel.

A **uniform brand** across all distribution channels can have positive spill-over effects (e.g. increased brand awareness, higher communication efficiency), provided that a combination of the product and channel-specific brands actually leads to a strengthening and not to a dilution of the brand message.[469] The brand message needs to be sufficiently versatile, so that new distribution and communication channels can easily be integrated. Brand versatility needs to be examined as to the question of whether there is a perceived fit between the parent brand and the brand extension. Higher perceived fit results when consumers identify explanatory links that make the brands (of each distribution channel) 'fit together' (coherence of brand usage). The main factors, that affect the formation of these explanatory links, are the dominant brand

---

[465] Kernstock, J., Brockdorff, B. and Schubiger, N. 2002, p. 592.
[466] Ennew, C. 1995a, p. 106.
[467] TECTEM 2001.
[468] Wirtz, B., Schilke, O. and Büttner, T. 2003, p. 48.
[469] Gulati, R. and Garino, J. 2000, p. 113; Krings, M. 2002, p. 419.

associations ('brand attributes' or 'brand images') and the nature of the brand-to-extension relationship. On the one hand, inconsistencies between the dominant parent brand associations and the brand-to-extension relationships may lead to low fit perceptions for a variety of reasons.[470] On the other hand, communication strategies that raise the salience or credibility of explanatory links can increase the number of potential extension categories for a brand. Therefore, effective communication strategies need to focus on the relevant associations that provide an explanatory link between the parent brand and the extension.[471]

The significant marketing costs for launching a new brand also represent an important argument for a 'one brand' strategy. For example, brand awareness, as established in the traditional channels, can be passed on to the Internet channel without incurring significant additional costs.[472] Studies have shown that when the perceived fit between a brand and an extension is high, consumers are likely to evaluate the new product or channel based on their attitudes towards the parent brand.[473] In fact, many incumbent insurance players have pursued this strategy, when they set up the Internet channel, while pure Internet players had to invest a significant amount in establishing the new brand.[474]

One well-known example of a global brand is AXA, which justifies its global branding policy by stronger brand equity and by the overall consistency of its internal and external communication.

> **AXA** pursues a global-brand strategy, since a "single brand means a stronger and more consistent brand. It gives everyone a sense of belonging" explains Claude Brunet, who is responsible for ensuring that all entities of the group use the same brand name.[475]

One consistent brand (or at least brand family) across all distribution channels and communication media represents a fundamental prerequisite for implementing a co-ordinated multi-channel distribution system. If different (sub-)brands are used for one brand family, the sub-brands need to be tightly managed and co-ordinated.[476] It is important that the brand system, which may include more than one brand, is established across all distribution and communication channels in a coherent manner (so-called crossover branding).[477]

Uniform branding also involves some risks, as it requires co-ordinated management of the distribution channels in order to avoid conflicting or contradictory brand messages being sent

---

470 Bridges, S., Keller, K. and Sood, S. 2000, p. 2.
471 Bridges, S., Keller, K. and Sood, S. 2000, p. 4.
472 Schramm-Klein, H. 2003, pp. 84-5.
473 Berghe, Van den L.A.A., Verweire, K. and Roelandt, P. 2001, p. 105; Bridges, S., Keller, K. and Sood, S. 2000, p. 2.
474 Lindstrom, M. 2002, p. 100.
475 Fleming, C. The Wall Street Journal, 28 January 2004.
476 Eierhoff, K. 2002, p. 355.
477 Kernstock, J., Brockdorff, B. and Schubiger, N. 2002, pp. 582-594.

out to the market[478]. This is shown by the example of a German insurer, who ultimately used channel-specific branding to avoid channel conflicts.

During the 1990s, a German insurer decided to set up a direct P&C insurer to target price-sensitive customers for P&C motor insurance products. The company was initially positioned under the company brand with the sub-brand 'direct', but this caused problems with the tied agent organisation, as the company brand was used for two different distribution channels at different price levels in the German market. As a result, the company decided to change the brand and re-launched it under a separate, 'neutral' brand name. The direct insurer incurred high costs to position the new brand.

The launch of a **separate brand** also has some advantages, e.g. to convey a fresh, young image, while maintaining the integrity of the 'established' brand and avoiding any negative spill-over effects.[479] The following examples illustrate that companies sometimes deliberately choose a new brand, if they want to access to a new customer segment, which shows significant differences in terms of customer behaviour compared to their established customers.

Egg is the UK online banking and financial services subsidiary of Britain's biggest insurer, Prudential. Egg grew out of Prudential Banking and was formed in 1996 to provide 'branchless' retail banking services via post and phone. Egg was launched by Prudential in June 1998 in response to changes in technology and the increasing impact of the Internet. Prudential has deliberately decided to position this new business model under a new brand name.[480]

The example of **First Direct**[481], the direct banking division of the highly respected HSBC bank, also shows that sometimes different brands are used where there are differences in segments served or differences in the association of the brands involved.[482]

Credit Suisse started to experiment with a multi-brand strategy when launching the discount broker 'youtrade', addressing customers who would not normally bank with Credit Suisse. In addition, their entire online activities are operated under the brand 'Direct-Net'.[483] However, these separate brands can also lead to confusion both in-house and among customers and the additional marketing costs may not be supported by the underlying business model in the long run.

Research by McKinsey has revealed that different customer segments ask for different brand properties. For customers with a high degree of experience in financial services and a general progressive behaviour, the brand is a status symbol. On the contrary, for more traditional customers with low experience in financial affairs, the brand reflects personal confidence and trust. In this case, the fundamental challenge for brand management lies in the management of customer segment-specific marketing strategies without diluting the overall brand values. Therefore, in certain cases it makes sense to maintain several brands to facilitate access to dif-

---

478 Lindstrom, M. 2002, pp. 241-2.
479 Kernstock, J., Brockdorff, B. and Schubiger, N. 2002, p. 590.
480 Berghe, Van den L.A.A., Verweire, K. and Roelandt, P. 2001, pp. 104-5.
481 See also Chapter 6.2, pp. 106-7.
482 Wright, M. and Howcroft, B. 1995, p. 225.
483 TECTEM 2002, pp. 61-2.

ferent customer segments[484], since multiple brands allow the company to pursue different market strategies depending on the targeted customer segment (price- vs. quality orientation).[485] The examples of AMB of the Generali Group as well as of Allstate illustrate how and why a multi-brand, multi-channel strategy can be implemented given the existence of entirely different and sufficiently large customer segments:

From a corporate perspective, **Allstate** pursues a multi-branding strategy in order to have access to multiple and different market segments: "*Reach out to more customers through a multi-channel, multi-brand, multi-product approach*". Allstate uses the concept of the 'brand family' for three distribution channels. The wholesale channel is served under the brand Allstate Financial. In addition, the worksite marketing is positioned as 'Allstate Financial Workplace Division'; thus the Allstate retail agents can also be used to identify new prospects for this distribution channel. In the retail sector, Allstate – as described – pursues a clearly co-ordinated multi-channel distribution channel, which is positioned under the umbrella brand 'Allstate Good Hands Network'. Allstate – via an acquisition – also has access to the independent agency market, which is considered to be entirely different from their own retail proprietary sales channel and serves a different customer segment. In order to avoid all confusion and to allow a different product and pricing strategy, this distribution channel is positioned under the brand 'Encompass Insurance'.[486]

Similarly, the **AMB group**, the German subsidiary of the Generali group, pursues a multi-branding strategy, as it intends to target entirely different customer segments with a differentiated product and pricing strategy. The distribution via the tied agents organisation is considered as the core or pivotal distribution channel, which is maintained by AM Versicherung, Thuringia, Volksfürsorge as well as Generali Versicherung. In total, around 11,000 full-time professional tied agents as well as around 80,000 part-time agents work in this distribution channel. The segment of customers with a high need for advice and demand for an ongoing relationship is serviced by the DVAG, the biggest independent financial distribution company in Germany. In the broker market, the AMB has around 17,500 broker relationships – in future Generali Lloyd will focus particularly on this distribution channel, especially on the life segment. Finally, COSMOS, as a direct insurer, is a market leader among the pure direct insurers in Germany and has been set up to address the more price-sensitive customers.

Although separate brands enable the financial services providers to target several customer segments with a differentiated product and pricing strategy, which is fully aligned with each customer segment, these advantages are also associated with a number of serious risks.[487]

- No focus of marketing activities possible; marketing activities are spread across different channels without any possible spill-over effects.
- Confusion of customers, when confronted with different brands of one company.

---

[484] Gulati, R. and Garino, J. 2000, p. 113; Meffert, H. and Schleusener, M. 2001, p. 142.
[485] Schramm-Klein, H. 2003, p. 84.
[486] TECTEM 2002, pp. 35-6.
[487] Fischer, T. 1998, p. 100.

- Customer segments served are not large enough to justify the additional marketing costs for a new brand.[488]
- Loss of control: additional complexity in communication and branding policy renders a uniform steering of the distribution system more difficult

Given these risks, an established company should only introduce new brands, if the new offering is significantly different from the traditional offering, a new target customer group is to be leveraged, different shareholders exist and where potential for an integrated branding and communication policy across all distribution channels is low. The risks of a multi-branding strategy are clearly illustrated in the example of Deutsche Bank.

The example of **Deutsche Bank 24** has shown that a multi-brand strategy in the same retail banking segment does not pay off. In fact, the retail customers themselves ask for crossover branding, as customers want to interact with Deutsche Bank 24 via multiple channels, while having the assurance of the brand quality of Deutsche Bank in all of these channels. Therefore, the launch of the newly branded financial portal Moneyshelf is an example of a failed brand introduction. In fact, the financial portal offered services, extremely similar to the existing services of Deutsche Bank 24, and, in addition, to a customer group, which at least overlaps with the clientele of Deutsche Bank 24.[489] Max Blue was introduced, as Deutsche Bank intended to target the self-directed investors, who do not feel attracted by the established Deutsche Bank Account or had migrated from Deutsche Bank to more aggressive e-players, e.g. Consors, during the e-Hype. However, in a subsequent review of the entire brand portfolio, the decision was taken to abandon the additional brands of Moneyshelf and Max Blue and to integrate the differentiated offerings of Deutsche Bank Private Banking, MaxBlue, Deutsche Bank Corporate Banking and Deutsche Bank 24 into one business model for Private and Business Clients under the one uniform brand of Deutsche Bank.[490]

Services with the dominance of intangible, interactive properties represent a much less standardised basis (than goods) for branding, especially since the customer actively participates in the entire service delivery process.[491] Therefore, a brand relationship does not exist in a vacuum, but develops over time in the customer interaction process to the extent that this communication process (in the sense of accessibility) becomes an integral part of the product and the brand.[492] As a consequence, the brand or rather the specific brand relationship develops in a **flow of brand contacts experienced** by the customer[493], so that the ultimate challenge lies in the effective co-ordination of this flow of brand contacts. These brand contacts can be grouped into four categories:[494]

---

488 Fischer, T. 1998, p. 95.
489 Kastenmüller, S. 2002, p. 606.
490 Neske, R. 2003, p. 4.
491 Grönroos, C. 2000, p. 286.
492 See Chapter 4.2, pp. 66-7.
493 Grönroos, C. 2000, p. 287-8.
494 Duncan, T. and Moriarty, S. 1998; Duncan, T. and Moriarty, S. 1997.

- Planned communication messages as a result of a planned marketing communication campaign.
- Product messages relate to information about the firm and its specific product offering.
- Service messages are directly linked to the service interaction and delivery process (the appearance, attitude and behaviour of service employees, the way systems and technology function and the environment - in short, all elements throughout the service delivery process[495]).
- Unplanned communication messages (all other messages, including word of mouth recommendations or the absence of communication)

Planning and managing the service process is at the heart of the branding process. The main task in the branding process is to manage communication and thus the service process in order to provide the customers with positive brand contacts, which ultimately create a favourable brand relationship, whereas the planned marketing communication efforts are only supportive activities in the creation of brand relationships.[496] In fact, planned communication cannot improve the brand if the image is affected by problems in the service delivery process. This idea has given rise to the emergence of the concept of **holistic integrated marketing communication**. The challenge is to manage all sources of messages about the company and its offerings in an integrated and consistent way along the entire interaction process with the customer ("Everything sends a brand message").[497] A marketing-based communication system, trying to avoid sending conflicting and overlapping messages to its various stakeholders, may be divided into three levels: corporate level, marketing and marketing communication.

Furthermore, it is important to understand that communication is interpreted as a two-way process, moving from mass customisation to more personalised, interactive communication.[498] Grönroos describes this two-way communication process as a relationship dialogue, requiring active participation from both sides to develop and maintain a dialogue. The **concept of relationship dialogue** reconciles the two concepts of integrated communication with the more general concept of relationship marketing. In fact, relationships are impossible without two-way communication.[499] In such a situation, the planned communication efforts and the com-

---

[495] See Chapter 4.3, p. 70.
[496] Grönroos, C. 2000, p. 291
[497] A classical example of an insufficiently co-ordinated brand communication process is the interaction of the customer with the tied agent and the call centre. Recommendations of the tied agent may be contradicted by the Call Centre advisor, since the latter does not know what messages the customer has already received from the tied agent when contacted by the customer. See also Diepen, van T. 2000, p. 38; Kastenmüller, S. 2002, pp. 609-10.
[498] Duncan, T. and Moriarty, S. 1998, p. 8; Grönroos, C. 2000, p. 264-284; Schultz, D. 1996, p. 145.
[499] Duncan, T. and Moriarty, S. 1998, p. 3.

munication aspects of the interaction process merge into one single, two-way communication process, i.e., the two processes merge into a **relationship dialogue** with the customer and the supplier or service provider as participants.[500]

A single distribution channel cannot enter into such a relationship dialogue with the customer. In implementing such a relationship dialogue, communication needs to be adapted to the specific channel requirements, as not all communication channels are equally effective in building a trust-based relationship; for example, consumers trust traditional media significantly more than the Internet.[501] The example of Allstate shows how the combination of distribution channels can effectively be used in order to provide the customer with a very integrated communication and branding strategy.

> **Allstate** has positioned its retail distribution channels under the Allstate brand with the marketing slogan '*Allstate Good Hands Network*'. The Allstate brand will in future be associated with additional attributes (Internet competency, direct distribution, etc.). Allstate will market its branded products through exclusive agents, direct mail, through the Client Information Centre (Call Centre) and over the Internet. Customers can choose when, where and how they want to access the company and will always receive the same products and services at uniform price levels across all distribution channels. Edward M. Liddy, Chairman and CEO of Allstate, has implicitly mentioned the value of an integrated communication strategy when formulating the value proposition of the new strategy: "*The value is in the convenience of conducting business anytime, anywhere, any way and in the reassurance of having the local presence of a professional insurance agent available as needed*".[502]

The overall implications for an integrated communication concept or of the insight "Everything sends a brand message" have further been defined by Berry:[503]

- Tracking the buying patterns and overall relationship of existing customers
- Customising services, promotions, and pricing to customers' specific requirements
- Co-ordinating or integrating the delivery of multiple services to the same customer
- Providing two-way communication channels
- Minimising the probability of service errors and breakdowns
- Augmenting core service offerings with value extras
- Personalising service encounters.

A powerful, overall IT system for storing relevant customer data represents a fundamental prerequisite for such an integrated communication approach and is an important competitive

[500] Grönroos, C. 2000, p. 281.
[501] Hess, J. and Huckemann, M. 2002, p. 64; Lindstrom, P. 2002, p. 71.
[502] Allstate Press Release on November 11, 1999.
[503] Berry, L. 1995, p. 238.

advantage.[504] The development of establishing integrated communication has, in fact, been accelerated by the progress of technology. "Technology is creating the intersection of communication and distribution, which is the major thrust of the change in marketing".[505] In this context, CRM tools play an important role, as they are able to consolidate customer data across product lines, define the appropriate communication channels depending on the customer profile and help organise more targeted campaigns. A CRM database also keeps track of customer history, i.e., data is stored when a customer has been contacted. The quality of the customer contacts stored and the overall customer profile represents the primary prerequisite for any sales success and multi-channel distribution strategy.[506] The example of Mediolanum illustrates how information technology can effectively be used to implement a relationship-oriented distribution strategy across different distribution channels.

> **Mediolanum** is a life, mutual fund and direct banking operation, focussed exclusively on the Italian market. Its business model is predicated upon a multi-channel strategy, combining both 'high-tech' channels (telephone, Internet, teletext) and high-touch channels. Technology is leveraged to enable high-volume, low-complexity tasks to be carried out efficiently, while the network of highly qualified agents (about 4,441 at the end of May 2000) concentrate on advisory services. Mediolanum is leveraging technology and media to provide customers with a seamless experience and to empower its agents. At the start of each day, the consultants can download or upload information with the company's central server, updating all transactions undertaken by the customer the previous day. Thereby, the agent can take up any customer contacts via other distribution channels for follow-up discussions with his customers.[507]

In the insurance industry such a consistent combination of all distribution channels in a multi-channel communication centre does not yet exist.[508] Data is very often stored in different systems, so the consulting company Mummert concludes that the current state of customer communication does not have much to do with efficient, targeted development of a profitable customer relationship.[509] This statement also applies to the entire financial services industry. In the past, the industry has implemented 'point solutions' to satisfy the specific needs of a particular point of service/contact, such as ATMs, Internet services and call centers. Each of these point solutions helped create and perpetuate a 'siloed' approach to customer service and automation, with each silo doing similar business processes and requiring individual programming, ongoing maintenance and its own integration effort to communicate with back-office systems. Consequently, the primary challenge is to implement a solution that offers a ubiquitous view on customers. Institutions must synchronise data from these multiple inde-

---

504 Graf, T. and Wetzke, E. 2001, p. 589; Gronover, S. 2003, pp. 147-170; Sohler, M. 2003, p. 672.
505 Schultz, D. 1996, p. 140.
506 Ladwig, F. 2002, pp. 91-93; Sohler, M. 2003, p. 672.
507 Morgan Stanley Dean Witter, June 9, 2000.
508 Lammenett, E. and Meister, G. 2003, p. 102.
509 Leitzmann, C.-J. and Keese, O. 2000, p. 1142.

pendent channels and integrate it with other data sources within the company. This demands an open, layered architecture, based on industry standards and modular building blocks, to weave the disparate strands of data into a strong, coherent pattern of information and knowledge. The implementation of the multi-channel strategy of Allstate illustrates the concrete managerial and financial implication of such a postulate.

For the implementation of their multi-channel distribution strategy, in 2000 and 2001 **Allstate** invested about 250 Million USD in a new front-office System, combining the different distribution channels in order to ensure uniform and consistent operation of the distribution channels vis-à-vis the end customer.

Datawarehouse: a proprietary database storing all information about customer data

- **Universal Customer Profile**: This is a real-time marketing tool, storing prospective information about customers.
- **Intelligent Lead and Campaign Management System**, which is considered by Allstate as the most important element of their eCRM system. In this system, campaigns are designed and lists of potential prospect customers are created, which will be filed to the corresponding agents for further commercial activities. A specific score is computed for each lead, reflecting the propensity of the customer to buy the insurance product.
- **Business Engine Rule:** The business engine enables Allstate to define flexibly the rules for the management and execution of specific commercial campaigns. For example, the Business Engine defines the time (e.g. two days) given to each agent to react to a specific lead generated by the Lead and Campaign Management System. Thereby, Allstate expects to better exploit the synergies between multiple distribution channels, i.e., for example lead generation by direct channel and subsequent follow-up by agency channel. In fact, Allstate can now monitor the interactions between channels, so that agents can no longer just pay lip service to the central idea of multi-channel distribution, but have to live up to it.
- **Front End System**: All relevant information on customer leads or prospects is transferred to the front end system of the relevant agent. Allstate has one uniform front-end system both for the Call Centre as well as the agencies, storing all customer contact details. The agency gets a list of prioritised customer leads, prioritised by the customer's propensity to purchase the relevant insurance product.[510]

To conclude, ensuring the overall coherence of the brand message represents a fundamental challenge in a multi-channel distribution strategy, which goes far beyond the question of individual vs. uniform branding. Given the insight "everything sends a brand message" financial services providers need to set up integrated communication and branding strategies, which require, above all, powerful and uniform front-office systems storing all customer contact information across all channels. Given these financial, organisational and process related challenges, companies may tend to opt for a focussed multi-channel strategy, where each distribu-

[510] TECTEM 2002, pp. 38-9.

tion channel is clearly separated by a different brand and management of the brand flow is limited to one channel.

7.2 Customer Segmentation and Customer Management

Distribution is responsible for the management of the exchange processes with the customers, while adapting the channel systems as far as possible to the specific requirements of the customers. For this purpose, customers need to be grouped into clusters with more or less similar consumption behaviour; these clusters then represent the basis for the design and implementation of the appropriate distribution strategy.[511] As channels evolve to finer or changing customer demands, customer segmentation becomes increasingly important, ultimately leading to segments of one.[512] A number of criteria for effective marketing segmentation have been identified: measurability, accessibility (i.e., access to these customer segments), economic viability of segments as well as actionability (i.e., the degree to which effective marketing programmes can be designed and implemented to attract and serve the segments).[513] The challenge lies in identifying the dimensions along which customer needs and behaviour vary.

A large number of studies suggest that financial services companies still have considerable challenges to overcome in analysing and using customer information and in their ability and desire to segment their customers.[514] This is also supported by the results of the first part of the benchmarking study. In the first phase of the benchmarking project (survey based on 38 returned questionnaires), more than half of the companies indicated that they segment their customers based either on their existing or future value. Less than 20% of companies also segment their customers based on their consumer behaviour.[515] This clearly shows that the implementation of a co-ordinated multi-channel system will also involve significant work on the review of this segmentation process, since customer value is not a good indicator of actual customer behaviour with respect to the use of distribution channels.

It can generally be stated that any distribution strategy first of all needs to rigorously segment customers based on their existing and future profitability. It is only then possible to allocate customers to different distribution channels in order to ensure an optimal fit between customer profitability and the distribution costs of each channel. Therefore, a segmentation based on

---

511 Gronover, S. 2003, p. 72; Hientzsch, R. and Bormann, S. 2003, p. 746; Wheeler, S. and Hirsh, E. 1999, p. 96.
512 Wheeler, S. and Hirsh, E. 1999, p. 10.
513 McKechnie, S. and Harrison, T. 1995, p. 46.
514 Huges, T. 2001, pp. 222-231.
515 Tectem 2002.

customer profitability is a prerequisite for any customer retention decision.[516] This profitability based segmentation approach has been taken forward by the customer lifetime concept.

The use of the **customer lifetime concept**, i.e., the computation of the total value of the customer including the expected future new business, enables the company to evaluate the overall balance of the customer portfolio as well as to prioritise its marketing and distribution activities on those customers with the highest customer potential. The problem for the computation of customer lifetime value is the availability of the raw data. This often requires significant investments in data warehouse applications to put together all necessary data.[517] A study among German retail banks has shown that only 3% use customer lifetime values, since prospective customer data as well as additional data (e.g. cross-selling, cancellation, referral rate) are often not available. The same study also confirmed that the majority of German retail banks (about 53%) use different distribution and communication channels depending on the level of customer profitability. While low-margin customers are dealt with in Call Centres or Self-Service units, high-margin customers are more actively taken care of in specific advisory banking centres.[518]

The conclusion that banks adapt their channel strategy to the customer value was also confirmed by the benchmarking partners. The examples of Nordea, Credit Suisse and Citibank shows that their customer segmentation, based on clear profit indicators, has clearly driven the design of their multi-channel distribution strategy.

> **Nordea** has segmented its customer base into four categories. Each customer segment is linked to clear economic benefits, which are openly disclosed to the customer in letters as well as brochures. The following diagram reflects the segmentation approach of Nordea, which was introduced (or refined) in March 1999:

---

[516] Grönroos, C. 1993, p. 10.
[517] Belz, C. 2002, p. 128; Peter, S. 1997, p. 274.
[518] Wiedmann, K.-P., Buckler, F. and Siemon, N. 2004, pp. 50-1.

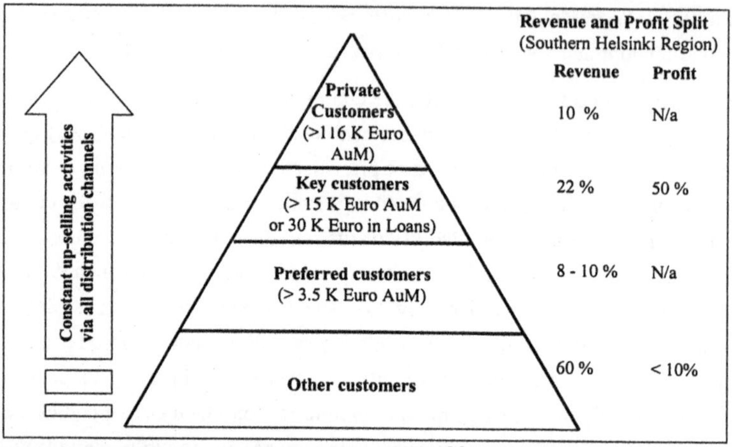

Figure 35: Customer Segmentation Approach of Nordea[519]

In the top segment, the private banking customers all have their personal financial advisors. In addition, they have access to all other direct distribution formats, most notably Call Centre and the Solo services. Furthermore, Nordea focuses on the segment of so-called key customers, who have free-of-charge access to the Internet platform 'Solo' and, as result of this pricing strategy, about 80 % of the key customers use Solo services. They can also contact their bank advisors at the branch office or a dedicated advisory team at the Customer Contact Centre. These bank advisors take care of about 600 to 700 customers and are supposed to contact their customers once or twice a year. The group below represents the preferred customers.

The obvious misfit of revenue and profit contribution, as illustrated by the Southern Helsinki region, clearly underlines the strategic challenge for Nordea. Given the distribution of its customers across the four segments, Nordea had no other option but to move aggressively into low-cost, efficient online and self-service processes. The Solo transaction platform is one way of bringing costs down, which is especially crucial for the mass customer segments with only limited up- or cross-selling potentials.[520]

In retail banking, **Credit Suisse** has divided its customers into four customer segments purely based on the profitability of the customer segment as approximated by the assets under management. This segmentation provided the basis for the customer care programme and their profit-based controlling of sales activities, e.g. customers below CHF 50,000 are exclusively managed via a Call Centre on a rigorous cost basis. Additionally, these customer segments are positioned in a matrix based on customer profitability and customer loyalty, while customer loyalty is measured by the number of customers per cluster having left the bank in the last quarter. The objective then is to bring customer clusters into more profitable segments.[521]

---

[519] TECTEM 2002, p. 88.
[520] TECTEM 2002, pp. 88-9.
[521] TECTEM 2002, pp. 63-4.

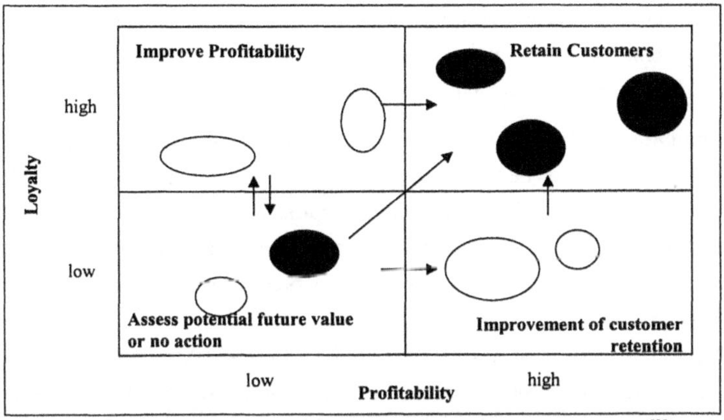

Figure 36: Value-based Marketing and Customer Segmentation at Credit Suisse[522]

At **Citibank Germany**, customer segmentation is based on their current and future 12-month profit potential; longer periods are deliberately not taken into account. Each week, the branches calculate the additional incremental profit potential of their respective customer base over the next twelve months. All distribution channels have access to the profit potential of the customers and take this into consideration when dealing with the customer. At Citibank, customer segmentation is actively used for the management of the customer interaction process. Customers with a high, 12-month customer potential, for example, receive preferential treatment at the Call Centres.[523]

However, the profitability analyses of customer groups represent 'filter criteria', i.e., a criterion to separate profitable from non-profitable customers, but not a basis for defining marketing strategies for specific customer segments.[524] Since co-ordinated multi-channel distribution strategies intend to align channel strategies with the customer behaviour during the different phases of the customer buying cycle, additional segmentation approaches need to be identified to segment customers based on their channel behaviour, preferably during the different phases of the customer buying cycle. Customers can then be grouped into respective segments characterised by similar consumption behaviour and expectations as to how the interaction with the financial services provider should be.

For financial services, customer segmentation can further be classified into four groups: geographic, demographic, socio-economic as well as psychographic methods for customer segmentation. However, one overall customer segmentation criterion does not exist for segmenting customers, since customer behaviour is multi-motivated and multi-determined.[525]

---

522 TECTEM 2002, p. 64.
523 TECTEM 2002, p. 54.
524 Bäte, O., Esser, M. and Staar, S. 2002; Gronover, S. and Bach, V. 2000, p. 15.
525 McKechnie, S. and Harrison, T. 1995, pp. 47-8; Müller, H. 1993, p. 261.

In the next paragraphs, an overview of possible customer segmentation methods is given. The objective of these segmentation approaches is to align the marketing and distribution strategy with the defined customer segments and their respective preferences and behaviour.

- **Geographic segmentation** approaches take into account regional differences, differences between cities and countryside; these distinctions may reflects differences in behaviour and economic wealth. Although this segmentation approach can easily be implemented due to the availability of data for segmentation, it only represents a first basis and is not sufficient on its own for the development of specific marketing strategies for each identified customer segment.[526]
- **Socio-demographic segmentation approaches** are based on variables, such as sex, age or civil status of the customer.[527] Segments, such as 'youth' or 'pensioners', may be formed. These segmentations are easy to implement and provide first indications about possible future consumer behaviour. However, research has shown that socio-demographic twins may in fact have entirely different expectations and needs in the area of financial services.[528]
- **Socio-economic variables** refer to income, professional activities and educational background. Net income is an important indicator for the demand for insurance products. It is important to note that (socio-)demographic attributes can explain the existence of specific insurance needs, but do not explain the individual preferences and consumption behaviour towards the selection of insurance products.[529] For example, although income is an indicator of rising interest in financial advisory services, young people with certain aspiration levels may show the same interest in sophisticated advisory services.[530]

The concept of the **customer life cycle** represents a combination of demographic and socio-economic segmentation criteria, e.g. age, profession and expected future wealth. Typically, customers are further segmented based on the individual phase of their life cycle, which may be divided into the following phases: foundation, set-up, stabilising, reduction phase (children grow up) as well as pensioners. The demand for financial services in the different phases of the customer life cycle varies quite significantly. A number of empirical studies confirm the superiority of this segmentation approach, which can be complemented by additional socio-

---

[526] Gronover, S. and Bach, V. 2000, p. 9; Müller, H. 1993, p. 150.
[527] Heinrich, D. 2002, pp. 106-7.
[528] Bäte, O., Esser, M. and Staar, S. 2002; McKechnie, S. and Harrison, T. 1995, p. 47.
[529] Müller, H. 1993, p. 200.
[530] Bäte, O., Esser, M. and Staar, 2002.

economic variables.[531] The concept is relatively straightforward and is particularly suitable for companies with a very focussed marketing approach (e.g. MLP).[532]

MLP is a typical example for a segmentation of a customer life cycle concept. Since their customers represent a relatively homogeneous group (all their customers have a university degree), MLP can use the indicator of the net annual income of the household, as this indicator correlates very clearly with the different phases of the customer segments. Customers in each segment are served by an advisor of the same age group in order to create multiple links between the customer and the advisor.

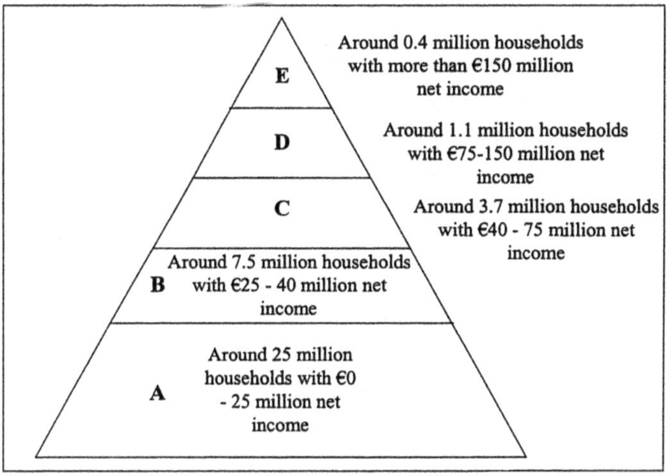

Figure 37: Customer Segmentation Approach of MLP[533]

On the lowest level, the customer may have an extremely low income, but, thanks to their education, have positive economic prospects. On the level B and C, when customers become older, the MLP advisors also have more attractive commission income. On the level E, customers, who earn very high salaries, are taken care of by extremely specialised advisors.[534]

Although demographic and socio-economic segmentation variables are important indicators for identifying customer segments with significant sales potential, they do not explain in what way these customer segments should be addressed. Evidence shows that demographics are poor predictors of customer behaviour, since they are descriptive rather than causal factors. In fact, people with the same demographic characteristics can have markedly different lifestyles, preferences and behaviour.[535]

---

531 McKechnie, S. and Harrison, T. 1995, p. 50; Müller, H. 1993, pp. 151-174.
532 Gronover, S. and Bach, V. 2000, p. 10.
533 Hypovereinsbank 2001, pp. 53-4.
534 Hypovereinsbank 2001, pp. 53-4.
535 McKechnie, S. and Harrison, T. 1995, pp. 47-8.

Consequently, psychographic approaches (e.g. attitudes, opinion, personality structure, value, etc.) are gaining in importance, as they try to explain differences in customer behaviour patterns as well as customer preferences (Why do customers prefer a specific distribution channel, insurer, product, etc. ?). 'Attitudes' represents an important criterion within the psychographical segmentation approaches. Attitudes is a theoretical concept, which is difficult to clearly define and includes aspects, such as general values and opinions about people, companies, products, etc.. This construct is often sub-divided into the following three aspects: (i) affective dimension (emotional attitude towards a product), (ii) cognitive dimension (knowledge about the product) as well as (iii) behavioural dimension (readiness to act).

Psychographic segmentation approaches have led to the emergence of life-style concepts. Based on a multivariate analysis, the **life-style concept** combines various dimensions together to cluster customers according to the way customers behave and organise their lives. This approach is more consistent with the complex process of buying financial services. Although the underlying traits of each life-style remains stable over time (e.g. motives), certain customer behaviour may depend on changes in the environment.[536] Consequently, some experts even believe that, in the insurance and financial services sector, all efforts to segment customers according to clearly defined criteria have failed, as customer awareness and preferences also change overtime.[537] One response to this criticism is to classify customers in underlying fixed segments and sort them into variable market groups on the basis of behaviour in order to tailor distribution channels to particular target groups.[538]

At the beginning of the 1990s, the Allianz Group performed a well-known study together with Sinus based on a fundamental study of about 2,000 people as well as a representative survey of 6,000 people. They came up with 12 overall customer life-style typologies, which can be used to adapt the distribution, communication and service policy more clearly to the needs, expectations and behaviour pattern of each customer segment.[539] The idea to segment customers according to fundamental beliefs and behaviour has now been implemented by some best-practice multi-channel providers, as illustrated by the examples below.

Charles Schwab[540] introduced a customer classification, which is now widely used to describe customer behaviour when buying investment products

- **Self-directed**: these customers are comfortable with managing their own finances and do not feel the need for face-to-face advice. They tend to be price conscious, and therefore natural online customers. This group is believed to account for no more than 15%.

---

536 Müller, H. 1993, p. 259.
537 Lehmann, A. 1998, p. 197-8.
538 Leichtfuss, R. and Mattern, F. 1996, p. 46.
539 Müller, H. 1993, pp. 227-260.
540 Umbau, G. 2003, pp. 20-1.

- **Comfort seekers/Validators**: these customers can be self-directed for portions of their portfolio, but they call for advice and guidance when they need to validate what they have done and when they need to be sure they are still on track. This segment, which represents the biggest group, making up about 50%, is the typical customer segment for a co-ordinated multi-channel distribution strategy.
- **Delegators**: these customers are advice seekers and essentially outsource their financial affairs to an advisor. They are traditionally the domain of financial advisors. The share of this group is believed to decline to 30% by 2004.

Deutsche Bank has developed eight customer segments based on the life stage of the customers, the revenue potential as well as the individual context of the customer (married, single, etc.). These customer segments are grouped into three sections: Private Clients, Private Investors as well as Business Clients with different sales and channel approaches depending on customer potential and customer needs.

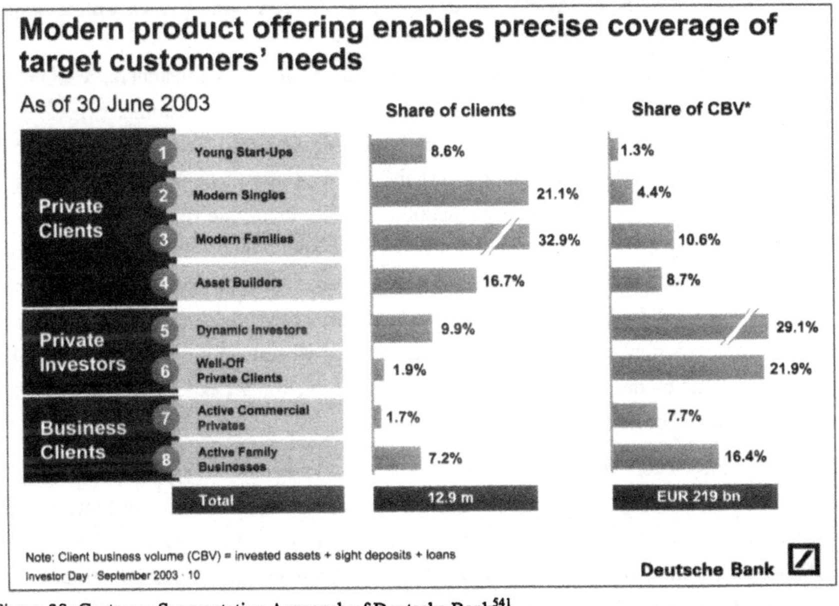

Figure 38: Customer Segmentation Approach of Deutsche Bank[541]

While private clients are served based on standardised products in a multi-channel environment, private banking offers more relationship based advisory services to both private Investors and Business Clients.[542] The example of Deutsche Bank shows how economic and behavioural segmentation variables can be combined and used for the design of an appropriate service and distribution strategy.

---

541 Neske, R. 2003, p. 10.
542 Neske, R. 2003, p. 10.

In 1994, **Allstate** undertook a large-scale study on consumer behaviour for the purchase of P&C products. They concluded that US customers can be classified into three groups based on behavioural and attitudinal criteria.

- The first group comprises so-called **Company Believers**, who feel attracted by the emotional and imaginary aspects of a specific brand.
- The second group refers to the so-called **Relationship Valuers**, appreciating the personal, long-last relationship with their agents or brokers.
- The third group comprises the **Self-directed pragmatists**, who undertake the bulk of their transactions in an efficient way via direct access to the company.

Allstate uses this customer segmentation approach for their marketing campaigns and for the definition of the appropriate service levels and communication channels for each customer group. While the first and second group (Company Believers and Relationships Valuers) account for about 80 % of the customer basis, the self-directed pragmatists account for about 20 % of the customer basis. With its distribution strategy, Allstate specifically targets the first two segments, while also being able to make a sales proposition to the third group.[543]

Based on a standardised conjoint analysis with more than 2,000 consumers, McKinsey has come up with a customer segmentation based on two dimensions: customer experience with financial products as well as their fundamental attitudes. The first dimension, 'customer experience with financial affairs', which can further be refined into three sub-sections 'weak', 'medium' and 'strong', can be captured by a maximum of about 10 questions. While customers in the weak category only have very limited knowledge about financial products, a short-term investment horizon and are averse to risk, customers with high experience with financial products have a solid financial knowledge and actively search for finance information. Since the 'customer experience with financial affairs' primarily captures the existing finance know-how, this dimension has a significant influence on the customer's expectation as to the appropriate product and channel mix.

The second dimension 'attitude' (fundamental beliefs), which can be split into the category of 'conservative' and 'progressive', can be ascertained on the basis of five questions. Conservative behaviour is characterised by a strong orientation to the status quo, compliance with social norms as well as scepticism about any changes. Conversely, progressive attitudes are reflected in emphasising one's own professional career, status symbols or the general wish for self-affirmation. This second dimension 'overall attitude' (fundamental beliefs) does not have a direct impact on financial needs, but rather on the preferred communication and advice processes in the interaction with the financial services provider.[544] It is interesting to note that each customer segment emphasises different aspects in the customer buying cycle.

---

[543] TECTEM 2002, p. 40.
[544] Bäte, O., Esser, M. and Staar, S. 2002.

The following figure sums up this segmentation approach.

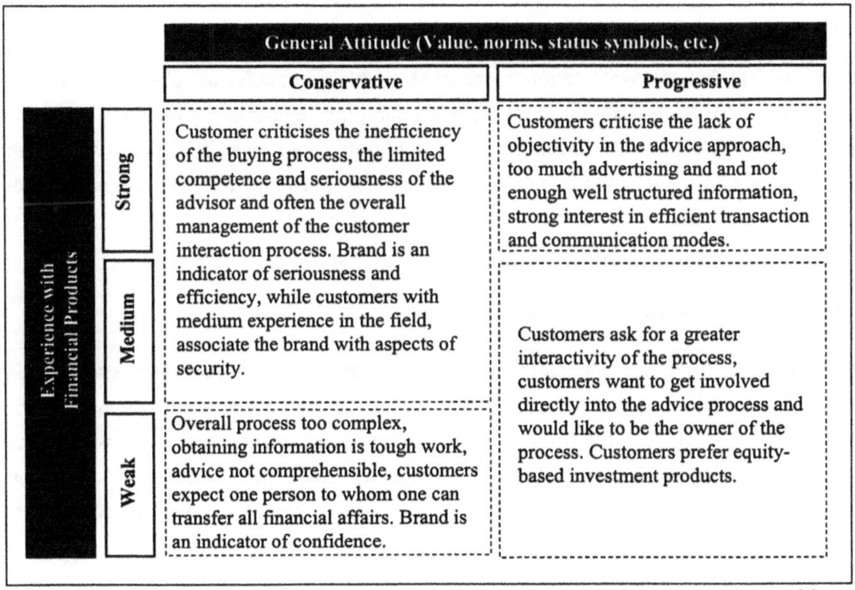

Figure 39: Two-Dimensional Customer Segmentation Approach for Financial Services (McKinsey)[545]

While the customer's experience with financial products determines his overall, specific financial services needs (e.g. unit-linked product vs. classical life insurance contracts), the attitudinal dimension defines how he intends to interact and communicate with the financial services provider, ranging from extreme high demands for interactivity and efficiency to the demand to have one personal advisor taking care of all issues. These six clusters, derived from the two segmentation dimensions, are not evenly distributed in the population. The conservative consumers with very low experience with financial products represent the largest group of 35%, while conservative customers with high experience only represent about 2 % of the total population.

To conclude, the distribution of customer typologies across the customer basis ultimately determines the appropriate distribution strategy. While financial services providers with a large amount of low-margin mass customers are forced to invest in low-cost distribution channels to service these customers as efficiently as possible, other companies may invest in the advisory competence of their tied agents, since they have a significantly smaller, but highly profitable customer base. In other words, while in some cases it may make more sense to optimise

[545] Bäte, O., Esser, M. and Staar, S. 2003.

one existing distribution channel, other customer segments require the improvement and extension of service time in the Call Centre distribution channel rather than a real-time exchange of customer data across all distribution channels.[546]

While profitability-based segmentation approaches enable companies to separate the profitable customers from unprofitable customers, psychographic segmentation methods (e.g. attitudinal concepts) help to cluster customers based on similar customer behaviour, which can be used firstly to analyse whether customers really ask for more than one distribution channel and secondly to design the multi-channel distribution strategy.

7.3 Product Offering and Product Positioning

In order to design effective product strategies in the context of multi-channel strategies, it is important to understand that the type of financial product appears to be a key influential factor for channel selection. In fact, the **level of buyer involvement**, namely the complexity of the product and the perceived risk associated with its purchase, determine the customer's selection of the distribution channel. "Respondents across all segments agreed that the degree of product complexity determines channel choice".[547]

High product complexity leads to an increase in experience and credence factors, so the customer bases his assessment more on other external factors, such as image and reputation as well as on service quality (i.e., relationship quality) itself. For complex products, there is a lack of voluntary need recognition, which means that these services need to be sold rather than bought. On the contrary, the lower the degree of service complexity, the greater the potential role of search qualities in adding value, so advice can be more easily evaluated and appreciated for less complex services. Consumer are more willing to become involved in a search process, so direct distribution channels represent attractive alternatives for the consumer. In addition, the price also becomes more important in less complex situations as consumers are more capable of weighing price against potential benefits.[548]

It can, thus, be concluded that it is necessary to align the product properties with the characteristic of the individual distribution channels. Face-to-face distribution channels seem to be very appropriate for complex, low-involvement products (e.g. life insurance, disability), where it is most important to establish a trust-based relationship with the consumer, who may not have the financial knowledge to fully understand the 'technical' product elements or the

---

[546] Bäte, O., Esser, M. and Staar, S. 2002.
[547] Black, N., Lockett, A., Ennew, C., Winkelhofer, H. and McKechnie, S. 2002, p. 167.
[548] Devlin, J. 2001, p. 654.

interest in getting involved.[549] Conversely, easy to understand products can be sold via direct distribution channels. However, in order to ensure that financial services products can be sold across a variety of channels, it is also important to streamline the product portfolio and reduce the self-made complexity of these financial products. Products, which are sold via multiple channels, should therefore be easy-to-understand, attractive and directly respond to key customer needs. In addition, standardised products allow the customer or the agent to key in all information required by himself and thus allow seamless processing of the contracts, so that efficiency gains can be realised simultaneously.[550]

With reference to Haller's, Belz' and Grönroos' product understanding,[551] it was illustrated that financial services can be broken up into a bundle of services and product features, which are directly or indirectly related to the core product. Customised marketing intends to tailor the product bundles to the extent possible to suit the individual needs of the customer, which can vary by customer segment and distribution channel. The objective is to differentiate the product and thus to add value for the customer. Service differentiation in the case of retail financial services is a function of service features, advice, support as well as corporate branding. Service features include everything which is made available to the consumer in terms of the particular service features and characteristics and the benefits these may bring to consumers. Advice refers to the advice and assistance offered to consumers which relates to the knowledge, skill and expertise of the service provider. Finally, support refers to elements of functional service quality such as attitudes and behaviour of staff, access and flexibility, reliability and trustworthiness, service recovery and tangible factors.[552]

Therefore, the same core product can be made available in different distribution channels, but with varying support and service features. Alternatively, the core competence of different distribution channels can be combined to further enhance the product features, e.g. the convenience and accessibility of direct channels combined with the advice function of the traditional, face-to-face channels. In fact, as illustrated by Grönroos' Service Concept, accessibility is an important product feature, as the access routes available should support the customers' requirements for information, advice, purchase and subsequent servicing. Providing multiple access routes is particularly important in a relationship-oriented sales strategy, where the key task is to maintain the moments of truth process with the customer. It can thus be concluded that co-ordinated multi-channel strategies can significantly enhance the product offering via service differentiation by combining different distribution channels throughout the customer

---

549 Black, N., Lockett, A., Ennew, C., Winkelhofer, H. and McKechnie, S. 2002, pp. 167-8.
550 Schneider, G. 1997, pp. 376-8.
551 See Chapter 4.2, pp. 66-7.
552 Devlin, J. 2001, p. 649.

buying cycle. The distribution strategy itself thereby represents an integral part of the product itself. The following examples show how distribution channels can actually add value to the core product 'retail financial services'.

> At **Citibank Germany**, the call centres focuses on the efficient management of all transactional services, including the arrangement of meetings in the branches. As a result, the branch offices have more time to give advice to the individual customers in face to face meetings.[553]

> **AXA Germany** set up a Call Centre in the 1990s to support the tied agent sales force particularly in the area of standard, recurring transactions or service requests. The idea was to provide 24 h availability to the customer, so overall service quality is increased, which should lower the customer's likelihood to switch insurer. In addition, the tied agents do not need to maintain availability by telephone in their individual offices and they can therefore concentrate entirely on generating new business for the company.

The positioning of products in the different distribution channels is therefore not only a question of product complexity and perceived risk, but also a question of the right combination of the different distribution channels throughout the buying cycle. The following 'product - channel' sums up the process of cross-channel product positioning.

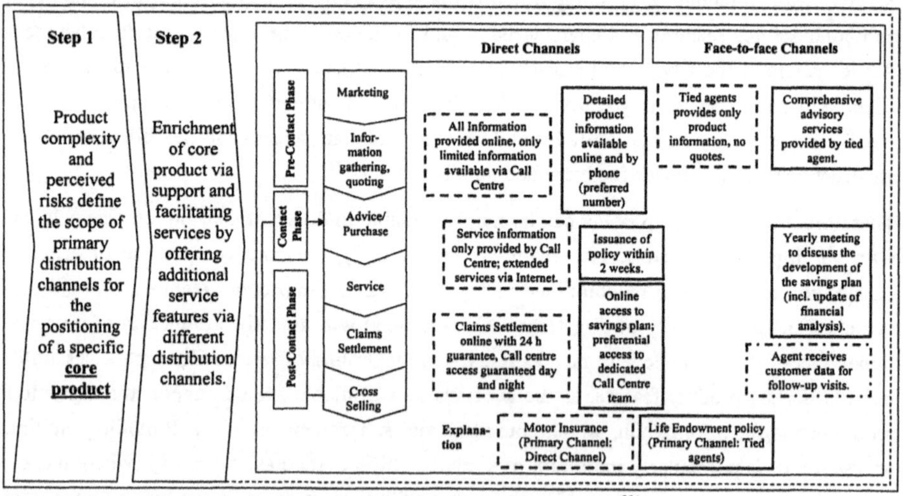

Figure 40: Product Positioning in a Co-ordinated Multi-Channel Environment[554]

Product development and positioning may proceed through two stages. In the first stage, the features of the core product define the potential scope of distribution channels for positioning the product based on the two criteria of product complexity and perceived risks. While a clas-

[553] Buschbeck, P. 2003, p. 473.
[554] Own Illustration.

sical endowment (life) policy is primarily positioned in the face-to-face channels (especially due to the provision of advisory services), a retail motor policy can primarily be sold via more efficient direct channels in a highly competitive distribution environment. Although a product is positioned in terms of its primary distribution channel, in a second step, facilitating or support services can be added in specific phases of the buying cycle. In the figure above, a motor policy, sold primarily via direct channels at competitive prices, may be enriched by support services in the Call Centre (e.g. 24 h access to Call Centre), while the owner of the life policy may have access to his account via the Internet or can contact the Call Centre for specific advisory services. Distribution thereby becomes part of the product 'retail financial services'. Product development needs to take the explicit integration of the different access points into account when designing the product.

In order to make sure that the provision of supplementary services via different distribution channels actually adds value from the customer's point of view, it is necessary to review step 2 of product positioning via multiple channels in more detail in order to find out whether the customer really expects certain facilitating services via a different distribution channel and whether he is willing to pay for these additional services. Here, one can use the so-called 'House of Quality' concept, which has been developed by the literature on quality management, more specifically by the concept of the Quality Function Deployment.[555] The **House of Quality** comprises two levels. On the upper level ('the first house'), customer requirements for specific products are matched with the different phases of the buying cycle in order to identify the most relevant phases of the buying cycle from the customer's point of view. This matching of customer requirements with the phases of the buying cycle is then used for the subsequent analysis. On the second level ('the second house'), one can determine which distribution channels are most relevant to fulfil the customer's requirements. It is important to undertake this analysis separately for each target group. The House of Quality thus proposes a very structured process for prioritising all initiatives related to the introduction or development of new and existing distribution channels by combining both the customer and management perspective.[556]

---

555 Eversheim, W., Eickholt, J. and Müller, M. 1995, pp. 65-75; Nevries, P. and Segbers, K. 2003.
556 Nevries, P. and Segbers, K. 2003.

House of Quality 1: Customer Requirements

	Info. Coll-ection	Advice	Trans-action	After-sales services	Termi-nation	Comp. Adv. (mgt.view point)	Impor- tance (customer view point)
Flexibility	9	5	9	5	5	3	10%
Trust	9	9	9	9	9	1	35%
Indivdual	1	1	1	1	1	5	25%
Long-term orientation	1	5	1	1	1	1	10%
Self-initiative	1	5	1	9	1	5	20%
Overall importance	**8,2**	**11,4**	**8,2**	**15,0**	**7,0**		
In command of the processes	**3**	**4**	**2**	**3**	**2**		
Management Priority (abs.)	**24,6**	**45,6**	**16,4**	**45,0**	**14,0**		
Management Priority (rel.)	**17%**	**31%**	**11%**	**31%**	**10%**		

House of Quality 2: Channel Mix

	Internet	Call Center	Branch	IFA	Broker	Mgt. Priority
Information Collection	9	5	5	5	5	17%
Advice	1	1	5	9	9	31%
Transaction	5	5	5	5	5	11%
After-sales services	1	5	9	9	9	31%
Termination of business relationship	1	1	5	1	5	10%
Management Priority (abs.)	**2,8**	**3,4**	**6,2**	**7,1**	**7,5**	
Management Priority (rel.)	**10%**	**12%**	**23%**	**26%**	**28%**	

Scale 1 (Evaluation of importance)
1: low importance, 5: medium importance; 9: high importance
Skale 2 (competitive advantage. and in command of the process)
1: strong position or strong command of processes vs. 5: weak position or weak command of processes

Figure 41: House of Quality - Basis for the Definition of the Channel Mix to Enhance Product Positioning[557]

In the first part of the analysis, customer requirements for specific financial services need to be identified, based on either existing surveys or on customer self-assessment. These customer requirements, which are limited in the example to five items (ranging from flexibility to self-initiative) then need to be weighed on a scale of 100%; various empirical methods (e.g. conjoint analysis) could be applied to establish how customers prioritise their own requirements. The mapping of customer requirements with the different phases of the buying cycle represents the most crucial task and should be undertaken by experts, who understand both the customer requirements and the different phases of the buying cycle. The relative importance of these customer requirements needs to be assessed for each phase of the buying cycle. In the figure above, high importance is indicated in the matrix of customer requirements and process phases using 9, while 1 represents low importance. In a final step, the customer point of view is complemented by the management view: management is asked to assess to what extent the company fulfils these customer requirements compared to competitors (better (1) or worse (5) than competitors).

557 Illustration based on Nevries, P. and Segbers, K. 2003.

The multiplication of each customer requirement with its relative importance for each process phase, the relative advantage compared to competitors as well as the customer's overall weighing of customer requirements then produce the weighted importance of each phase of the buying cycle. In this scoring approach, it is ensured that process steps with high importance in terms of customer requirements receive higher scores. In addition, the inclusion of the competitive position in the scoring ensures that particularly weak processes (compared to competitors) will also receive some attention. In addition, management needs to assess to what extent the company is in command of the different phases of the buying cycle, ranging from (1) very strong command of the processes to (5) very weak command of the processes. The overall scoring then results from the multiplication of customer requirements by the degree to which the company is in command of the processes. Thereby, the overall score of priorities is computed. In the example, the process phase 'advice' received the highest score, as this process ranks high in importance from the customer's point of view, yet the company only has poor command of this process.

As a result of this first step, the company can now prioritise the different phases of the buying cycle. These findings can be used to establish which distribution and communication channels most effectively address the different phases of the buying cycle. For this purpose, the same methodology is used in the second house of quality. In this case, the different phases of the customer process and their relative importance are matched with the distribution channels. In this mapping, 9 indicates that this channel can strongly support the particular phase of the buying cycle, while 1 indicates relatively low support of a particular phase. These scores are then multiplied by the outcome of the first house of quality (called 'management priority' in the above figure). The final scores then indicate the relative importance of different distribution channels for fulfilling customer needs. In the example, a product which is predominantly positioned via the Internet and the Call Centre, would not be very effective to meet customer requirements. With respect to a specific core product, the House of Quality can therefore indicate which distribution channels can be combined with the primary distribution channel to most effectively enhance product value for the customer. The House of Quality can therefore be considered to complement the 2-step approach for product positioning across distribution channels.

To conclude, product positioning and decisions on distribution channels are strongly interlinked. Distribution is, in fact, part of the financial services product itself. Multi-channel distribution system can therefore significantly enhance value for the customer. However, this requires product positioning to define the optimal 'product-channel' fit in a two-step process the. In a first step, the core product features (product complexity and perceived risks) define the primary distribution channel(s) and only subsequently, in a second step, the value of the product can be enhanced by offering support or facilitating services via different distribution channels throughout the different phases of the buying cycle. The 'House of Quality' approach can be used to identify the right channel mix to position support and facilitating services for a given product and target customer segment.

7.4 Cross-Channel Pricing of Products

As competition has intensified, price competition in retail financial services has become a more important and visible aspect of marketing strategies. In fact, pricing has become a key decision variable in the operational configuration of the distribution system and should be viewed comprehensively to prevent arbitrage across channels and to keep one channel from dominating other important channels.[558]

Research by McKinsey based on interviews with 2,000 customers has revealed that, from the customer's point of view, the price does not play an important criterion as long as it remains within a 10% corridor of the average price. Insurers can only compensate for a 20% price increase by providing a significant bundle of other value-enhancing services.[559] This finding is actually backed up by some other empirical findings regarding consumer evaluation of retail financial services. It is argued that price does not represent a particularly important variable in most people's decision-making process, since a reasonable price is more a prerequisite than a determining factor. Service aspects, such as speed and access, play a more important role.[560] In fact, providing multiple access points to the customer is one way of enhancing service and convenience for the customer and justify different pricing levels in the various distribution channels.[561] This argument shifts the discussion from pricing to customer value. In fact, the reason for employing alternative distribution channels is to offer new forms of value to the customers, e.g. the availability of the service provider 24 hours a day. Ultimately, the channel-specific value proposition should, in the consumers' eyes, be worthy of the price.

From a company perspective, the pricing decision represents a fundamental decision, as it not only determines the degree of internal tension and conflicts between distribution channels (i.e., the implicit fear of internal cannibalisation), but it also has significant consequences for the company's profit, as illustrated by the example of Charles Schwab.

The example of **Charles Schwab** illustrates that pricing is probably the key variable for defining both short-term and long-term economic success. In January 1998, Charles Schwab decided to

---

[558] Wheeler, S. and Hirsh, E. 1999, p. 150.
[559] Bäte, O., Esser, M. and Staar, S. 2002.
[560] Devlin, J. 2001, p. 642.
[561] Ramsay, J. and Smith, M. 1999.

abandon the established differentiated pricing system and to offer one price (i.e., $ 29.95 per trade) to all its customers for Internet trading with full access to all service options. The company was very concerned about the short-term cannibalisation effect, since offline customers would open up online accounts to benefit from the low-cost, high service Internet trading. However, the decision was justified by the fact that, in the long run, the company could not maintain two separate service levels and, in addition, given its higher customer base as a multi-channel provider, Charles Schwab could never compete on price in the pure online segment, with competitors such as E*Trade or DLJdirect.[562]

Once the new uniform price for Internet trading had been implemented, an unexpected high number of customers migrated to the Internet, so pre-tax income declined by 16% in the first quarter 1998 together with a decline in share price by 18%. However, by the end of 1998 the situation changed significantly as a result of a strong increase in the number of overall trades. In fact, online trades outnumbered trades made through its call centres by nearly a 4 to 1 margin, helping Schwab maintain its margins due to the efficiency advantages of the online channel.[563]

To conclude, the pricing decision of Charles Schwab had a fundamental impact on their business model. The uniform pricing for Internet trades for all customers actually gave rise to a significant increase in volume. Price thus represents an important variable for managing customer's channel behaviour, but one needs to pay special attention to the economic effects of the pricing system. It is important to note that Charles Schwab justified the uniform pricing for online quotes for all customers by the expected benefits of the volume effect (i.e., digression of unit costs) as well as by its strategic positioning as a multi-channel provider in the market, so pure online providers were not considered to be direct competitors.

Generally speaking, in a multi-channel environment, a company can choose between three alternative pricing strategies:

- **Pricing autonomy of each distribution channel**: each distribution channel can determine its own pricing depending on channel economics, customer expectation and the competitive environment. Price competition is even warranted and helps to increase the overall efficiency of the distribution system. This pricing system is used in the case of focussed multi-channel distribution systems, where each channel has full autonomy to define its pricing.
- **Overall management of the pricing system**, while allowing for price differences among distribution channels due to different channel economics.
- One **uniform pricing level** across all distribution channels which reflect the average channel economics. The direct distribution channels thereby indirectly subsidise the more labour intensive distribution channels. For a uniform pricing system, it is important to have a very clear understanding of the expected sales volumes by channel, as changes in

[562] Harvard Business School 1999, pp. 14-5.
[563] Harvard Business School 1999a, p. 3.

the channel mix may otherwise cause rising unit distribution costs and uniform prices would then no longer generate the expected profitability margins.

In the first phase of the benchmarking project (survey based on 38 returned questionnaires), about half of the companies indicated that they pursue a differentiated product and pricing strategy, which has primarily been justified by customer expectations and, to a lesser extent, by the avoidance of channel conflicts or by the improvement of profitability.[564] In a survey among 41 German companies, especially insurance companies, banks and retail distribution, only 23% indicated that they used channel-specific pricing to a large extent.[565]

In general, a **uniform pricing model** generates lower financial performance than channel-specific performance, since differences in the price-demand curves[566] as well as different channel costs (sales, transaction and service costs) cannot be leveraged. However, companies often decide in favour of uniform pricing for the sake of transparency and simplicity[567] as well as to avoid all possible political tensions (i.e., conflicts) and cannibalisation among distribution channels. In the context of co-ordinated multi-channel strategies, it is often argued that the low-cost channel could not exist without leveraging the core competence of the high-touch and more cost intensive channels. These arguments are used to justify cross-channel subsidisation.[568] However, it has to be recognised that there are substantial differences in distribution costs among the different distribution channels, as illustrated by the following figure of relative distribution costs among 33 European life insurers, where the cost of the own sales force is indexed at 100%.[569] Insurers, with a clear dominance of the tied agent channel, may opt for a uniform pricing system in order to guarantee the organisational acceptance of the tied agents channel. This is an extremely crucial aspect, as the successful implementation of a co-ordinated multi-channel distribution system, where the core competencies of each distribution channel are combined to optimally leverage the customer potential, requires very tight co-operation across the distribution channels.[570]

---

[564] TECTEM 2001, pp. 3-4.

[565] Wirtz, B., Schilke, O. and Büttner, T. 2003, p. 48.

[566] This refers to the fact that customers accept different price levels, depending on the service properties of each distribution channel.

[567] Hardock, P., Wübker, G. and Lauszus, D. 2003, pp. 100-1.

[568] Schneider, G. 1997, pp. 378-80.

[569] Maynard, P. 2001, p. 33.

[570] A European P&C insurer has given up its separate direct distribution structure, as the numerous conflicts between the tied agents sales force and the direct distribution channel made all co-operations impossible and resulted in a financially unfavourable situation. The tied agents channel granted discounts to their customers to compete with the pricing structure of the direct channel, while the direct channel incurred higher losses, since the purely direct sales volume did not have the critical size to support the cost structure.

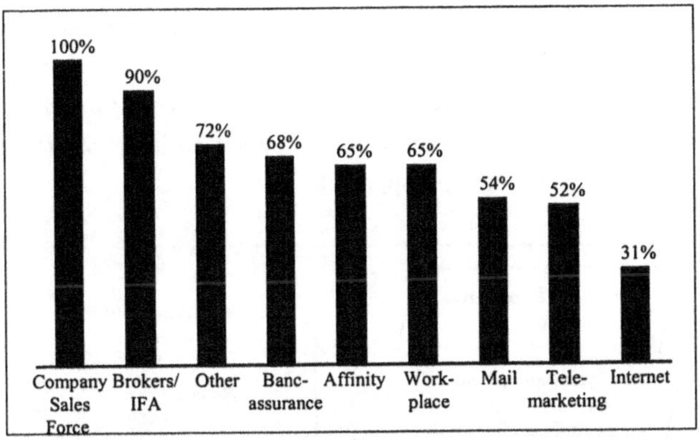

Figure 42: Relative Distribution Costs (Survey among 33 Life Insurers in Europe)[571]

The decision in favour of a uniform pricing system has to be offset against the fact that important profit margins are given up up-front. The example of AXA Germany illustrates that uniform pricing still allows some degree of differentiated pricing, as long as these differences are explained by differences in the underlying products.

> **AXA Germany** opted for a uniform pricing strategy across all channels in order to ensure that all distribution channels work together optimally and keep cannibalisation to a minimum. It is important to note that a uniform pricing strategy does not mean that all products are offered in all distribution channels. A second, low-cost, low-service product line was introduced to cater for the needs of different customer groups. The specific product features of this product line, the lower commission rate as well as reduced insurance cover give rise to a cost advantage and, thus, allow lower pricing; the price difference between the two lines is about 20-40%.[572] This dual product strategy has proved to be quite successful with 180,000 policies in 2004, which is more than twice the volume of the previous year. The low-cost product line supports the growing market segment for price-oriented consumers.[573]

Although **channel-specific pricing systems** make sense from an economic point of view, since difference in channels costs are fully recognised in the product prices, differentiation in prices can seriously destabilise the entire socio-political structure and processes of the distribution system. In case of a channel-specific pricing system, there should, therefore, at least be some degree of product differentiation to avoid channel conflicts and intra-channel cannibalisation. However, product differentiation across channels only works when there are meaningful differences regarding the value chains of products in different distribution channels. As long as a higher price reflects more service and thus higher customer value, customers will be loyal to a particular channel, but if the service is unnecessary or can be obtained at a lower

[571] Maynard, P. 2001, p. 33.
[572] Schmidt-Kasparek, U. 2003.
[573] AXA Germany, 2004, p. 12.

cost, customers will cross to the low-price channel.[574] However, it would be incorrect to argue that by shifting to a perspective of customer value, the entire problem of pricing across channels can be solved. Therefore, a concept of a consistent cross-channel management of pricing needs to be developed, where both the consumer and company/market positions are to be taken into account. The following figure illustrates this approach.

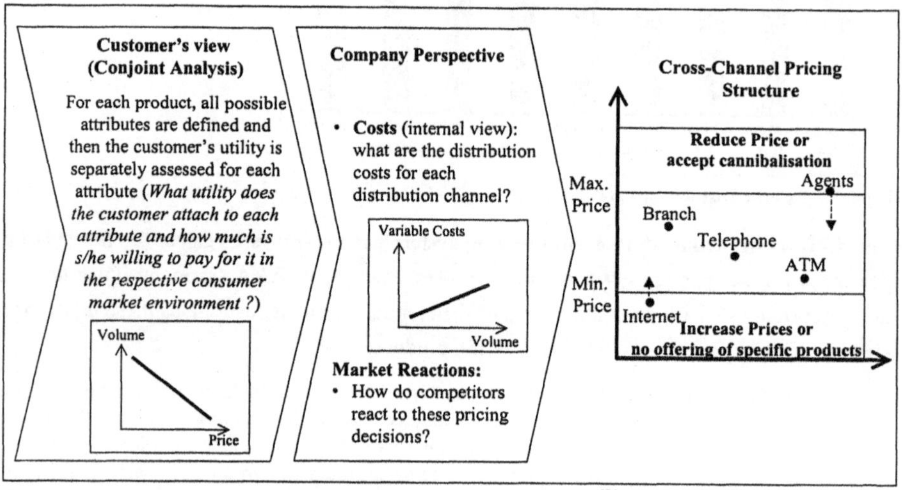

Figure 43: Concept for a Consistent Cross-Channel Management of Pricing[575]

First, the optimal, overall, cross-channel pricing level needs to be assessed based on customer preferences, channel economics as well as on competitors. Customer preferences can best be captured by a conjoint analysis: customers are asked to value different offers regarding his own preferences, while each offer comprises different attributes. The customer's utility determines his willingness to pay for a specific service and can thus be used to derive a price-demand curve. The customer compares the utility of the service with the sum of the monetary and non-monetary sacrifices he is willing to make.

As there are significant differences regarding the distribution costs in the distribution channel, a customer-oriented approach to pricing needs to be complemented by an assessment of the cost structure and the potential market reactions to any pricing decisions. The price-demand curve, derived from the customer preferences, coupled with the cost analysis of each distribution channel, enables the service provider to define the optimal price to maximise its profits in each channel. While in practice the cost advantage resulting from the use of different distri-

574 Anderson, E., Day, G. and Rangan, K. 1997, pp. 64-5.
575 Hardock, P., Wübker, G. and Lauszus, D. 2003, pp. 101-2.

bution channels is often passed to the end customer[576], it would be more appropriate to define the pricing level jointly on the basis of customer utility of each distribution channel and the actual channel costs, so that part of the cost advantages stays with the service provider. Thirdly, competitors and their behaviour need to be taken into account regarding price differentiation across distribution channels and in terms of potential market reactions, when the pricing decision is taken. Once the channel specific prices have been defined, co-ordinated multi-channel distribution systems requires overall management and reconciliation of the pricing structure across the different distribution channels. The pricing structure should reduce cannibalisation effects to a minimum and thus political friction between the distribution channels. One way to manage the pricing system is to define a minimum and maximum price band for all distribution channels.[577]

In the preceding paragraphs, it has been assumed that each financial service can be priced separately. However, given the intangible and interactive nature of financial services, financial services often involve a bundling of different implicit services, which are not separately priced, so a clear-cut profit analysis for each service is extremely difficult. One of the reasons for this is that financial services demand long-term customer relationships, involving several services, so that implicit pricing strategies seem to be more appropriate and allow for cross subsidies. Although financial services providers start to charge specific fees for the use of certain services, most of the products are implicitly priced, e.g. the life insurance premium includes fees for the remuneration of the internal administration costs. Implicit pricing has the general effect that services are over-supplied and consumers over-use some services such as transaction facilities. In fact, the consumer is, in addition, generally unaware of the costs that different patterns of consumption behaviour impose upon banks, so there is no incentive for the customer to use more efficient distribution channels.

Cross-subsidies across distribution channels imply a misallocation of resources because they tend to encourage over-use of under-priced services and under-use of over-priced services. Therefore, there is a general trend towards explicit pricing, where explicit charges aim to recover at least part of the costs incurred by the customers who use the service. If explicit transaction charges were differentiated to reflect the marginal costs of different transaction media, explicit charging would create an environment conducive to the development of the most efficient distribution system in the long run.[578]

It can, thus, be concluded that if multi-channel distribution intends to reduce costs by transferring customers to other distribution channels, the pricing of these services needs to be made

576 Schüller, S. and Riedl, M. 2000, p. 829.
577 Hardock, P., Wübker, G. and Lauszus, D. 2003, pp. 101-2.
578 Ennew, C., Watkins, T. and Wright, M. 1995, pp. 157-163; Harrison, T. 2000, pp. 192-4.

explicit and customers should be given financial incentives to use those distribution channels, which are advantageous to the financial services provider.[579] The example of Nordea and Citibank show that the explicit pricing of services can significantly help to transfer customers to those distribution channels, which exhibit more favourable cost-benefit relationships.

Nordea uses its explicit pricing strategy to migrate customers into less expensive channels for transactions. While, over the past three years, manual transactions decreased by about CAGR 16.4%, the amount of online based transactions increased by about 23%. Nordea has succeeded in reducing the total amount of manual transactions in the past three years by about 14 million transactions in Finland, which involves costs savings in the branch offices of at least € 6 million.

The pricing of the Internet service represents a good example of explicit pricing. Nordea's management emphasises the fact that Internet services constitute real value-enhancing services for the customer and, therefore, should be priced separately. Consequently, customers using the Solo services for e-payments pay about 1.70 Euro per month, while the branch charges about 3.40 Euro for processing manual payment transactions. In addition, preferred customer segments (for example the preferred or key customers) receive discounts of 100% and 50 % respectively for a multitude of additional services (e.g. access to Solo market place). The entire price system, with its differentation based on channels and customer segments, is actively published in the sales brochures.[580]

Citibank Germany has introduced an explicit pricing strategy for brokerage services with a differentiation based on transaction volumes and distribution channels in order to move the customer to more low-cost distribution channels. In addition, they started to credit some money to the customer's accounts for transfers entered via the Internet.[581]

Transaction Fees	Internet & Brokerage	Citi Sales Direct	Branches
Minimum Fee	€ 9,71	€ 30,68	€ 30,68
< 50 K Euro	0,20%	0,30%	0,40%
50 K Euro < x < 100 K Euro	0,10%	0,25%	0,35%
> 100 K Euro	0,05%	0,20%	0,30%

Figure 44: Explicit Pricing System for Brokerage Services at Citibank Germany[582]

To conclude, pricing is an important variable for the configuration of the distribution channels. While a uniform pricing system may foster cross-channel interaction and the referral of customer leads, the customer's utility of different distribution channels as well as differences in channel costs are not leveraged at all. Therefore, multi-channel distribution systems may need to move towards introducing at least some level of price differentiation across channels (within certain price bands) to maintain and increase distribution margins. In addition, some services could be priced explicitly. Customers understand that in a multi-channel environment prices can differ as long as they reflect differences in service levels. However, there are cer-

579 Llewellyn, D. and Drake, L. 1995.
580 TECTEM 2002, p. 82 and 88.
581 TECTEM 2002, p. 55.
582 TECTEM 2002, p. 55.

tainly limits to fully exploiting the different channel economics within a co-ordinated multi-channel system. Therefore, in cases where the customer segments are significantly large, a differentiated pricing strategy could be implemented in the context of a focussed distribution system. In this case, the channel-specific distribution margins should be superior to the benefits of a co-ordinated distribution approach.

7.5 Change Management - Transformation of Customer Behaviour

While, in the previous sections, important variables for the operational configuration of the multi-channel distribution system have been discussed, the behavioural aspects of channel usage by customers has, so far, been left out. However, the question is crucial as to how actual customer behaviour can be fully aligned with the multi-channel distribution system. This specifically refers to the question of how customers could be encouraged to use alternative, new distribution channels.

Distribution channels are rigid and stable because of powerful, persistent inertia. Changes in distribution channels come slowly, partly because the inherent complexity of the many links, which connect value-adding functions in a channel, obscure the need for change. However, the pressure for change will ultimately overcome this inertia in distribution channels.[583] As a result of the persistent inertia in distribution channels, transformation processes require time. The importance of time in change programmes is also confirmed by the example of Nordea, believing that their long-term 'step-by-step' approach in introducing and replacing distribution channels is one of the key reasons for the success of their multi-channel distribution system.

> **Nordea's** successful multi-channel distribution strategy is clearly marked by a long-standing history of adding new distribution channels, while gradually moving out of existing distribution channels by lowering the attractiveness of these distribution channels. This is, for example, the case with the slightly old-fashioned ATMs, which, compared to the new PC-based terminals 'Solo', are relatively out of date and user unfriendly.

[583] Anderson, E., Day, G. and Rangan, K. 1997, p. 59; Hughes, T. 2001, pp. 222-231.

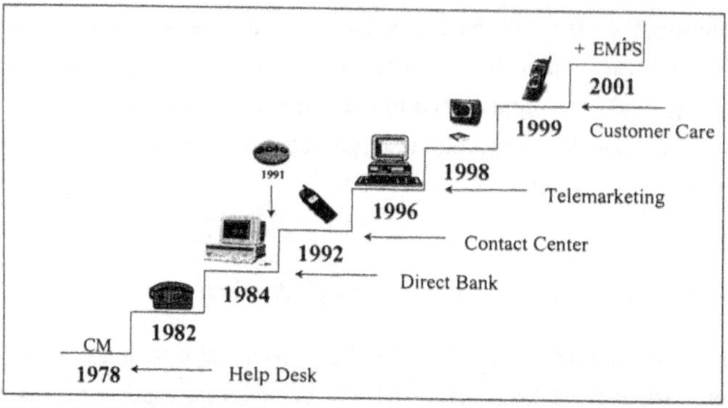

Figure 45: Nordea - Gradual Introduction of New Distribution Device and Channels[584]

Nordea considers this 'incremental' evolution of the multi-channel distribution strategy as one of the key success factor in order to avoid abrupt socio-political disturbances or other issues.[585]

The example of Nordea shows that the information revolution has created opportunities and/or alternative ways of creating and maintaining relationships, but only if there is no 'technology gap' between the service provider and the customer. The fundamental challenge for the financial services provider is to overcome any potential 'technology' gap with respect to the end customer.[586] In the banking industry, the introduction of the ATM has shown that, although customers appreciate the introduction of a new distribution channel, they rarely give up using existing distribution channels. However, from a company's point of view the introduction of new channels is very often based on the assumption that traditional channels can significantly be sized down.[587] Active customer migration is thus crucial to ensure that new channels are fully adopted and used, so existing, cost-intensive distribution channels can ultimately be closed down. One way, as illustrated by the example of Nordea, is to demonstrate to the customer the convenience and ease-of-use of the new and alternative distribution channels, while the level of service is deliberately reduced for other channels.

Past experience regarding the introduction of new distribution channels has shown that customers often fear that they cannot correctly perform the tasks required to obtain a service from a machine and have fears of personal or financial losses. Consequently, one of the key lessons learnt has been that customers first need to be educated.[588] The example of Charles Schwab

---

584 TECTEM 2002, p. 84.
585 TECTEM 2002, p. 84.
586 Lang, B. and Colgate, M. 2003, pp. 29-37.
587 Howes, G. 1999, p. 27. The same applies to Internet Banking. Internet is only a cheap distribution channel if customers can be persuaded to use it and other channels (such as branches) can be scaled back. In many cases, this has not materialised as most banks need to maintain their existing channels while developing the Internet as a new channel at substantial cost. See Li, F. 2002, p. 153.
588 Leblanc, G. 1990, p. 37.

shows that customer education plays a pivotal role in familiarising customers with new communication and transaction media.

> **Charles Schwab** actively managed the integration of the Internet in its service offering. The company held over 10,000 seminars in the year 2000 to familiarise its customers with the Carles Schwab website.[589] The experience gained in these courses was then used in order to develop an online course on Capital Market Investments, where new and potential customers can receive information about the online services of Charles Schwab. "We needed to take some of the fear out of investing and making people feel capable", explained J. Lecuyer, Vice-President of Charles Schwab. "Training its customers represents a strategic objective, since we believe that well trained customers are more loyal and open for other services".[590]

In order to ensure that new automated distribution channels unfold their true cost saving potential, it is important to understand why customers are reluctant to migrate to these new distribution channels. Among the factors that contribute to the poor adoption rate are channel design issues, customers perceptions and attitudes as well as implementation issues. An empirical study undertaken at a large US retail bank, which intended to migrate customers to call centres, has evaluated different methods to migrate customers to a call centre. It has been revealed that more customised, high-touch methods, e.g. a guided demonstration of the new distribution channels by staff members and an immediate attempt by the customer to use the new service media, were significantly more effective than more anonymous communication initiatives. However, the study also showed that communication options to support the migration process differ across customer segments, primarily depending on the age of the customer. In addition, the process of migrating customers to the new distribution channels is a long-term communication process, otherwise customers revert back to their 'established' consumption habits. Therefore, promotions and financial incentives need to be established to promote sustainable change in channel usage.[591] As shown in the previous section, pricing is one of the most important variables to promote change.

Experience at Citibank Germany has also shown that active change management has to take place in order to effectively reach the objectives of the multi-channel distribution strategy: customers need to be familiarised with the alternative or newly positioned distribution channels. New distribution channels can only be introduced with marketing pull factors (pricing and convenience for the customers) and not only exclusively with IT push factors. Ultimately, customers change only if the barrier for change is relatively low. Customers moving into the desired direction need to be rewarded, while misbehaviour should be penalised over time.[592]

---

589 Lindstrom, M. 2002, p. 23.
590 Aldrich (2000) www.learningcircuits.org/jul2000/aldrich.html (1.5.2001).
591 Sarel, D. and Marmorstein, H. 2002, pp. 254-266.
592 TECTEM 2002, p. 55.

Citibank Germany has established a very comprehensive change programme and identified the following success factors for its customer-focussed change programme:

- It is important to set up attractive, intuitive systems with top-quality user interfaces and good performance so that the customer has an interest in using them
- Staff members need to provide a good introduction regarding the use of new distribution channels or communication devices, explaining things several times if necessary.
- The bank staff need to accept customer behaviour and should convey this impression in a credible manner.
- The non-users of new distribution channels need to be clearly identified in the IT systems, so that staff members can contact them actively (even several times, if necessary).
- The price system should encourage customers to change their behaviour. For example, Citibank introduced a handling charge of 1.50 Euro per transfer handed over the counter to branch staff, while the customer received a credit of 0,15 for each transfer undertaken via the Internet.[593]

The result of the Citibank change programme with respect to the introduction of the Citibank Express Terminals, which were introduced to reduce the amount of manual transactions, was striking. After its introduction in February 2000, about 70% of money transfers were already performed in so-called 'unmanned' distribution channels by the end of 2001.

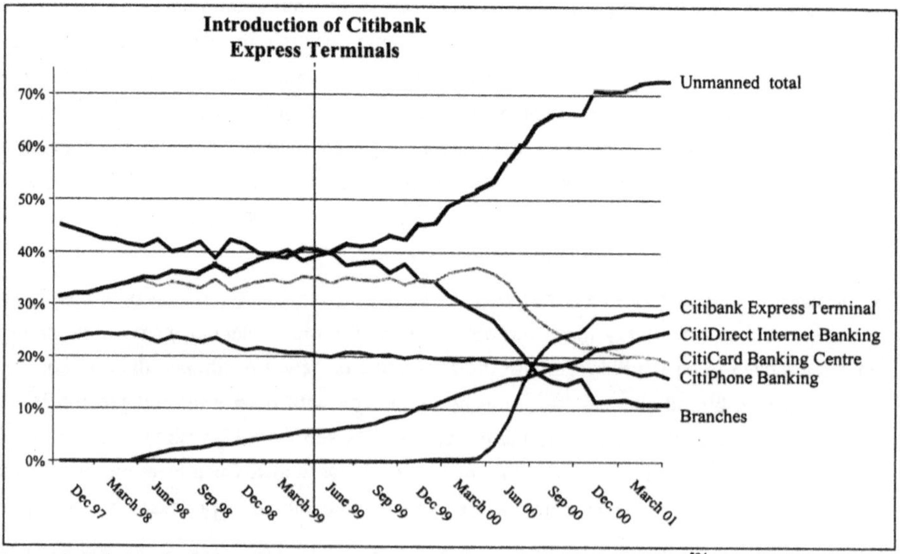

Figure 46: Citibank - Evolution of Money Transfers via Different Distribution Channels[594]

[593] TECTEM 2002, p. 55.
[594] TECTEM 2002, p. 56.

To conclude, it is important to note that transformation of customer behaviour takes time and needs to be accompanied by a comprehensive change management programme. While pricing, higher convenience or other marketing push-factors will certainly help to change customer behaviour, active customer training by the established distribution channels - preferably in the form of face-to-face demonstrations - is an important prerequisite in order to reduce the technology gap between the customer and the new distribution channels.

7.6 Conclusion

The objective of the chapter was to identify and analyse some of the key variables for the configuration of the multi-channel distribution system with respect to the end customer (external fit of the distribution system). The following main conclusions can be taken from this chapter:

- The **branding and communication process:** co-ordinated multi-channel providers opt for a uniform branding concept, where all distribution channels contribute to the strengthening of the brand and substantial marketing costs for separate brands can be avoided. Separate brands should only be used in case of significantly large and clearly separated customer segments. However, in retail financial services, branding and communication is not only limited to planned external communication, but involves all messages the service providers sends out via its distribution channels to the end customer. This insight that 'everything sends a brand message' calls for an integrated communication strategy. The more distribution channels are in place, the more complex the implementation of such an integrated communication strategy, which requires powerful IT front-ends to store and exchange all relevant customer data. Companies may, therefore, want to opt for a focussed multi-channel system, where the complexity of managing the communication process can be limited to the individual distribution channel, which is separated by its own brand and branding (i.e., communication) policy.
- **Customer Segmentation**: In order to fully align the distribution system with customer behaviour, customers need to be grouped into clusters with similar channel behaviour. Profitability-based segmentation approaches are important for identifying the most important profit pools, but do not indicate channel behaviour and, therefore, need to be complemented by additional segmentation techniques. However, the traditional socio-demographic or socio-economic approaches are not helpful to predict channel behaviour. More hybrid customer segmentation approaches (psychographic segmentation or life style segmentation concepts), e.g. based on the customer's knowledge of financial affairs and general attitudes, are more effective and used by best-practice companies.
- The **product offering** is one of the key variables for defining the structure of the multi-channel system. More complex products, where the customers perceive high risks, are

more appropriate for personal, face-to-face distribution channels, while less complex products are suitable for direct distribution channels. However, the question of product positioning goes far beyond this aspect of the core product, since financial services involve a large number of support and facilitating services. Product positioning in a multi-channel environment, therefore, is a two step process. First, the scope of primary distribution channels for each (core) product needs to be established (e.g. based on product complexity and perceived risks). Secondly, it has to be seen whether the value of the product can further be enhanced if additional distribution channels are added at specific stages of the customer buying cycle to offer support or facilitating services. The decision to add distribution channels (and thereby increase overall distribution costs) is driven by the question of whether from the customer's point of view the value of the service can further be enhanced by providing additional distribution channels to the customer. The 'House of Quality' provides a powerful instrument to assess this.

- The correct **pricing of the product** represents a crucial prerequisite for the socio-political stability of the distribution system, but also for the economic attractiveness of the distribution strategy. Although a uniform pricing system seems the easier solution to avoid all channel conflicts and ensure active channel interaction, this is certainly not the best alternative from a purely economic point of view due to large differences in distribution costs across channels. In fact, pricing should take customer preferences for different distribution channels, channel costs as well as competitors' behaviour into account. One solution for a co-ordinated multi-channel system is to fix a price brand, where price differences among the distribution channels are justified by clear differences in the service offering of each channel. In case of clearly different distribution margins across channels and the existence of different customer segments, a focussed distribution system is more appropriate. Furthermore, **explicit pricing** for at least some services may be one way of implementing some level of price differentiation in a co-ordinated multi-channel system. Explicit pricing represents an effective way of migrating customers to more efficient, low-cost distribution channels.

Although these operational elements are crucial for the management of the distribution system, they may not pave the way for the actual **transformation of the distribution system**. Distribution systems exhibit a high level of inertia and stability, so the transformation of customers takes time. Customers need to be actively familiarised (i.e., trained) in order to reduce the technology gap between the customers and the new distribution media. Successful companies do not go for an abrupt change in their distributions system, but seem to prefer a step-by-step approach, which is complemented by some hard marketing push-factors, especially financial incentives, to change customer behaviour or other convenience factors.

8. Internal Fit of the Distribution System

While, in the preceding chapter, the operational constituent elements of the external fit of the distribution system have been identified and analysed, i.e., the fit between the customer, intermediary and the financial services provider, focus now shifts towards the internal perspective. Firstly, this refers to the organisational design of a multi-channel distribution strategy. Secondly, the chapter deals with the question of whether customers are 'owned' by a specific distribution channel or by the distribution organisation as a whole and, linked to the question of customer ownership, how the different sales channels are remunerated in such a way that cross-channel interaction actually takes place (in the case of co-ordinated multi-channel organisation). Finally, similar to the preceding chapter, an analysis of how the internal transformation of a distribution system, i.e., behaviour of the channel members, can actively be managed, will follow.

8.1 Internal Structure and Processes of Multi-Channel Distribution Systems

The need to integrate new distribution channels into the existing organisation (e.g. marketing, sales, finance, etc.) also makes multi-channel distribution an important organisational problem.[595] However, compared to the management of ongoing channel relationships, the organisation of distribution channels has received less attention.[596] In order to ensure the overall economic, but most importantly socio-political stability and continuity of the distribution channel it is important to align the organisational structure of the management of the distribution system with the fundamental strategic objectives.

In the case of a **focussed distribution system,** the organisational arrangement is clear: each distribution channel is managed separately, preferably in an independent legal entity or as an autonomous profit centre. Sourcing and marketing functions are performed by each distribution channel. A timely reaction to market changes thanks to more direct decision-making as well as easier financial control and charging systems represent the most important advantages of such a decentralised organisational approach.[597]

Co-ordinated multi-channel distribution strategies require that processes across distribution channels be clearly co-ordinated, thereby ensuring that no inconsistencies exist in the supply of information to the customers as well as in the information shared about the customers. Consequently, distribution channels have to be organised in such a way that they are

---

[595] Ladwig, F. 2002, pp. 76-82.
[596] Frazier, G. 1999, p. 232.
[597] Ladwig, F. 2002, p. 80.

clearly customer-centric and no longer product-oriented: the various channels and processes behind these channels have to be properly co-ordinated to guarantee uniformity in services delivery.[598] Fundamental marketing processes, such as customer segmentation, the design of marketing plans as well the management of all marketing activities, need to be properly managed across all distribution channels. A dedicated unit for channel steering (so-called channel manager or channel management)[599] allows the implementation of a uniform and consistent communication and service strategy vis-à-vis the end customer, easier control of all channel activities and also avoids parallel marketing activities. A central unit for channel management is also crucial for the implementation of holistic, integrated communication strategies: cross-functional management teams monitor messages for strategic consistency and ensure the overall coherence of all brand contacts.[600] In a survey among 41 German companies, especially insurance, banks and retail, more than three quarters of the companies interviewed indicated that a dedicated organisational unit had been created to co-ordinate the distribution channels.[601] The example of John Hancock Financial Services illustrates the importance of such a central unit for channel management.

> Peter Mawn, senior vice president of **John Hancock Financial Services**, identified the organisational arrangement as the most important success factor of Hancock's co-ordinated multi-channel distribution strategy: "Perhaps the most important [thing] is that our retail sales operations - including channel management, product development and process development - reports to one individual who oversees all the channels and communicates a common vision. Channel managers meet regularly to work toward the shared goal of allowing issues and cross-channel opportunities to be explored and capitalised on".[602]

Despite the obvious benefits of a more centralised organisational structure, this question needs to be very thoroughly investigated in the context of the specific organisation. While integrated teams can better align strategic objectives, find and exploit and share knowledge, separate teams for each distribution channel can focus more sharply, innovate more freely and avoid contaminating one business model with another.[603] The following figure summarises the organisational set-ups for a focussed and co-ordinated multi-channel strategy.

598 Diepen, T. v. 2000, p. 47.
599 Ladwig, F. 2002, pp. 79-83; Macchi, M. 2002, p. 131.
600 Duncan, T. and Moriarty, S. 1998, pp. 8-10.
601 Wirtz, B., Schilke, O. and Büttner, T. 2004, p. 47.
602 Mawn, P. 2001, p. 10. Word in bracket [...] inserted by the author to read the quote more easily.
603 Gulati, R. and Garino, J. 2000, p. 113.

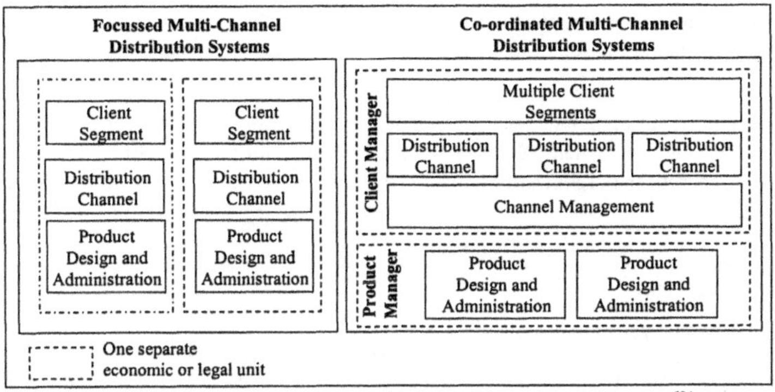

Figure 47: Organisational Structures for Multi-Channel Distribution Systems[604]

In the case of a co-ordinated multi-channel structure, front-office 'distribution' (also known as Client management) is focussed on customer relationship management, while the back-office is organised by product categories with a clear focus on product development and product administration. Although product groups and distribution channels are no longer one organisational unit, the tasks and responsibilities of different units must remain connected to maintain an effective overall business process. Product groups still need a connection with the market, although they are no longer directly responsible for distribution channel and customer related issues. This demands a number of important changes. Rules need to be defined as to how to deal with certain transversal processes, e.g. the processing of customer complaints. When redefining the processes, it is important to decide which of the three dimensions of customers, distribution channels and products should be leading in developing and organising processes.[605] The separation of product manufacturing and customer servicing also has implications for measuring financial profitability.[606]

The implementation of such a bifurcation of the organisation into a customer relationship unit as well as a product (i.e., operations) unit can best be illustrated by the organisational structure of AXA Germany. In fact, AXA Germany decided to implement an organisational structure where the fundamental activities of product design, processing and administration (so-called operations management) are separated from the management of the client relationship via multiple channels (so-called client management).

AXA Germany has defined its organisational structure along the classical value chain. On the one hand, the Operations Manager is responsible for product development, product processing and product administration. On the other hand, the Client Manager deals with customer management

[604] Own illustration based on Diepen, T. 2000.
[605] Diepen, T. v. 2000, p. 55.
[606] Diepen, T. 2000, p. 52; See Chapter 9.1, pp. 172-3.

across all distribution channels. It is responsible for the distribution of the proprietary products and receives a comprehensive, market-based compensation for its distribution activities from the Operations Manager.

After this new organisational structure had been put in place, the organisational and process-related interfaces between the Product and Client Manager were established in order to ensure communication and co-ordination across the organisation units. These interfaces are illustrated in the figure below:

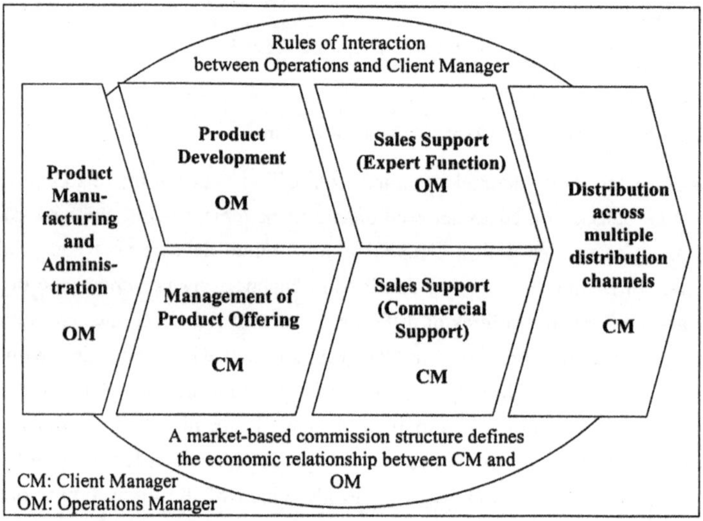

Figure 48: AXA Germany: Interfaces between the Product Manufacturer and the Distributor[607]

The Client Manager has set up its own unit for managing the processes of introducing new products in the various distribution channels (so-called Management of Product Offering). Thereby, it has been ensured that client management can establish a very structured process between the various Product Providers and the channels distributing these new products via multiple distribution channels. This unit thus allows an overall management of all the commercial activities across all product groups. In addition, the process of sales support has clearly been defined. While the Client Management provides first-level sales support, the Operation Management takes care of the more product specific questions and provides more detailed support for the distribution channels.

The **ERGO Group (Germany)**, aggregating the retail insurance activities of the Munich Re Group, offers a similar example of a separation of product manufacturing and distribution. In 1996, Vorsorge Leben, belonging to Victoria, a subsidiary of the ERGO group, was set up as an 'insurance factory' to produce white label insurance products, which brokers, banks or other financial services providers can distribute under their own label.[608]

---

[607] Own Illustration taken from company interviews.
[608] Hypovereinsbank 2001, p. 25.

One of the fundamental risks of such a bifurcated organisational structure is that there is a complete lack of communication and co-ordination across organisational units. As a result, product manufacturing becomes completely 'alienated' from market developments and distribution channels units no longer take any aspects of product processing or product profitability into account. Therefore, organisations need to share relevant information in order not to suffer from organisational chimneys. Formal information connectedness facilitates the exchange of information and reduces the conflicts that inhibit communication. One possibility to mitigate this risk is to set up cross-functional teams. However, in order to ensure the effectiveness of cross-functional teams, they must have the authority to reallocate budgets and the team members should have overlapping personal targets.[609] Cross-Channel commitments must be communicated across the organisation through the resource allocation (budgeting) and performance management process. In fact, the amount and type of resources devoted to the respective distribution channels across global product markets represent a highly important decision for many firms.[610]

> **AXA Germany** has recognised the importance of cross-functional teams, which have the necessary authority in terms of resource allocation across distribution channels in order to ensure that the company achieves its overall objectives. Therefore, they have set-up so-called transversal committees, where high-ranking decision-makers from different units of the company (i.e., distribution, product manufacturing, IT, HR and Finance) meet on a bimonthly basis to discuss and resolve all operational issues within the constraints of the overall budget and targets of the company for a specific business unit.

To conclude, financial remuneration systems need to be aligned with the organisational structure. Co-ordinated distribution approaches generally give rise to higher organisation complexity, because, on the one hand, the multiple distribution channels need to be co-ordinated via a dedicated unit to ensure the consistency of all customer contacts, and on the other hand, the organisation is generally split up into a client and product/process management. Furthermore, cross-functional teams may be set up to maintain the overall connectedness of the organisation and are also responsible for the resource allocation process within the company based on certain defined corporate targets. All this organisational complexity can be avoided in the case of focussed multi-channel distribution strategies, where there is very often a simpler and linear organisational relationship between the distribution channel and the product units.

---

[609] Duncan, T. and Moriarty, S. 1998, pp. 10; Hayden, J. 2000, p. 45.
[610] Frazier, G. 1999, p. 235.

8.2 Customer Ownership and Remuneration of Distribution Channels

Co-ordinated multi-channel distribution systems give rise to a number of problems, which can be avoided altogether in the case of focussed multi-channel distribution systems. If multiple channels contribute to overall sales success, it needs to be defined which distribution channel owns the customer relationship and, more importantly, how channel members are compensated for their contribution to overall sales success. One of the reasons for a focussed multi-channel distribution is the fact that the question of customer ownership and sales compensation is such a politically tense subject, that a clear and complete separation of the distribution channels - at least on the distribution side - seems to be the best solution. In a co-ordinated multi-channel environment, the question of customer ownership is one of the most widely debated subjects, since it is most closely related to the issue of channel compensation.[611] In fact, the remuneration system represents the most effective controlling instrument for the distribution of financial services, particularly in the tied agent channel.[612] If the remuneration of sales success is not sufficiently defined, all the envisaged benefits of the distribution system fall apart, as channel members are more concerned with internal fights than with an optimal serving of customer needs.[613] It is, therefore, important to address the issue of channel compensation together with the question of customer ownership, since channel compensation has, at least in the past, always been linked to the question of customer ownership. Within a co-ordinated multi-channel environment, it is therefore necessary to address the following two issues:

- **Customer ownership**: Are customers managed centrally or allocated to the respective lead channel?
- **Remuneration of sales success or contribution to sales success**: Are channels remunerated only for their 'own' sales success or is their contribution to the overall sales success of a customer relationship across multiple channels also taken into account.

Although it is often debated which of the multiple distribution channels 'owns' the customer relationship, one has to bear in mind that, in the first instance, the customer himself chooses the distribution channel at his discretion. "If a bank designing a multi-channel organisation persists in assuming that a channel can own customers, it is deluding itself about how customers use banks and the range of choices they enjoy".[614] However, although this statement is certainly valid from the customer's point of view and reflects the fundamental reasoning of

611 Hientzsch, R. and Bormann, S. 2003, p. 746.
612 Müller, H. 1993, p. 98; Stern, L.W., El Ansary, A.I. and Coughlan, A., 1996, p. 289.
613 Krotsch, S. 2002, p. 188; Ladwig, F. 2002, p. 93.
614 Holmsen, C., Palter, R., Simon, P. and Weberg, P. 1998, p. 84.

co-ordinated multi-channel distribution strategies (i.e., co-ordinated multi-channel systems leave the channel choice to the customer), the question of customer ownership, nevertheless, needs to be resolved from a purely internal point of view. In fact, a clear and unambiguous definition of customer ownership is crucial for safeguarding the internal socio-political stability of the distribution system and, thus, represents a prerequisite for the successful functioning of the entire distribution system.

In the first phase of the benchmarking project (survey based on 38 returned questionnaires), around 34% of companies indicated that customers are allocated to that distribution channel, which was responsible for the initial customer acquisition, while only 20% stated that customers are managed centrally and 13% indicated that customers are forwarded to other distribution channels for cross-selling purposes. The rest mentioned diverse criteria for solving the issue of customer ownership in a multi-channel distribution system.[615] In the further course of the benchmarking project, it could be confirmed that customers are often allocated to a lead channel, while the other channels have access to these customers for specific marketing campaigns, often with prior notification of the lead channel about these campaigns. This conclusion can also be corroborated by other studies.[616]

It is important to understand that the question of customer ownership can often be solved or de-emphasised by establishing clear and open communication between distribution channels regarding the operational aspects of cross-channel customer relationship management. For example, AXA Germany has set up so-called multi-channel committees to ensure open communication between the direct channel and the face-to-face distribution channel.

> **AXA Germany** has set up a 'multi-channel' committee, where all multi-channel campaigns are discussed between representatives of the tied agents organisation and the direct channel, in order to ensure that all channel members can jointly design the cross-channel marketing campaigns. Thereby, it is ensured that the tied agent channel actively takes up the commercial offers or leads, generated by call centre staff or direct mailings, in their face-to-face discussion with the customer. In addition, multi-channel agreements have been signed between the tied agent channel and the company, where the rights and obligations of all channels involved are clearly defined. For example, the tied agent has been given the right to exclude a maximum of 10% of his customers from multi-channel campaigns and, in addition, another 20% of customers, specifically selected for a campaign. Thereby, AXA Germany has succeeded in receiving an overwhelming acceptance of their new multi-channel system by the tied agents organisation.

Trust and clear respect of the rules of co-operations are also the underlying reasons for successful channel co-operation between the direct channel and the IFA channel at Scottish Widows.

---

615 TECTEM 2001.
616 Gronover, S. 2003, pp. 142-4.

Scottish Widows, originally a mutual life company focussed on the independent adviser market, demutualised and became part of Lloyds TSB, one of the UK's big high street banks. As a result of this acquisition, Scottish Widows products are now accessible through IFAs, through the 2,600 sales staff at Lloyds TSB branches as well as via call centre and web site. This mixture of bancassurance and independent advisers is bound to give rise to channel conflicts. However, Scottish Widows pays special attention to fully complying with a strict code of conduct regarding customer relationships, where the IFA has exclusive access rights, as explains the responsible Brand and Network Development Director: "The IFA has exclusive access rights and we work hard at following this to the letter ... We might agree with an IFA that we will mail his clients. If a client takes up the offer, the IFA gets a commission cheque for doing no work at all. The secret is openness, communication and involvement".[617]

The example of Scottish Widows also emphasises the importance of the underlying commission system, i.e., the question of how channels are compensated for their sales success. Surveys indicate that, in the insurance industry, the remuneration of tied agents is deemed to have the most important impact on the effectiveness and efficiency of the tied agents distribution channel.[618] Therefore, one fundamental challenge in co-ordinated multi-channel distribution systems is to ensure that the compensation systems of each distribution channel are fully aligned.[619] Generally speaking, the remuneration system fulfils two important functions:

- **Compensation** of the channel members for their sales efforts based on a transparent commission system.
- **Steering** of the distribution systems by providing financial or non-financial incentives (e.g. bonus payments or sales rewards) to achieve certain strategic sales targets, e.g. cross-channel customer servicing.[620]

In multi-channel environments, the channel members dealing with the customer no longer perform all channel functions and they can, thus, not expect to receive a traditional margin or commission. Ideally, channel members are compensated only for the functions they perform[621]. Compensation should be awarded on the basis of the degree of each channel member's participation in the marketing flows and each channel member's contribution to the generation of relevant service outputs in the channel system.[622] This approach can deprive the traditional channels of substantial commission income and, as a consequence, these channels are not likely to transfer customers to other distribution channels for additional sales activities. Therefore, each of the channels involved needs an incentive to maximise the client relationship for the company across all possible access points. This objective may be achieved by two

617 Maynard, P. 2001, p. 89.
618 Gerhardt, M. and Doerfner, O. 2002, pp. 277-9; Weigelt, O. and Engler, K. 2003, pp. 282-4.
619 Hientzsch, R. and Bormann, S. 2003, p. 746.
620 Damm, P. 1993, pp. 47-59.
621 Anderson, E., Day, G. and Rangan, K. 1997, p. 67.
622 Stern, L. W., El Ansary, A. I. and Coughlan, A., 1996, p. 289.

different options. One way is to include the target of cross-channel servicing of customer needs in remuneration via the sales plan or via bonus payments. In order to ensure the effectiveness of these financial incentives, it is important that at least 25% of overall annual remuneration is linked to this strategic objective.[623]

A second option is to modify the underlying commission system, which needs to evolve from a more transaction-focussed to a Customer Lifetime Value-oriented system, where the channel is remunerated based on the annual value creation of his customer portfolio.[624] The Customer Lifetime Value captures the expected overall discounted profit of a particular customer relationship resulting from current in-force policies as well as expected new business. The idea is that channels should be measured and rewarded based on customer profitability (e.g. overall annual increase in customer value). In order to foster cross-channel interactions, the channel, that has acquired the customer, may be remunerated for the value, this channel could extract from the customer relationship on a standalone basis. Thereby, the direct channel is rewarded for having established the customer relationship and, at the same time, is given a financial incentive to pass the customer on to a face-to-face channel, where the customer value for the company can further be enhanced by additional cross-selling activities.

An analysis of the remuneration system of the companies inside the scope of the benchmarking study shows that the remuneration system has been designed in such a way that cross-channel interactions are actively encouraged. For example, similar to the approach taken by Scottish Widows, Allstate credits some reduced commission to its tied agent force for business, which has been concluded via a direct distribution channel. Citibank introduced the concept of shadow accounting where sales success is credited to the channel responsible for the sales activity as well as to the lead channel.

> The **Allstate** remuneration system for its co-ordinated multi-channel approach is based on two fundamental characteristics. First, clear positioning of the tied agent channel as the lead channel, receiving commission income for all business contracted with their customers or with new customers living in their region. Secondly, a remuneration system, which is fully aligned with the company objectives.
>
> The central incentive for the agents is the compensation system. Business, concluded by the agents, will be remunerated at 10 % (preferred auto), 8 % (sub-standard auto), 20 % (new business property) as well as 10 % (renewal business property). If the business is processed and concluded via a different distribution channel, then the agents receive a 2% service fee and, in the case of additional, successful cross-selling activities, this commission goes up from 2% to 3.5 %.
>
> The remuneration system for the Call Center agents is entirely different, as Call Center agents are directly employed by Allstate. Thus, they receive a fix salary and supplementary social benefits. In

623 Reindl, E. and Blum, R. 2003, pp. 1490-1492.
624 Stern, L. W., El Ansary, A. I. and Coughlan, A., 1996, p. 289.

addition, a team-focussed reward system has been established based on sales success. The team awards are relatively small and more oriented towards recognition of success than compensation.[625]

At **Citibank**, the branches represent the lead channel and receive all future earnings less costs incurred in the other channel. However, in order to ensure active involvement of all channels in the customer interaction process, a shadow accounting has been introduced where both the lead channel as well as the distribution channel, responsible for a specific transaction, are credited for sales success. It is thereby ensured that the different distribution channels actively work together.[626]

It can be concluded, that mechanisms have to be found where channels are encouraged to work together. This may be achieved by crediting sales success partially or totally to all distribution channels involved for their shared involvement in the customer service process (e.g. by means of shadow accounting) or by charging the distribution costs incurred to the lead channel to ensure a consistency between commission income and total distribution costs.[627]

Furthermore, commission system itself needs to reflect the different distribution costs and level of services rendered by the respective channel. Traditionally, the commission system for insurance products is linked to the percentage of premium or to the sum insured and distributors receive up-front commissions for the entire period of the contract. A first step in the evolution of the compensation scheme is to link the commission systems to profit measures (rather than sales volume).

AXA Germany has introduced a new remuneration system, where sales success rigidly takes into account the underlying economics of its business and forces agents to concentrate on the maintenance and pruning of the portfolio, as the commission income is also computed, based on the portfolio of insurance contracts.

Although this shift from volume to profit based compensation represents an important first step, it does not resolve the issue that the channel mix itself has a significant impact on the overall product profitability. For example, there may be significant negative consequences on profitability, if a product which has been designed for the tied agent channel, where a seamless processing of contracts is possible, is, in reality, predominantly distributed via the broker channel with high back-office manual work for the insurer. Such a situation could have serious effects on the overall product profitability of the insurer. It is, therefore, necessary, that the commission scheme takes different channel costs into account. This view on channel compensation requires a two-step approach. In the first instance, a gross distribution margin needs to be computed. In a second step, based on the overall costs of the specific channel, one can then calculate the net distribution margin to be passed on to the channel member for compensation of sales activities.

---

[625] TECTEM, 2002, pp. 41-2.
[626] TECTEM, 2002, pp. 53.
[627] Stone, M., Hobbs, M. and Khaleeli, M. 2002, pp. 47-8.

By linking the compensation of the individual distribution channel to an explicit distribution margin, it is much easier to manage and measure the financial performance of the different distribution channels and also to add new distribution channels. Differences in compensation of the distribution channel can, in this case, be explained by significant differences in channel costs. So-called resource allocation patterns, as illustrated in the following figure, help to find the right balance of compensation for the distributor and the support functions.

	Career Agents	Brokerage Companies
Compensation of distributors	40%	50%
Management Compensation	10%	12%
Field Expenses	23%	15%
Other Benefits	10%	0%
Head Office Costs	17%	23%
Total	100%	100%
Total Distribution Costs in Euro	190	170

Figure 49: Resource Allocation Patterns[628]

Support functions include all indirect cost positions (e.g. marketing material, lead generation programmes, training, etc.), which need to be taken into consideration when defining the proportion of the distribution margin to be paid to the distributor. However, this approach requires the overall product margin be broken up into a distribution and a production margin.[629] As shown later, it is therefore necessary to have different profit & loss statements for the manufacturer of financial services products and the distributor.

Finally, modification of the remuneration system often involves an increase in the complexity of the IT systems, which, in turn, leads to a high degree of manual work in the calculation of the remuneration schemes.[630] Some insurers, therefore, seek technology-based flexible solutions to handle multiple and distinct remuneration systems. Software providers offer rule-based systems that allow carriers to align compensation with the business strategy by implementing new compensation requirements (such as complex teaming arrangements, asset-based compensation, role-based compensation and third-party selling agreements).[631]

To conclude, the question of customer ownership can first be resolved by a transparent allocation of customers to a specific lead channel and, secondly, by establishing very clear and open rules in respect of customer contacts between the different channels. Openness and trust are the key success criteria in this context. Once the question of customer ownership has been

---

628 Wellborn, J. 2000, p. 26.
629 Wellborn, J. 2000, p. 26.
630 Gerhardt, M. and Doerfner, O. 2002, pp. 277-9; Reindl, E. and Blum, R. 2003, pp. 1490-1492.
631 Hollander, D. and Coleman, M. 2000, p. 185.

resolved, the remuneration system also needs to be aligned with the strategic objectives of the multi-channel distribution system, as the remuneration system is the most important variable for influencing the sales behaviour of the various distribution channels. The remuneration system has to include financial incentives (either via the commission system or via bonus payments) to ensure that cross channel co-operation takes place. In addition, the remuneration system also has to take the different channel costs and service levels into account. This aspect can best be brought into the remuneration system by breaking up the product margin into a distribution and manufacturing margin. However, once a remuneration system has been designed, it also needs to be implemented. Switching the remuneration system of the established distribution channels towards a new system represents the real and fundamental challenge.[632] The next section therefore illustrates the challenges related to the actual transformation of a distribution system.

8.3 Change Management: Transformation of the Behaviour of Internal Customers

Management's interest in changing the distribution system is an important factor for change.[633] This implies that the implementation of a multi-channel distribution system predominantly needs to be pushed forward by top management. However, in the retail financial services industry, especially in the insurance industry, the most fundamental challenge is to receive the organisational acceptance of the financial intermediaries, most notably from the self-employed tied or captive agents. Fundamental distribution projects have failed because of the lack of support from financial intermediaries.[634] The concern of the tied agent channel is that their commission income will decrease. The following extracts from financial analysts notes clearly underline this very important aspect of actively managing the interest of the financial intermediaries in any transformation process of a distribution system.

> "The main barrier to insurance companies using alternative distribution channels has been the concern that this could weaken their major source of revenue: tied agents".
>
> "The biggest execution risk Allstate faces is not in the development of an Internet and client platform, but is the degree of organisational acceptance of its agents".
>
> "One of the primary obstacles that the insurance/financial services industry faces in implementing an Internet-based distribution model, is how to maximise the online distribution channel without disrupting existing sales agent channels and relationships".[635]

---

[632] Reindl, E. and Blum, R. 2003, pp. 1490-1492.
[633] Mols, N. 1999, p. 297.
[634] See Chapter 6.3, pp. 111-2.
[635] Quotes taken in the order as mentioned above from Fox-Pit (May 2000), Goldman Sach (November 1999) and Strategic Research Institute quote taken from PR Newswire June 12, 2000.

The concept of relationship is not limited to the end customer, but also covers the internal relationships, most notably between the employer and the employees. This aspect is also known under the concept of internal marketing, which is based on the belief that a company needs to sell its ideas first to employees before selling its services to external customers, i.e., satisfying the needs of internal customers upgrades the capability to satisfy the customers. For example, Sales Improvement Councils could be enacted to act as a cultural change force within the organisation.[636]

One of the key elements of internal marketing is training[637], which is considered as one of the most essential factors to reduce channel conflicts.[638] Training refers, on the one hand, to the correct handling of new technical devices (e.g. Internet, WAP Mobile, PDA) as well as to a thorough understanding of the overall strategic ideas of multi-channel distribution. Successful multi-channel providers, such as Charles Schwab, have taken training very seriously:

> When, in 1998, **Charles Schwab** merged its online and offline brokerage facilities into a click-and-brick strategy, they also tried to gain the acceptance on the expanded Internet offering from its customer service representatives. They gave each of its 4,000 phone and branch representatives Web access and training. Moreover, Schwab included a measure of customer migration to the Internet as one of the handful of components that determined team-based bonuses for its customer services representatives.[639]

It is interesting to note that Charles Schwab combined training with some financial incentives for the teams. The following example illustrates that training is not limited to cognitive knowledge about new technical devices, such as the Internet, but also includes some experience-based elements. At the DAB bank, a German direct bank, the management intended to get across the message that the new distribution concept requires customer contacts to be correctly documented in a cross-channel CRM database.

> The **German direct bank DAB** has initiated a very comprehensive change management programme. In order to foster the shift from a transaction-oriented to a sales-oriented bank, the DAB has launched so-called customer partnerships. Each staff member personally takes care of a defined group of customers. Via these contacts, employers develop some understanding of the customer needs as well as experience how important it is to document all customer contacts well.[640]

Many staff feel threatened by the Internet, particularly if they do not have a personal relationship with the new media. It is therefore important to communicate to the established distribution channels, that they will not be replaced by, but rather supported by the additional distribution channels. It is imperative to resolve these issues, as distribution strategy often fails be-

---

636 Shemwell, D. and Yavas, U. 1998, p. 295.
637 Belz, C. 2001, p. 78.
638 Ladwig, F. 2002, pp. 83-5; McDonald, L. 1999, pp. 88-99.
639 Harvard Business School 1999a, p. 2.
640 Sohler, M. 2003, p. 674.

cause the staff in the different distribution channels continue to work separately, not co-operatively and, ultimately, dysfunctionally. Everyone thus needs to understand the whole company story and appreciate the importance of their role in the organisation.[641] This also explains why the Citibank has placed so much emphasis on communication by nominating so-called 'Champions' for each bank branch. The overriding question of the Citibank change programme has been the question "What's in it for me?", i.e., what are the individual benefits of the new distribution strategy from the point of view of the individual employee? The entire communication efforts have been centred around the aspect of explaining to the employee just how the new distribution strategy can actually facilitate the work of the individual employee.

Citibank Germany has identified the following guidelines for employees for its transformation programme:

- To dispel initial fears (e.g. via Workshops)
- To give confidence to people that jobs will be maintained
- To credibly communicate management commitment
- To define responsibility (name transaction champions and Internet champions)
- To provide information on the new technology and the concrete benefits for staff (*'what's in it for me?'*)
- To integrate the new communication devices or channels into the selling process
- To define and track specific goals at branch level (transparency of profit figures for the entire bank down to the branch level)
- To ensure success transfer from successful teams to less successful teams
- To provide promotions and competitions
- IT supported sales process (e.g. integration of the use of new distribution channels into form for opening of current account)

Citibank Germany respected these guidelines when introducing ATMs and Citibank Express Terminals in the branches; Citibank considers the Express Terminals as a separate distribution channel. Staff very quickly appreciated the time-saving aspects of these terminals, so they could concentrate on their actual sales activities. In order to promote the exchange of experience, staff from different branches were linked up for a weekly telephone conference. Branches could learn from each other, resulting in the desired spill-over of best-practice to other branches.

A similar strategy was pursued when introducing the Internet channel:

- Organising workshops to facilitate the introduction of CitiDirect in all sales unit
- Appointment of an 'Internet champion' in each branch office
- Transparency on key performance indicators on the level of bank headquarters, broken down to branch level.
- Organisation of regular telephone conferences with the Internet Champions in each branch office
- IT Integration of the sale of Internet banking in each and every process of opening an account

Citibank Germany concluded that, in all their change programmes, they always laid emphasis on communicating to the established sales channels that the new channels will not be positioned as

[641] Lindstrom, M. 2002, p. 242.

competing channels, but as support channels. The fundamental idea of this philosophy is summed up in the following figure.[642]

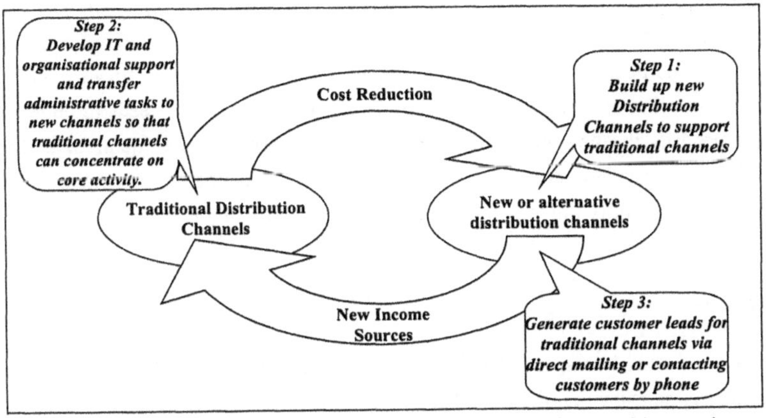

Figure 50: Citibank Germany: Channel Strategy - Simultaneous Reduction of Costs and Increase of Income[643]

The figure illustrates that the traditional and new channels are seen in a kind of mutually beneficial relationship (virtuous circle of the interplay of different distribution channels). In the first step, new channels are built up to provide support functions to the branches, which can reduce their administrative costs and can concentrate on the core activity of advising people on their financial situation instead. In a second step, the new channels are requested to generate additional sales leads for the branches, whereby the branches can generate additional fee income. It is interesting to note that Citibank uses the fundamental objectives of a co-ordinated multi-channel strategy for communicating their new strategy internally.[644]

It can be concluded from the Citibank example that openness of communication and active confrontation of all employees involved with the new distribution channels are very important in this transformation process. Citibank actively communicated on the mutually beneficial relationship between branches and the new distribution channels, which only renders it possible to simultaneously reduce costs and exploit new sources of income. However, given the inertia of distribution channels, the example also underlines the necessity to introduce some elements of competition to make sure that all channel members meet the new requirements of the distribution strategy.

To conclude, the transformation of distribution systems represents one of the key management

642 TECTEM 2002, p. 55-6.
643 TECTEM 2002, p. 48.
644 TECTEM 2002, p. 48 and 55.

tasks. The interest of the financial intermediaries clearly needs to be aligned with the objectives of the new distribution approach. In this context, the remuneration system certainly plays an important role, but it needs to be accompanied by some other elements (e.g. legal status, reporting lines, etc.). In addition, internal marketing is crucial for the new distribution channel: clear communication in respect of the new strategy and training of all people involved with the customer are vital aspects thereof. Each channel member needs to understand the individual benefits the new distribution strategy brings for the individual. In addition, certain team-based bonus programmes or other elements of competitions among channel managers help to successfully implement the transformation programme.

8.4 Conclusion

In this chapter, the internal perspective of multi-channel distribution strategies has been analysed along three dimensions: (i) the overall organisational structure, (ii) the question of customer ownership and, related to this, the overall remuneration system as well as (iii) the concrete process of managing the transformation process of the distribution system.

It can generally be concluded that, from the internal perspective, these issues only arise to some small extent in the case of a **focussed multi-channel distribution system**. This is not surprising as this distribution approach is usually chosen when the market segments are relatively large and stable and/or the internal socio-political structures and processes are not likely to successfully support any transformation towards tighter co-operation among the distribution channels. Therefore, in a focussed distribution system, the organisational implications are very straightforward, as each distribution channel is organised separately with a clear and linear relationship between customer segments, distribution and product management. The question of customer ownership does not arise and the remuneration system is, of course, to be aligned with the interests of the respective distribution channel.

In case of co-ordinated multi-channel systems, the following internal dimensions need to be actively designed:

- **Organisational Structure**: To ensure the overall consistency of all customer contacts, it is helpful that all channels are governed by a central channel management unit. Clear customer focus across multiple channels may also lead to a bifurcation of the traditionally integrated service providers into two separate units, i.e Client Management and Product Management. While the Client Manager can focus on the overall management of the customer contacts via multiple channels, Product Managers focus on the important tasks of product development and product administration. The overall connectedness of the organisation could be ensured by setting up transversal teams with corresponding budgetary authority.

- The **remuneration system** is the best driver for change. In a first step, the question of customer ownership needs to be clearly resolved, as customer ownership is considered to be the fundamental prerequisite for safeguarding the financial revenues for the financial intermediaries, especially for self-employed agents or brokers. In practice, customers are usually allocated to a lead channel, but with clear access to these customers via other channels. It is important that all commercial campaigns are discussed among the channels in advance and all formal rules of customer contact are fully complied with. Mutual trust that these rules are respected is a very important success factor. The remuneration system can encourage cross-channel interaction via bonus payments or via the underlying commission system itself. One option is to credit a reduced service or commission fees to the lead channel for business acquired by other distribution channels. In order to be able to flexibly add new distribution channels as well as adapt the remuneration system to the actual economics of each distribution channel, the remuneration margin should explicitly take the distribution costs of each channel into account.

However, all of these efforts only unfold the true potential of the distribution strategy, if the **transformation process** is clearly and actively managed; this particularly applies to the tied agent channel. Therefore, all channel members have to be fully introduced to the new distribution concept. This certainly requires extensive training to familiarise all channel members with the new sales concepts and tools. In addition, each channel member needs to understand the individual benefits (What's in it for me ?). This experience- and trust-based learning, coupled with some degree of team-based competition, help to successfully manage the transformation process.

Now the internal and external dimension of multi-channel distribution system have been analysed in depth, the final chapter of this part will deal with the appropriate financial steering system.

9. Financial Steering of the Distribution System

Successful channel management also requires the implementation of appropriate measurement systems, containing a mixture of financial and non-financial information, which are to be linked to the business unit strategy.[645] The actual challenge lies in a fair and transparent evaluation of the contribution of the different distribution channels to overall sales performance.[646] As stated in the second part, one of the major challenges relates to the simultaneous management of the economic as well as socio-political variables of the distribution channel. Fears of cannibalisation as well as internal conflicts, which are often fuelled, in the case of insurers, by the tied agents organisation, need to be addressed very proactively, as they could otherwise disrupt the entire distribution system. The key to managing these channel conflicts is the rapid identification of conflict through open communication with sales associates and business partners, periodic evaluation of performance and trends (including quality trends) to distinguish between true conflicts and vocalised complaints.[647] Therefore, a performing financial steering system is not only important for safeguarding the economic performance, but also for ensuring a certain level of socio-political stability.

9.1 Management of Distribution Systems as Profit Centres

In a multi-channel organisation, it is crucial to allocate accountability for the profit and loss statement to the responsible people as well as to closely track the key economic drivers of the business as well as identify potential synergies between distribution channels.[648] Consequently, an increasing number of companies use the profit centre concept as the basis for a clear financial evaluation of the sales and profit contribution of each distribution channel. In the US, companies with career agency system have separated manufacturing from distribution by establishing a profit and loss statements for distribution. In doing so, these companies hope to make distribution performance easier to understand and subject to more disciplined management.[649] The following example of a specialised life distribution company in Germany shows the clear benefits of such a profit-based company steering.

> A **German life insurer** manages its specialised, advice-oriented sales force in a separate legal entity. In the past, the focus had been on optimising the costs of this distribution company and any negative result had been financed by the insurance carrier via a year-end lump sum commission payment. This situation has now changed significantly. As of today, the distribution company is

---

645 Ramsay, J. and Smith, M. 1999.
646 Schwanitz, J. 2001, p. 590.
647 McDonald, L. 1999, pp. 88-99.
648 Holmsen, C. Palter, R., Simon, P. and Weberg, P. 1998, p. 85; Macchi, M. 2002, p. 123.
649 Fenton, J. and Williams, C. 2003, pp. 14-5.

managed as a true profit centre, which, similar to a third-party distribution company, receives commission income from the insurance carrier, which needs to suffice to finance both internal costs as well as the commission payments to the sales force. The distribution company has identified three important value drivers: commission income, commission pay-out as well as overall internal costs. The focus of steering this company is entirely based on the management of these three drivers. Consequently, the profit centre of the distribution company has been broken up into separate profit centres for each local service centre, which can clearly see its contribution to the overall contribution to the profit of the entire company. As a result of this change in the company steering, the after-tax result was improved significantly, while the agent productivity increased.

Frese has identified the following two prerequisites for the successful management of distribution channels with separate p&l accounts:

- The distribution channel needs to have direct market access, so that all income can be directly allocated to this channel
- The distribution channel needs to be in command of all factors, which influence the financial success of the channel.[650]

It can, thus, be concluded that only distribution channels with direct market access can be managed based on the concept of profit centres. Distribution channels, which tend to fulfil support functions (e.g. information functions), can therefore only be managed as cost centres, as financial income can hardly be allocated to these channels.[651]

The design of the profit concept is different for focussed and co-ordinated multi-channel distribution systems. In the case of focussed distribution channels, these channels are very often managed in separate legal entities, as is the case for the AMB Group in Germany or the Allstate Independent Financial Advisor Channel (Encompass).[652] If, these distribution channels are maintained in one company, but are still managed separately, it is often relatively easy to allocate costs and benefits to each distribution channel, as they are not very much intertwined in terms of structure and processes.

The situation is significantly different, if the distribution channels are deeply integrated into the entire company. Especially in the insurance industry, it is very often the case that the distribution company is not separated into its own legal entity, but constitutes an integral part of the insurance carrier. Nevertheless, in such a case, it is all the more crucial to have a clear picture about the profitability of the distribution channels on a standalone basis. In a first step, it is therefore necessary, at least for internal monitoring purposes, to clearly separate all costs

---

[650] Renggli, 1997, p. 19.
[651] Bohnenkamp, P. 1999, p. 33.
[652] See Chapter 6.2, pp. 101-3.

and commission income for the distribution company. The example of AXA Germany, where the distribution function is part of the insurance carrier, shows that this is possible.

> **AXA Germany** set up a profit & loss statement for its distribution function, which is not separated in a different legal entity, but only exists for internal steering purposes. Market-oriented price agreements have been negotiated between the client manager (distribution) and the product manufacturer based on an arm's length principle. The client manager receives commission income based on its sales volume, which needs to be sufficient to finance both the commission payments to the agents as well as all internal costs of the distribution function. The profit centre is structured as a 'contribution margin', where different margins are computed based on a decreasing possibility of directly allocating distribution costs to a particular distribution channel.

If a number of different distribution channels are involved in the customer buying processes, it is difficult to allocate sales success correctly to these channels, as customer processes are spread across a number of different channels and are not stable over time, as they depend on the customer's individual decision to establish contact with the financial services provider. Given this phenomenon, there are basically two possibilities of allocating costs and benefits to the different distribution channels. In case of the existence of lead channels (e.g. the branch office in retail banking or the tied agent channel for some insurers), it is often the case (also as a result of the legacy of IT systems) that all revenues are allocated to the lead channel despite the customer's use of multiple channel, thus overestimating revenues, while distribution costs are significantly underestimated.[653] In this case, the lead channel can be managed as a profit centre, while the other distribution channels are kept as cost centres. Alternatively, cost and benefits are allocated to the channel, according to their 'actual' contribution to sales success. In practice, costs are then often charged to the lead channel on the basis of certain consumption patterns, so that there is no longer any mismatch between commission income and true overall distribution costs, which are to be seen in connection with total revenues.

In order to avoid the usual problem of the 'arbitrary' allocation of overheads or indirect costs, costs could be allocated to the distribution channels based on the underlying customer processes.[654] This idea of activity-based costing[655] has been taken up for multi-channel distribution in the sense that cost allocation is based on the interaction points along the customer process from the first-time inquiry to the final purchase. Schwanitz proposes the use of so-called **'customer touch points' (CTP)**, where a CTP is defined as one individual interaction between the customer and the financial services provider. Thereby it is possible to compute 'cost per CTP' for each channel, which could then be allocated to customer processes and ultimately to the corresponding lead channel, where all costs and commission income could be matched.

---

[653] Holmsen, C., Palter, R., Simon, P. and Weberg, P. 1998, p. 85.
[654] Gronover, S. and Bach, V. 2000, p. 11.
[655] Coenenberg, A. G. 1999, pp. 220-230.

This approach requires a clear tracking of customer behaviour across channels, as illustrated by the following figure.

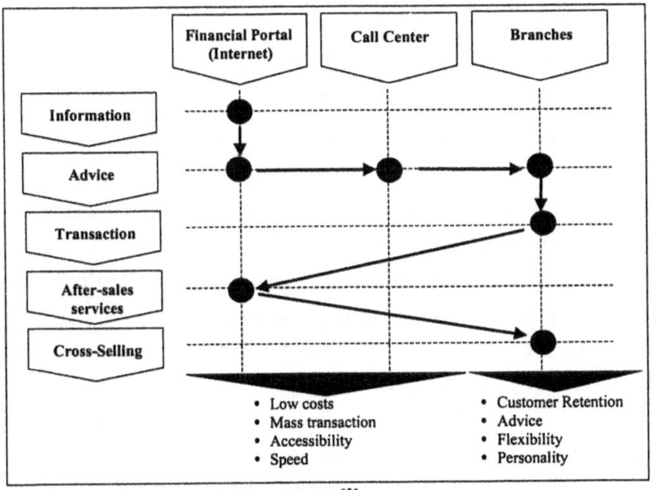

Figure 51: Customer Touch Points Matrix[656]

The customer may start his search in the financial portal, where at some point in time, he is referred to the Call Centre for additional information. The Call Centre provides the requested information and passes this lead on to the branch for a follow-up, where the customer has a face-to-face meeting some days later and subsequently completes the transaction. In a later period, he is given access to his accounts via the financial portal where he is informed about potential additional products. Cross-selling activities are undertaken by the branches.

The figure clearly illustrates that, depending on his preferences, the customer himself defines the actual 'multi-channel' business process for establishing contact with the financial services provider. The next customer may define an entirely different business process, which is related to the same customer request. Since there are no standardised, multi-channel business processes, e.g. for the acquisition of a life contract, these customer touch points represent the only possible basis for the allocation of costs. This requires customer activities to be tracked entirely in terms of product inquiry, time and length of the customer's interaction with a particular channel. In the Internet, log files and web controlling allow for such a perfect tracking of customer activities. In the other distribution channels, appropriate data has to be identified to track customer activities. These customer touch points can then be used to

---

656 Schwanitz, J. 2001.

allocate the costs to the corresponding lead channel of the customer, and, on the other hand, to calculate the costs of the various multi-channel business processes. In a second step, it can then be assessed whether the costs of these multi-channel processes are justified by the customer benefits. It is also possible to aggregate the data in such a way as to analyse the degree of cross-channel interaction (so-called migration matrix). A migration matrix shows to what degree customers of a specific lead channel use other channels.[657]

However, based on the results of the benchmarking study as well as on additional interviews, it can be concluded that the allocation of costs based on the tracking of customer processes is a rather complex endeavour and is associated with significant investments. Consequently, activity-based costing based on customer processes is hardly used in the financial services industry. Companies look for more practical solutions instead. Nevertheless, various possibilities are explored of how to allocate the distribution costs of those channels, which provide customer service or generate customers leads, to the primary channels. For example, one German insurance company is currently discussing charging a certain fee for each customer lead generated by the direct channel and referred to the tied agent channel. In this model, costs are charged to the lead channel irrespective of the question of whether these qualified leads will be converted into customers. The benchmarking partners explore other ways of monitoring their distribution channels. Citibank uses shadow accounting, where they allocate the benefits of customer success to all distribution channels involved in the sales process. Alternatively, Nordea maintains the lead channel as a profit centre, while the costs of the other distribution channels are charged to the lead channel.

In **Nordea**'s multi-channel banking strategy, the branch offices represent the lead channel and all customers are allocated to a specific branch office, which is managed as a profit centre. All transactions and services, the customers use of other distribution channels (e.g. Call Centre, Solo services), are charged to the branch office. For this purpose, internal unit prices have been established for each transaction type – these prices are reviewed and negotiated with the regional offices on an annual basis. In addition, overhead costs or direct marketing costs are not directly allocated to each branch, but are included indirectly in the internal unit-prices. In general, the regional offices decide whether they participate in any commercial activities, organised by headquarters, and only in case of participation do they get charged the corresponding costs for these commercial campaigns.[658]

At **Citibank**, the branches also represent the lead channel and, therefore, all future earnings from a newly acquired customer are credited to the branch, irrespective of the distribution channel, which has undertaken this transaction. Generally, about 70 to 80% of future earnings are credited to the branch. Shadow accounting has been established in order to fully reflect the performance and sales

[657] Schwanitz, J. 2001, pp. 589-95; Schwanitz, J. and Krugmann, B. 2002, pp. 20- 22; Schwanitz, J. and Ahr, H. 2002, pp. 26- 28. See also Bohnenkamp, P. 1999, pp. 31-3.
[658] TECTEM 2002, p. 85.

success of each sales channel; both the lead channel (i.e., the branch) as well as the channel responsible for the specific transaction are rewarded for sales success. [659]

9.2 Analysis of the Efficiency and Effectiveness of the Distribution System

One of the fundamental risks in the development of multi-channel distribution strategies is that the company invests heavily in connecting the multiple distribution channels via a powerful CRM database or in extending the distribution network even further without analysing ex ante whether the customer is willing to pay for these significant investments either in the short or long run. Since multi-channel strategies often entail significant investments at the beginning, both on the IT side as well as in the overall reorganisation of the distribution system, it is advisable to test the sustainability of these IT investments during the design phase.[660]

One possibility to test the **economic sustainability of the channel investment** is to use the concept of **target costing.**[661] This concept is illustrated by the following figure.

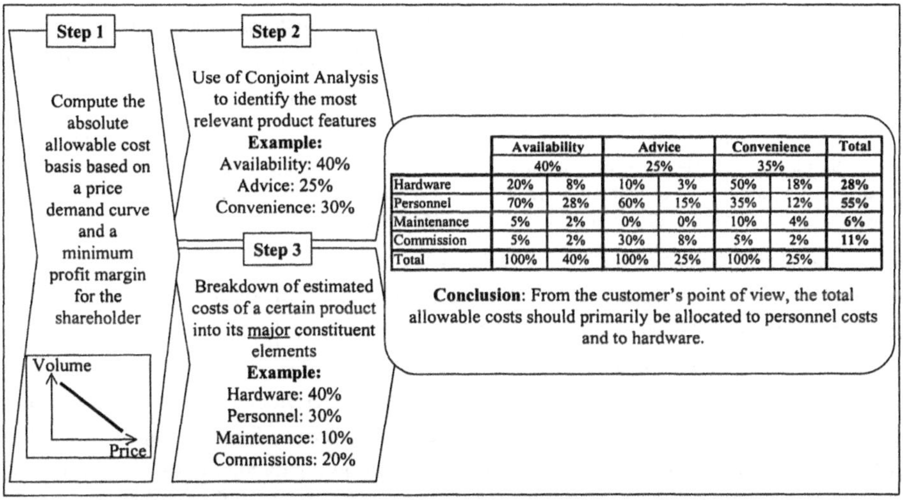

	Availability		Advice		Convenience		Total
	40%		25%		35%		
Hardware	20%	8%	10%	3%	50%	18%	**28%**
Personnel	70%	28%	60%	15%	35%	12%	**55%**
Maintenance	5%	2%	0%	0%	10%	4%	**6%**
Commission	5%	2%	30%	8%	5%	2%	**11%**
Total	100%	40%	100%	25%	100%	25%	

Figure 52: Use of Target Costing for Defining the Relevant Dimensions for a Distribution Concept based on the Customer's Requirements[662]

Based on a best-estimate of the price-demand curve (i.e., an estimate of expected income at varying price levels), it is possible to estimate the overall commission or fee income, which

---

[659] TECTEM 2002, p. 53.
[660] Nevries, P. and Segbers, K. 2003.
[661] See Hummel, T. 1998; Ziegenbein, K. 2002, pp. 243-50.
[662] Own illustration based on Nevries, P. and Segbers, K. 2003.

can be generated from a new channel concept. Given a certain minimum profit margin, this price-demand curve then computes the allowable cost basis. The Conjoint Analysis can subsequently be used to identify those customer requirements, which the channel concept should address at a given price level (in the figure the customer requirements 'availability', 'advice' and 'convenience' were chosen). At the end of this process, a limited number of product features may remain, which are most relevant to the product from a customer's point of view. In a last step, it is necessary to assess to what extent these customer requirements are specifically met by the most important constituent elements of the channel concept (in the example Hardware, Personnel, Maintenance and Commissions).[663]

While the 'House of Quality' prioritises the allocation of financial resources to different distribution channels, the concept of target costing specifically addresses the questions of intra-channel investments; both concepts adopt a clear customer perspective. Although target costing is certainly not the only instrument to assess the economic sustainability of the overall investment, it may give a first indication whether the expected benefits and costs remain in a sensible and acceptable relationship. Target costing will also help to adapt the channel concepts to the expected profit potential of the different customer segments. While profitable customers can have more access to labour-intensive distribution channels, less profitable customers can only be managed by direct channels if margin requirements remain constant.

In retail banking, **Credit Suisse** has divided its customers into four customer segments based purely on the profitability of the customer segment. This segmentation provided the basis for their distribution strategy. To maintain a certain profit level, customers below CHF 50,000 are exclusively managed via a Call Centre on a rigorous cost basis.[664]

While the profit centre represents a solid basis for monitoring the overall efficiency of the distribution system, **additional financial and non-financial indicators** need to be controlled to be in a position to assess whether the distribution strategy enables the financial provider to achieve its strategic and financial targets.[665] This financial assessment needs to be undertaken both prior to and after the implementation of a multi-channel distribution system based on a number of limited indicators. These indicators need to be derived from the targets of the distribution strategy, e.g. increase in revenues or reduction in distribution costs.[666] Indicators of profitability or effectiveness are to be assessed, either via an external benchmarking or based on a time series analysis, and could include, for example, the following items for each channel and over the entire distribution system: e.g. number of products per customer, numbers of cross- and up-sales, costs per sale as well as sales and marketing costs per customer and ana-

---

663 Nevries, P. and Segbers, K. 2003.
664 TECTEM 2002, p. 64.
665 Bohnenkamp, P. 1999, pp. 33-4.
666 Bohnenkamp, P. 1999, pp. 33-4; see Chapter 5.2.1, p. 82.

lysed by source.[667] In a survey among 41 German companies, especially insurance, banks and retail, the majority of the companies interviewed indicated that they use key performance indicators to manage their distribution channels.[668]

The mere computation of these indicators is of no use, if they are not regularly used when discussing the financial performance with the channel members. It is important to include these indicators in scorecards and link them to the remuneration system. The example of Allstate illustrates the importance of financial indicators being actively used for the management and remuneration of the sales force.

The tied agents of **Allstate** are governed by a contract, which can be terminated with a 90 day notice period. Inside the contract, there is a manual defining the commission system, which can be changed in a more flexible manner at a 90 day notice period. Agents' performance is monitored on four criteria:

- New financial service premium : 15,000 to 20,000 US new business financial services products
- Premium growth (based on a policyholder basis)
- Loss ratio below 65 %
- Compliance with regulation and company policies

If over a period of two years, the agents does not fulfil these criteria and no significant improvement compared to the previous year can be observed, Allstate will terminate the contract. In case of missing the targeted loss ratio, immediate actions are taken. However, in 2001, only a total number of 110 tied agent relationships were terminated.[669]

The following two examples of Deutsche Bank and Citibank provide further practical examples of how a distribution system needs to be financially controlled in order to ensure that the distribution objectives are actually met. A clear focus on a few financial indicators and a rigorous review of these numbers seem to be the key success factors.

Deutsche Bank has developed performance monitoring, which is based on a weekly monitoring of performance as well as on a monthly review of the individual achievements compared to the target. On a quarterly basis, the distribution units are then ranked on a European basis.[670]

---

[667] Weigelt, O. and Engler, K. 2003, pp. 282-284.
[668] Wirtz, B., Schilke, O. and Büttner, T. 2004, p. 47.
[669] TECTEM 2002, p. 41.
[670] Neske, R. 2003, p. 17.

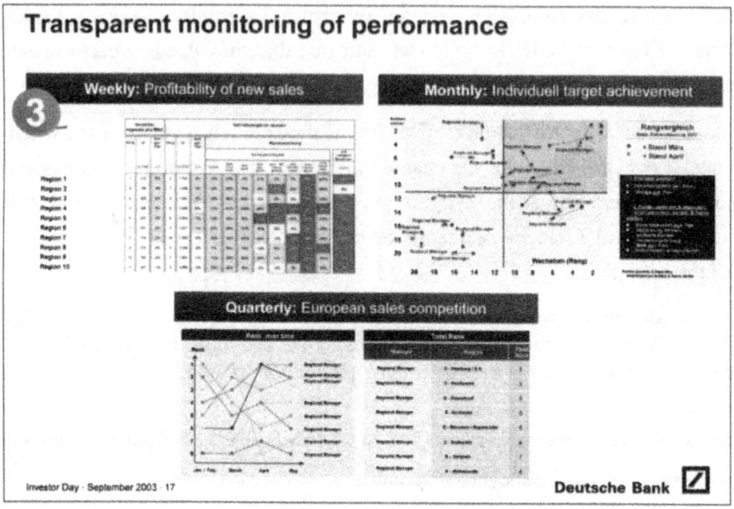

Figure 53: Deutsche Bank - Elements of Monitoring of Sales Performance[671]

The steering of sales activities at the **Citibank** in Germany is based on the following measures: customer profitability, product profitability, channel profitability as well as productivity. In addition, each sales employee receives information as to the expected profit potential within the next 12 months. All information is stored in a high performing management information system, which is updated daily and can be accessed by all sales people.[672]

Nevertheless, the financial steering of a distribution system cannot entirely be limited to an exclusive analysis of the variations of the bottom-line result of a profit centre or to a rigorous ex-ante or ex-post analysis of certain financial indicators. These important financial drivers need to be complemented by other, non-financial indicators, which is particularly important when the company pursues a relationship-oriented distribution strategy. In this case, the company needs to have a clear picture whether the fundamental elements of the relationship strategy (especially the 'ongoing management of truth process') are actively lived up to by all channel members. In addition, these non-financial indicators are of particular importance in those distribution channels, which do not generate their own commission income, but rather provide information or refer customer leads to other distribution channels. These indicators include customer-focussed measures, innovation and learning measures.[673]

Since the function of the non-financial KPIs is to measure the degree to which the primary targets of the distribution strategy are actually realised, the following list illustrates the poten-

---

[671] Neske, R. 2003, p. 17.
[672] TECTEM 2002, p. 54.
[673] Stone, M., Hobbs, M. and Khaleeli, M. 2002, p. 47.

tial scope of indicators. In practice these KPIs need to be derived from the overall distribution strategy and its specific targets:

- **Service Index**: For each customer-related process, a service index needs to be computed regularly, based on the customer's evaluation of the important service features (customer satisfaction) as well as of the quality of the services rendered. The objective would be to maintain the service index on a high level for those services, which the customer considers most important.[674]
- **Multi-Channel Process Index**: KPI measuring the operational capacity of each distribution channel. Based on the customer touch point matrix, this analysis could be complemented by the number of different channels, each customer segment uses on average.
- **Multi-Channel Interaction Index** (e.g. referral of customers across channels): Amount of customers, who were referred from one channel to a different distribution channel, or percentage of customer leads converted into customers. The idea of this indicator is to assess the degree to which the channels actively co-operate, share information about customers and transfer customers to other channels.
- **Specific Channel Performance Indicators:** Waiting time in Call Centres, speed of answering customer requests, Website Performance, etc.
- **Customer Channel Preferences**

The transparent and regular monitoring of channel performance is certainly more important than the mere existence of a performance measurement concept itself, which is often too complicated and not well accepted by the distribution units. The examples of Citibank and Deutsche Bank show that weekly monitoring of sales performance as well as some degree of competition among the distribution channels or unit is crucial to ensure the long-term success of any multi-channel distribution strategy.

[674] Layr, W. and Dahlem, C. 2001, pp. 72-4.

9.3 Conclusion

The last chapter dealt with the effective steering of distribution systems and the following conclusions can be drawn:

- **Steering of distribution system based on profit centres**: The management of a multi-channel distribution system requires the existence of a clear financial basis, preferably in the form of a profit centre, since channels can be held clearly accountable for their distribution activities. It is often the case that only the lead channel in a co-ordinated multi-channel distribution system is managed as a profit centre and thus receives all revenues and costs for its clients, while the other (support) channels are managed as cost centres.
- **Allocation of costs and benefits in a multi-channel distribution system**: One of the central problems relates to the correct allocation of distribution costs to customers and thus lead channels. Since customers define the customer processes for themselves in a co-ordinated multi-channel system, methods taken from the concept of activity-based concept could be used in the form of a Customer Touch Points matrix to compute costs per customer process and allocate them to the respective customer. However, this approach has not yet been tested in practice.
- **Distribution Efficiency and Effectiveness**: Prior to its introduction, the overall economic viability of a new channel concept needs to be assessed (e.g. by using the concept of target costing) given the significant investments required for multi-channel distribution strategies. It is crucial to find out whether the customers really ask for specific elements and are willing to pay for these services.
- **Financial and non-financial Steering of the Distribution System**: After implementation, financial steering of the distribution system based on a profit centre should be complemented by a limited number of financial and non-financial indicators. Non-financial indicators should help to monitor whether the strategic distribution targets will actually be realised. This is particularly important in the case of a relationship-oriented distribution strategy. Finally, it is important to rigorously integrate the financial steering of the distribution system in the entire management process: any significant deviation from certain indicators must give rise to clear actions, which are also clearly visible in the distribution channels.

The clear implementation of such a steering system is crucial to ensure that the envisaged strategic and financial benefits will also be realised.

IV. Conclusion

Changes in the Distribution Landscape for Retail Financial Services

The retail financial services industry, comprising all companies fulfilling customer needs for financial services, is undergoing a major transformation phase initiated by a number of different change factors. The deregulation of the industry, particularly the insurance industry, the capital market crisis and the increased competition of new market entrants (often from other industries) have weakened the competitive position of some financial services companies.

Three fundamental change drivers have been identified and analysed in this dissertation. First, the **distribution landscape for financial services**, which is rather heterogeneous, is characterised by a high degree of competition and dynamic change. In Germany, the classical tied agent is believed to continue to lose market shares, while bancassurance concepts as well as the IFA channel are expected to increase their market shares, both in the insurance as well as mutual fund business. The classical retail bank is under extreme cost pressure, with the result that new branch concepts need to be developed. Value-creating advisory activities need to be strictly separated from administrative tasks, which must be shifted to low-cost channels.

In addition, changes in the distribution landscape are also fuelled by a fundamental change in **customer behaviour**. Consumers are better informed and decide just how, when and where they purchase personalised product solutions; convenient and easily accessible distribution channels are greatly appreciated. As consumer behaviour today is characterised by dynamic, erratic and often unpredictable actions, customers can no longer be assigned to any particular distribution channel. Studies in retail banking confirm that retail banking customers will, in future, use a combination of up to three distribution channels and these multi-channel customers will be even more profitable than customers using only one distribution channel.

The **Internet** represents the third major change driver and has an impact both on the supply and demand side. On the one hand, the Internet has increased competition by providing customers with greater market transparency; it has also influenced consumer behaviour by setting new service standards regarding the instant availability of information and reactivity of the service provider. On the other hand, the Internet has changed the competitive landscape by enabling new players, often from other industries (e.g. process and service providers) to enter the financial services market as well as by enabling companies to explore new business models (e.g. creation of fund platforms by mutual fund providers)

One response to market pressure to increase customer orientation and reduce distribution costs is the establishment of a fully co-ordinated **multi-channel distribution system**, in which the consumer can interact with the financial service provider anytime, anywhere and in any way. While low-margin business and administrative processes are transferred to low-cost distribution channels, the high-touch channels could concentrate more strongly on strengthening the customer relationships. For certain value-creating processes, financial services providers could move away from management of individual transactions to ongoing management of the process of truths with the customer (so-called relationship marketing approach). In doing so there could be an increase in customer retention and better leveraging of the cross-selling potential, while the efficiency of distribution systems increases. Multi-channel distribution could, therefore, be considered as a new business model which allows players in the financial services industry to escape from the continuous efficiency trap.

Identification of the research questions for this dissertation

Given these changes in the financial services industry, practitioners and academics agree that distribution plays a very important role in creating competitive advantages for the financial services company and in ensuring long-term corporate financial performance. Distribution thus plays an integral part in the management of the exchange processes and in safeguarding the long-term company performance and, consequently, represents an important function within the overall management process.

Since the financial services industry is confronted with the simultaneous task of intensifying customer relationships and reducing distribution costs, it is no longer a question of whether to manage multiple distribution channels, but rather a question of how to manage a multi-channel distribution system. Some academic research has been undertaken to structure and analyse the fundamental issues of multi-channel distribution systems as well as to identify the different ways of co-ordinating multi-channel distribution channels based on the theory of transaction cost analysis and relational exchange. As a result, one can generally distinguish between market- vs. rules-based co-ordination forms for multi-channel distribution systems. However, emphasis has been placed – implicitly or explicitly – on the distribution of goods rather than services, thus not taking note of the particular characteristics of services, let alone financial services. Therefore, a systematic analysis of the fundamental strategic and operational dimensions of multi-channel distribution systems in the area of financial services has not yet been performed.

This dissertation has taken up these fundamental, open issues, raised both by the professional and academic world, and has responded to the following two research issues: (i) identification of the most important dimensions of multi-channel distribution systems for financial services and (ii) description and analysis of the relevant operational elements of multi-channel distribution systems for financial services. The usefulness of these findings for the professional world has been at the centre of this research project. Consequently, qualitative research methods, particularly case studies, have been used to develop a very thorough understanding of the phenomena of multi-channel distribution systems. It is believed that case studies best capture the complexity of the research subject and its context and take into account the fact that a comprehensive theory of the co-ordination and configuration of multi-channel distribution systems for financial services does not yet exist.

Major dimensions of multi-channel distribution systems for financial services

Distribution manages the exchange process (marketing flows) between the customer and service provider, while distribution channels are viewed as a system of interdependent agents and institutions. In this context, distribution has two fundamental tasks: configuration and co-ordination of the multi-channel distribution system. However, in order to fulfil these tasks, it is necessary to identify the important dimensions of distribution systems, which can then be used as a basis for the co-ordination and configuration of multi-channel distribution systems for financial services.

Financial services are generally characterised by a high degree of intangibility and need to integrate the customer into the service delivery process; financial services are, to a large degree, embodied in the service delivery process with the customer (i.e., the interaction process with the customer). In this process, information asymmetries between the service provider and the customer arise from the dominance of credence and experience elements in financial services. These information asymmetries give rise to uncertainty, so trust in the service provider represents a very important element. Distribution, linking both parties together, can mitigate this uncertainty by appropriate management of the exchange process. Furthermore, retail financial services have to be defined over and above the core product to include other support and facilitating services into the value proposition. In the concept of the augmented service offering, Grönroos has extended the scope for defining services even further: the accessibility of services, the interaction with the service organisation as well as customer participation are all important product dimensions. It is important to understand that, in such a product definition, distribution becomes an integral part of the product itself and it is responsible for the management of the exchange process during the different phases of the customer's buying cycle. From the point of view of service management, Lehmann developed a concept for defining the degree of customer integration depending on the complexity of the product and the desired level and nature of the customer interaction process. Service management needs to answer the question of whether to manage the exchange process with the customer as an individual ('discrete') transaction or as a process of ongoing ('relational') exchanges.

Distribution has the overall task of configuring and co-ordinating the distribution system, whereby one needs to distinguish between the internal and external fit of a distribution system. The following figure sums up the most relevant dimensions for the analysis and management of multi-channel distribution systems.

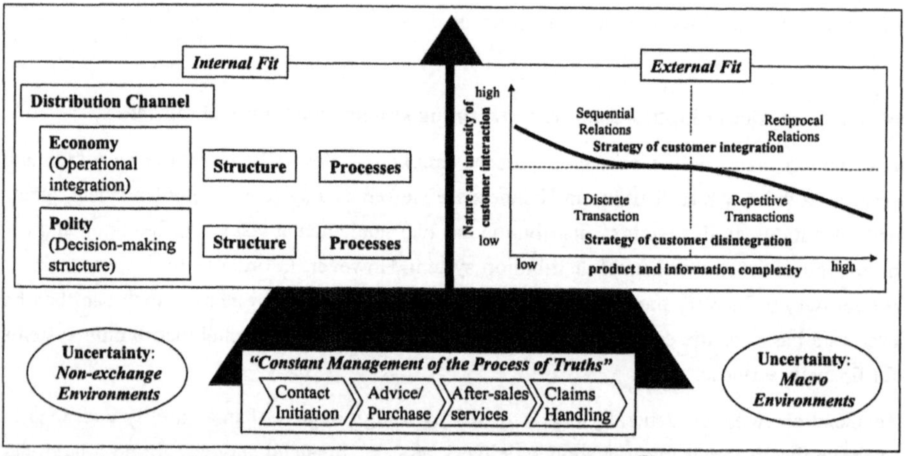

Figure 54: Comprehensive Framework for the Analysis of Distribution Systems[675]

The **internal fit** refers to the 'internal functioning' of the distribution system. Here, the Political Economy Paradigm has identified two important dimensions: the internal economic and operational integration of the distribution channels (economy) as well as the decision-making mechanisms (polity). Both dimensions can further be broken down into the two components of processes and structure. Economic structure refers to the way the distribution channel is organised and the degree of economic autonomy of the channel, ranging from fully independent distribution channels organised in separate legal entities to completely integrated distribution channels. Each economic structure of a channel also requires specific internal economic processes, referring to the way marketing functions are shared among channel members and resources are allocated and controlled across distribution channels. The second important dimension relates to the polity of distribution channels, which refers to the allocation and use of authority and power (i.e., potential for influence) as well as to the decision-making mechanisms within the distribution system. The socio-political structure is defined by the power-dependence relations, while the socio-political processes refer to the relationship of co-operation or conflict between and inside the distribution channels. In the case of financial services, most notably insurance services, particular attention needs to be paid to the management of the internal conflicts (socio-economic processes) as well as to the distribution of power (socio-economic structures).

[675] Own Illustration.

The **external fit** refers, above all, to the appropriate fit between the service provider and the customer. The way this external fit can be achieved depends, on the one hand, on the product complexity (i.e., product properties) as well as on the intended nature and intensity of customer interaction on the other hand. Lehmann's framework for the development of two generic service strategies for customer integration and disintegration provides a more concrete definition of the concept of the 'external customer fit'.

Furthermore, both the internal and external fit ultimately relates to the management of the exchange processes with the customer during the different phases of the customer buying cycle. The more the customer is integrated into the different **phases of the buying cycle**, the more the internal functioning of the distribution system is influenced by the customer interaction process. Creating the optimal context for customer interactions represents the ultimate distribution and service challenge. All corporate activities and capabilities have to be directed to this fundamental service task.

In addition, the PEP framework clearly points out that uncertainty, resulting from the **non-exchange and macro exchange environment**, also has an influence on the distribution system. In this context, multi-channel distribution systems can be seen as a possible vehicle for reducing environmental uncertainty, as the distribution strategy is based on a number of different distribution channels.

The strategic and financial context for distribution management

Distribution management is considered as part of general management, responsible for the planning, organisation, management and controlling of the distribution system. Therefore, distribution management needs to be embedded in the overall context of strategic management. The corporate strategy identifies the key value drivers of a business model (e.g. customer acquisition, customer retention) and constitutes the basis for the appropriate marketing approach, which has to design all aspects of the customer interaction process more specifically. This interaction process can either be seen as the ongoing management of an exchange process or as a one-off, distinct transaction. These two different views lead to entirely different marketing concepts. While transaction-oriented marketing focuses on optimising the individual exchange by limiting the degree of customer involvement to a minimum, relationship marketing believes that the customer extracts additional value from the on-going exchange processes itself. These two distinct marketing concepts clearly require different types of multi-channel distribution systems.

Different structures of multi-channel distribution systems

Multi-channel distribution systems can be classified on the basis of the two extremes of purely focussed vs. entirely co-ordinated multi-channel distribution systems. However, in practice, hybrid distribution systems are far more common, where, for each element of the distribution system, it has to be reviewed as to what extent this element needs to be particularly developed and maintained for one distribution channel or can be shared across all channels.

Focussed distribution systems can pursue a number of different strategies of price- and product-differentiation across their different customer segments and distribution channels, provided that the customer segments are significantly large and have very little overlap. The additional costs for maintaining separate distribution channels are justified by the possibility of realising higher margins in the different customer segments. The advantage is that new channels can easily be added without destabilising the remaining distribution system. In a highly uncertain market environment, a number of distribution channels can be maintained simultaenously to see how the market will develop. Nevertheless, in more stable markets the appropriate number of separate distribution channels needs to be reviewed.

Co-ordinated multi-channel distribution strategies try to leverage the customer potential of the existing customers more strongly. The idea is that the primary sales channel should be freed up from all non-sales or administrative tasks so that it can concentrate on concrete sales activities. In addition, other channels support sales activities throughout the entire buying cycle to ensure utmost customer integration. Thus, these channels also contribute to strengthening the customer relationship and thereby increase the value for the customers. In order to ensure optimal co-operation internally, there needs to be a low level of conflict, whereby the power is normally centred around the lead channel in this distribution system. Co-ordinated multi-channel strategies seem to achieve stronger customer retention, while reducing distribution costs at the same time. Despite these benefits, this distribution strategy is also associated with a significant increase in complexity and co-ordination requirements, which inevitably cause higher costs (IT costs, management costs, etc.). Therefore, this distribution strategy may only be possible in high-margin industries or in companies of a sufficient size and with a strong market position. In order to ensure that all distribution channels work together effectively, strong, centralised management of all channel activities is necessary.

The following table sums up the major results of this dissertation regarding the description of the most important dimensions of the two types of multi-channel distribution strategy.

	Focussed Multi-Channel Strategy	Co-ordinated Multi-Channel Strategy
Financial Targets	Primary focus on growth in new customers and on increase in market share.	Primary focus on profitability of existing customers, while realising synergies by sharing resources across channels.
Strategic Objective	Market Development : Each channel is focussed on a specific customer group.	Market Penetration : Strong focus on penetrating the existing customer base.
Marketing Approach	Dominance of transaction marketing with emphasis on efficient service delivery, except in the case of a niche strategy (e.g. low number of serviced customer).	Dominance of relationship marketing: Ongoing management of the customer exchange process, all channels manage the customer relationship.
Internal Economy	**Structure**: Each distribution channel organised in a separate company with clear contractual agreements with product suppliers. **Processes**: High degree of decentralisation - with clear management autonomy within the constraints of the defined corporate targets.	**Structure**: complete vertical integration of all distribution channels, clear definition of channel roles, carefully designed governance structure. **Processes:** Focus on products, "end of pipe" philosophy; Low degree of customer integration.
Internal Polity	**Structure**: equitable distribution of power across different channels; more successful channels have easier access to capital. **Processes**: Clear conflict among channels due to price discrimination and cannibalisation, channels need to be as separate as possible.	**Structure**: Clear dominance of one channel (lead channel); strong and powerful managers necessary to manage channel conflicts **Processes**: Co-operation is vital to leverage the customer base across all channels; some conflict necessary to avoid complacency.
External Environment	Highly uncertain environment: a portfolio of different channels can help to respond to any unexpected change in consumer behaviour.	Strategy responds to constant changes in consumer preferences; this uncertainty is partially absorbed by providing multiple channels

Figure 55: Specification of the Major Dimensions of Focussed vs. Co-ordinated Distribution Systems[676]

Now that the two distinct types of multi-channel distribution systems have been analysed from a top-down, strategic perspective on the basis of a comprehensive framework for the analysis of distribution systems, operational management requires clearer identification of the most relevant operational elements of the distribution system.

The operational elements of multi-channel distributions - External Fit

Branding is one of the most complex issues in channel management, but it is, nevertheless, essential to differentiate the service offering in the eyes of the consumers. One can generally decide between uniform branding across all channels or channel-specific branding. This decision is driven by the degree to which the attributes of an existing brand can be extended to new distribution channels and by the strategic positioning of the individual channels. Furthermore, the additional marketing costs for a new brand need to be taken into account. How-

[676] Own Illustration.

ever, branding is not confined to the brand itself, but includes all messages sent to the customers. The insight that "everything sends a brand message" calls for an integrated communication strategy. The more distribution channels in place, the more complex the implementation of such an integrated communication strategy. A co-ordinated multi-channel distribution system requires active and integrated management of the customer communication processes via all access points. High IT investments in integrated front-office systems are necessary to store all relevant customer data in the various channels. Companies may, therefore, want to opt for a focussed multi-channel system, where the complexity of managing the communication process can be limited to the individual distribution channel. Each distribution channel is separated by its own brand and branding (i.e., communication) policy.

Channel management needs to understand customer preferences for channel usage, so an appropriate **segmentation of the customers** is crucial to ensure an optimal fit between the customer and the service provider. If the service provider has an intimate knowledge of customer preferences for specific channels and their usage in various situations, the distribution channels can be aligned more effectively with customer behaviour. Profitability-based segmentation approaches are important for identifying the major profit pools and for allocating customers to specific distribution channels, but they are not helpful in predicting channel behaviour; this also applies to the traditional socio-demographic or socio-economic segmentation approaches. Behavioural or psychographic approaches, for example based on customer's knowledge in financial affairs and general attitudes (fundamental beliefs), are more effective.

Once the overall communication strategy has been defined and implemented and the targeted customer segment has been identified, the **product and pricing strategy** then needs to be designed. Generally speaking, co-ordinated distribution systems ask for a uniform product and pricing system, whereas focussed distribution systems have the advantage that the product and pricing questions can be determined separately for each distribution channel based on customer preferences, price elasticity, distribution costs as well as competitors. More complex products, where the customers perceive high risks, are more appropriate for personal, face-to-face distribution channels, while less complex products are suitable for direct distribution channels. However, the product offering goes far beyond the positioning of the core product in a specific distribution channel; it also includes the positioning of support and facilitating product elements in the various distribution channels. The combination of different distribution channels to enhance the value of the core product for the customer is one of the fundamental advantages of co-ordinated multi-channel distribution systems.

The correct **pricing of the product** represents a crucial prerequisite for the socio-political stability of the distribution system, but also for the economic attractiveness of the distribution strategy. Although a uniform pricing system seems to be the easier solution in a co-ordinated multi-channel environment in order to avoid all channel conflicts and to ensure active channel interaction, this is not the best economic solution. It is better to fix a price brand, where price differences among the distribution channels are justified by clear differences in the service offering of each channel. Furthermore, explicit pricing of certain services offers some possibility of introducing price differentiation and of encouraging customers to use low-cost distribution channels. In the case of clearly different distribution costs across channels and the existence of different customer segments, a focussed distribution system is more appropriate to better leverage the different channel and customer economics.

Pricing also represents an important instrument to **change customer behaviour** regarding channel usage. Distribution systems exhibit a high level of inertia and stability, so customers need to be actively familiarised (i.e., trained) with a newly configured distribution system. Staff members in the established distribution channels play an important role in the attempt to dispel customer fear vis-à-vis the new distribution channels. Finally, the following table sums up the major operational elements which ensure the external fit with the customer.

	Focussed Multi-Channel Strategy	Co-ordinated Multi-Channel Strategy
Branding / Communication	Separate branding and communication for each channel; brands are aligned with the different customer segments and distribution channels.	Brand needs to be versatile to allow one uniform brand across all channels; the flow of brand contacts needs to be managed across channels via an integrated communication strategy.
Customer Segmentation	Customers are segmented based on existing and potential profitability. Additional segmentation efforts to capture differences in channel behaviour are <u>not</u> necessary.	Segmentation based on existing and potential profitability;additional segmentation necessary to capture differences in channel behaviour.
Product Positioning	Products are separately positioned in each channel. The product properties need to be aligned with the properties of the individual channel.	Positioning of the core product complemented by additional services in other channels to enhance overall value; use of House of Quality to review whether these services add value for the customer.
Pricing	Each distribution channel has full autonomy in pricing products within the constraints of financial targets.	Uniform pricing or overall management of the pricing system (e.g. via a price band); a managed pricing system can exploit the different channel economics. Pricing to be derived from the distribution costs, the customer's utility of the services and competitors' behaviour; use of explicit pricing at least for some services.
Trans-formation	No Issue	Ongoing transformation better than abrupt changes: Customer training, granting of financial incentives and active involvement of the established channels help to change customer behaviour.

Figure 56: Description of the Major Dimensions of the External Fit of Distribution Systems[677]

[677] Own Illustration.

The operational elements of multi-channel distributions - Internal Fit

The appropriate **organisational set-up** represents a particular challenge for co-ordinated multi-channel systems. In order to ensure the consistency of brand and communication messages in the customer interaction processes, it is generally necessary to have a central unit with corresponding budgetary and disciplinary authority to ensure effective steering of the distribution channels. The shift from product-focussed to customer-centric distribution strategies may also lead to a bifurcation of the traditionally integrated financial services company into two separate units, i.e., client management and product management. While the client manager can focus on the overall management of customer contacts via multiple channels, the product managers concentrate on the important tasks of product development and product administration. However, the overall connectedness of the organisation needs to be very actively managed, e.g. by defining specific organisation interfaces and by setting up transversal teams with corresponding budgetary authority.

The **remuneration of the individual channels** for their sales activities represents one of the fundamental prerequisites for a stable and well performing distribution system. This is particularly challenging in co-ordinated distribution systems, where different channels are involved in the customer interaction process. It is therefore important to clearly define the question of customer ownership, which is directly linked to channel compensation, and, in this context, to define how different channels are remunerated for their commercial activities. In practice, customers are usually allocated to a lead channel, while all other channels have access to these customers. It is important that all commercial campaigns be discussed among the channels in advance and all formal rules of customer contact are fully complied with. One possibility is to set up dedicated multi-channel committees. The remuneration system can encourage cross-channel interaction via bonus payments or via the underlying commission system itself. In order to gain flexibility in adding new distribution channels as well as to adapt the remuneration system to the actual economics of each distribution channel, a gross distribution margin needs to be defined between the distribution unit and the product provider. This gross distribution margin can then be reduced by the actual distribution costs of each channel to define the net distribution margin (i.e., commission payments) for the individual channel.

However, all of these efforts to ensure the internal fit of the distribution system only develop its true potential if the internal **transformation process** is clearly and actively managed. Experience- and trust-based learning, coupled with some degree of team-based competition, can help to successfully manage the transformation process, where, in the end, all channel members are firmly committed to the new distribution approach. The following table sums up the major operational elements which ensure the internal fit of the distribution systems.

	Focussed Multi-Channel Strategy	Co-ordinated Multi-Channel Strategy
Organisational Structure	Each distribution channel is managed separately, preferably in an independent legal entity or as a autonomous profit centre. Sourcing and marketing functions are performed by each distribution channel.	Central unit for channel management with budgetary authority. The organisation is often bifurcated into product management and channel management; but explicit organisational interfaces between the units and transversal steering committees are necessary to ensure the overall connectedness of the organisation.
Customer Ownership & Remuneration	Generally no issue. Channel compensation has to be aligned with the underlying channel economics.	Customer are generally "owned" by the lead channel while all channels have access to the customers with clear respect of the formal rules of customer contact. Channels should only be rewarded for the distribution functions they perform. The lead channel often receives an overall channel compensation for their own customers regardless of their contribution to the transaction. Cross-channel interaction often promoted via bonus payments.
Transformation	Generally no issue since focussed multi-channel strategies are generally not confronted with the issue of directing customers to a new distribution channels.	Multi-channel distribution strategies should be positioned as win-win strategies for all channels. Open communication about the ratioanale of the distribution strategy, financial incentives, team experience and active management of the change process help to foster internal change.

Figure 57: Description of the Major Dimensions of the Internal Fit of Distribution Systems[678]

Financial steering and assessment of the distribution system

The management of a multi-channel distribution system also requires the existence of a clear financial basis, whereby cost or profit centres represent the most feasible basis. In practice, only the lead channel in a co-ordinated multi-channel distribution system is managed as a profit centre and, thus, receives all revenues and costs for its clients while the other (support) channels are managed as cost centres. One of the central problems in co-ordinated multi-channel systems relates to the correct allocation of distribution costs to customers and thus to the distribution channels which own the customer relationship. Little experience and knowledge exist as to the comprehensive calculation of the costs of multi-channel business processes since the customer defines the business process each time based on the arbitrary combination of the different distribution channels in the customer buying cycle. Some first concepts for the allocation of costs in a multi-channel environment with changing customer processes have been derived from the theory of activity-based costing.

Prior to the introduction of a new channel concept, the overall economic viability of the distribution concept needs to be evaluated (e.g. by using the concept of target costing) given the

678 Own Illustration.

significant investments required for multi-channel distribution strategies. An assessment of customer willingness to pay for the additional investments in distribution channels on a long-term basis is necessary. After implementation, the financial steering of the distribution system based on a profit centre should be complemented by a limited number of financial and non-financial indicators. Non-financial indicators should help to monitor whether the strategic targets of the distribution strategy will actually be realised. This is particularly important in the case of a relationship-oriented distribution strategy. Finally, it is imperative to rigorously integrate the financial steering of the distribution system into the entire management process: any significant deviation from certain indicators must give rise to specific actions which are also clearly visible in the distribution channels and in the entire organisation.

Final conclusion and research outlook

Finally, it can be concluded that this dissertation provides managers of financial services companies with an overall comprehensive framework which identifies the relevant dimensions for the co-ordination and configuration of multi-channel distribution strategies. This framework has been complemented by the identification of the relevant, operational elements which have to be taken into account when designing and managing multi-channel distribution channels. It is important to bear in mind that this dissertation has derived its major conclusions from the analysis of the current experiences of selected financial services players. Case-study research has been one of the fundamental research methods. The conclusions of this dissertation are thus relevant to the current economic and socio-political context of the financial services industry. The traditional concerns about these research methods, such as lack of rigour or the missing basis for scientific generalisation, are fully recognised.

Therefore, future empirical and theoretical research should focus on the validation of the major conclusions presented in this dissertation. In addition, this analysis, which has deliberately adopted the point of view of management of a financial services company, needs to be complemented by a detailed, empirical analysis of customer attitudes and expectations regarding multi-channel processes for financial services. This refers - among other issues - to the question of how the different constituent elements of financial services (core product, support and facilitating services, etc.) can best be positioned via multiple distribution channels. In addition, the question of how to change established customer behaviour with respect to channel usage also needs to be investigated further; here more empirical evidence is necessary. Furthermore, the financial management and steering of multi-channel distribution systems still represents a significant but still unexplored field of research. Consequently, a more comprehensive concept for the monitoring and financial evaluation of multi-channel business processes should be developed in more detail.

V. Bibliography

Achrol, R. S., Reve, T. and Stern, L. W. [1983]: The Environment of Marketing Channel Dyads: A Framework for Comparative Analysis. In: Journal of Marketing, Vol. 47, Fall 1983, p. 55-67.

Ackermann, W. [2001]: Wertschöpfungsstrategien auf Finanzdienstleistungsmärkten. In: Ackermann, W. (ed.): Financial Services- Modelle und Strategien der Wertschöpfung, Band 1, Institut für Versicherungswirtschaft der Universität St. Gallen, pp. 67-82.

Ahlert, D. [1991]: Distributionspolitik, 2nd edition, Stuttgart.

Ambros, H. [2001]: Multi-Channel - Strukturwandel im Retail Banking. In: Schmoll, A. and Ronzal, W. (eds.): Neue Wege zum Kunden - Multi-Channel-Vertrieb im Bankgeschäft, pp. 183-204.

Anderson, E., Day, G. and Rangan, V. K. [1997]: Strategic Channel Design. In: Sloan Management Review, Summer, pp. 59-69.

Andreassen, T. W. and Lanseng, E. [1997]: The principal's and agent's contribution to customer loyalty within an integrated service distribution channel – an external perspective". In: European Journal of Marketing, Vol. 31 No. 7, 1997, pp. 487-503.

Ansoff, H. [1965]: Corporate Strategy, New York.

Arndt, J. [1993]: The Political Economy Paradigm: Foundation for Theory Building in Marketing. In: Journal of Marketing, Vol. 47, Fall 1983, pp. 44-54.

AXA Germany [2004]: 2003 Annual Report, Cologne, Germany.

Arnold, P., Wheeler, B. and Abernathy, C. [1999]: Shopping for value: Insurance distribution in the information age. In: CPCU Journal Media, Fall, pp. 140-152.

Bagozzi, R. [1995]: Reflections on Relationship Marketing in Consumer Markets. In: Journal of the Academy of Marketing Science, Vol. 23, No. 4, pp. 272-277.

Bäte, O., Esser, M. and Staar, S. [2002]: Neue Strategien für Finanzdienstleister. In: Versicherungswirtschaft, No. 4, pp. 232-236.

Bäte, O., Esser, M. and Staar, S. [2002a]: Neue Strategien für Finanzdienstleister II. In: Versicherungswirtschaft, No. 5, pp. 304-307.

Bauer, H., Leach, M. and Grether, M. [1998]: Der Beitrag des Internet zum Relationship Marketing – eine theoretische und empirische Analyse. working paper No. 129, Mannheim.

Beisheim, O. (ed.) [1999]: Distribution im Aufbruch - Bestandsaufnahme und Perspektiven, München.

Bekier, M., Flur, D. and Singham, S. [2000]: A future for bricks and mortar. In: McKinsey Quarterly, No. 3, pp. 78-85.

Bekier, M. and Flur, D. [2000]: A future for bricks and motar, US Banker, New York, October, pp. 76-80.

Belz, C. (ed.) [1986]: Realisierung des Marketing, Festschrift zum 60. Geburtstag von Prof. Dr. H. Weinhold-Stünzi, St. Gallen.

Belz, C. [1995]: Dynamische Marktsegmentierung. Fachbericht für Marketing 95/2 des Forschungsinstitutes für Absatz und Handel an der Hochschule St. Gallen, St. Gallen.

Belz, C. (ed.) [1998]: Management von Geschäftsbeziehungen: Konzepte - Integrierter Ansätze - Anwendungen in der Praxis, St. Gallen, Wien.

Belz, C. [1998a]: Erkenntnis zum systematischen Beziehungsmanagement. In: Belz, C.: Management von Geschäftsbeziehungen: Konzepte - Integrierte Ansätze - Anwendungen in der Praxis, St. Gallen, Wien, pp. 17-126.

Belz, C. [2001]: Leistung für Kundenvorteile. In: Maas, P. (ed.): Integriertes Dienstleistungs-Management: Auf dem Weg zum Customer Value, St. Gallen, pp. 63-81.

Belz, C. [2002]: Marketing Update 2005 - Akzente im innovativen Marketing, St. Gallen.

Bennett, D. and Salazar, C. [2003]: Challenges in Assessing Distribution Effectiveness for Life Insurers. In: National Underwriter, Life & Health/Financial Services Edition, May 19, Vol. 107, No. 20, p. 36.

Benölken, H. and Wings, H. [2003]: Neue Strategien in geändertem Umfeld. In: Bankmagazin, No. 2, pp. 42-44.

Berger, A., Cummins, J., Weiss, M. [1997]: The Coexistence of Multiple Distribution Systems for Financial Services: The Case of Property-Liability Insurance. In: Journal of Business, Vol. 70, No. 4., pp. 515-546.

Berghe, Van den L.A.A., Verweire, K. and Roelandt, P. [2001]: How the economy is changing the financial services industry. In: Ackermann, W. (ed.): Financial Services - Modelle und Strategien der Wertschöpfung, Band 1. Institut für Versicherungswirtschaft der Universität St. Gallen, pp. 101-124.

Bergmann, G. [1988]: Strategisches Absatzkanalmanagement in Märkten mit hoher Nachfragemacht des Handels – Eine Bestandsaufnahme mit Beispielen aus der Möbelindustrie, Frankfurt.

Berman, B. [1996]: Marketing Channels, New York.

Bernskötter, H. [1991]: Gehört die Zukunft den "hybriden" Verkaufssystemen? In: Marketing Journal, Heft 2/91, pp. 122-129.

Berry, L. [1983]: Relationship Marketing. In: Berry, L., Shostack, G. and Upah, G. (ed.): Emerging Perspectives on Services Marketing, Chicago, pp. 25-28.

Berry, L. and Parasuraman, A. [1991]: Marketing Services, Competing Through Quality. New York, NY.

Berry, L. [1995]: Relationship Marketing of Services – Growing Interest, Emerging Perspectives. In: Journal of the Academy of Marketing Science, Vol. 23, No .4, pp. 236-245.

Bezold, T. [1996]: Zur Messung der Dienstleistungsqualität: eine theoretische und empirische Studie zur Methodenentwicklung unter besonderer Berücksichtigung des ereignisorientierten Ansatzes, Frankfurt am Main.

Bhattacharya, C. and Bolton, R. [2000]: Relationship Marketing in Mass Markets. In: Sheth, J. and Parvatiyar, A. (ed.): Handbook of relationship marketing, Sage Publications: California, pp. 327-354.

Biesel, H. [2002]: Kundenmanagement im Multi-Channel-Vertrieb - Strategien und Werkzeuge für die konsequente Kundenorientierung, Wiesbaden.

Bittl, A. [1998]: Image und Vertrauen als zukünftige Erfolgsfaktoren in der Assekuranz. In: Versicherungswirtschaft, No. 20, pp. 662-667.

Black, N., Lockett, A., Ennew, C., Winkelhofer, H. and McKechnie, S. [2002]: Modelling consumer choice of distribution channels: an illustration from financial services. In: International Journal of Bank Marketing, Vol. 20, No. 4, pp. 161-173.

Blommen, D. [1997]: Interorganisationale Macht und Abhängigkeit im Absatzkanal – Determinanten und Wirkungen, Aachen.

Böhler, J. [1992]: Betriebsform, Wachstum und Wettbewerb, Wiesbaden.

Bohnenkamp, P. [1999]: Controlling im Multi-Channel-Banking. In: Kostenrechnungspraxis, No. 43, Issue No. 1, pp. 30-34.

Bonnes-Valkyser, R. and Engels, C. [2003]: Neue Konzepte für den Filialbetrieb. In: Bankmagazin, No. 10, pp. 42-3.

Bonoma, T. [1985]: Case Research in Marketing: Opportunities, Problems, and a Process. In: Journal of Marketing Research, Vol. 55, January, pp. 1-9.

Bormann, S. and Hientzsch, R. [2001]: Vertriebskanäle im Umbruch. In: Versicherungswirtschaft, No. 21, pp. 1730-2.

Bridges, S., Keller, K. and Sood, S. [2000]: Communication Strategies for Brand Extensions: Enhancing Perceived Fit by Establishing Explanatory Link. In: Journal of Advertising, Vol. 29, No. 4, Winter, pp. 1-11.

Brunner, W. and Lutz, S. [2001]: Internet-Banking im "Konzert der Vertriebswege". In: Schmoll, A. and Ronzal, W. (eds.): Neue Wege zum Kunden - Multi-Channel-Vertrieb im Bankgeschäft, pp. 253-268.

Buhl, H. U. and Mellwig, N. [2002]: Der Einfluss des Internetvertriebs auf die Bank- und Versicherungsmärkte. In: Basedow, J., Meyer, U., Rückle, D. and Schwintowski, H.-P. (eds.): Europäisches Privatversicherungsrecht, steuerrechtliche Rahmenbedingungen im Versicherungswesen, Perspektiven und Entwicklungslinien im Versicherungsvertrieb: Beiträge zur zehnten Wissenschaftstagung des Bundes der Versicherten, Baden-Baden, pp. 173-197.

Buschbeck, P. [2003]: Die aktuelle Strategie der Citibank Privatkunden AG - Erfolgsfaktoren für 2003. In: Die Bank, No. 7, pp. 472- 476.

Büschgen, H. [1979]: Absatzwegepolitik. In: Bank und Markt, Year 8, No. 3, pp. 33-35; No. 4, pp. 29-31 and No. 5, pp. 29-31.

Cespedes, F. V. [1988]: Channel Management is General Management. In: California Management Review, Fall, pp. 98- 120.

Cespedes, F. [1988a]: Control vs. Resources in Channel Design: Distribution Differences in One Industry. In: Industrial Marketing Management, New York, Vol. 17, pp. 215-227.

Cespedes, F. V. and Corey, R. E. [1990]: Managing Multiple Channels. In: Business Horizons, No. 4/90, pp. 67-77.

Chen, J. [1997]: Insurance Calling. In: Best's Review P&C, August 1997, pp. 70-73.

Christensen, C. and Tedlow, R. [2000]: Patterns of Disruption in Retailing. In: Harvard Business Review, Vol. 78, No. 1, pp. 42-6.

Clercks, M. [1991]: Multidistribution in Europa – wo stehen wir und wo gehen wir hin? Manuskript zum Vortrag gehalten anlässlich des Swiss Broker Forum, 1991.

Choudhury, V. et al. [2000]: Web versus Agent: A Consumer Choice Perspective. In: International Insurance Society: The Power of Leadership in the Knowledge Millenium, Vol. 2000, pp. 136-150.

Coenenberg, A. G. [1999]: Kostenrechnung und Kostenanalyse, 4th edition, Landsberg/Lech.

Corsten, H. [1997]: Dienstleistungsmanagement, 3. Aufl., München, Wien.

CPCU [1999]: Shopping for Value: Insurance Distribution in the Information Age. In: CPCU Journal, Fall, pp. 140-152.

Cramer, J.-E. [1998]: Banken im Wettbewerb: Schlankheitskur gefragt. In: Bank und Markt, January, pp. 15-21.

CSC Ploenzke [2000]: Trendbericht Versicherung, Geschäftsbereich Versicherung, May 2000.

Cummins, J. D. and Weiss, M. A. [1997]: The Coexistence of Multiple Distribution Systems for Financial Services: The Case of Property-Liability Insurance. In: Journal of Business, 1997, Vol. 70, No. 4, pp. 515-546.

Damm, P. [1993]: Ertragsbarwertbezogene Vergütungspolitik von Versicherungsunternehmen zur Steuerung von Absatzorganen, Karlsruhe.

Day, G. [2000]: Capabilities for Forging Customer Relationships, Marketing Science Institute, Working paper, Report No. 00-118.

Delisle, E. [1993]: Versicherungsmarketing, Wiesbaden.

Devlin, J. and Wright, M. [1995]: The changing environment of financial services. In: Ennew, C., Watkins, T. and Wright M. (eds.): Marketing Financial Services, 2nd edition, Butterworth-Heinmann, pp. 1-32.

Devlin, J. [2001]: Consumer evaluation and competitive advantage in retail financial services. In: European Journal of Marketing, Vol. 35, No. 5/6, pp. 639-660.

Diepen van, T. [2000]: Multi-Channel Distribution in Financial Services. Impact of Electronic Distribution Channels on the Internal Organization. In: TIC -AMSTERDAM - Vol. 6, pp. 37-60.

Diller, H. [1995]: Kundenbindung als Zielvorgabe im Beziehungs-Marketing, Working Paper No. 40, Department of Marketing at the University of Nürnberg-Erlangen, Germany.

Dohmen, C. [2004]: Die Zukunft liegt im Supermarkt. In: Handelsblatt, 13 February 2004.

Donnelly, J., Berry, L. and Thompson, T. [1985]: Marketing Financial Services – a strategic vision, Homewood, Illinois.

Duncan, T. and Moriarty, S. [1997]: Driving Brand Value, New York.

Duncan, T. and Moriarty, S. [1998]: A Communication-based Marketing Model for Managing Relationships. In: Journal of Marketing, 62 (April), pp. 1-13.

Dwyer, F., Schurr, P. and Oh, S. [1987]: Developing Buyer-Seller Relationships. In: Journal of Marketing, Vol. 51, April, pp. 11-27.

Easingwood, C. and Storey, C. [1996]: The Value of Multi-Channel Distribution Systems in the Financial Service Sector. In: The Service Industries Journal, Vol. 16, No. 12, pp. 223-242.

Easingwood, C. and Coelho, F. [2003]: Single Versuch Multiple Strategies: Typologies and Drivers. In: The Service Industries Journal, Vol. 23, No. 2, March, pp. 31-46.

Eggert, U. [1997]: Konsumententrends, Düsseldorf.

Ehrler, B. [1999]: Kernkompentenzorientiertes Management der Versicherung - Strategien in Risiko- und Finanzdienstleistungsnetzen, St. Gallen.

Eierhoff, K. [2002]: Medienprodukte über alle Kanäle für mehr Kunden - die Click-and-Mortar-Strategie der Bertelsmann AG. In: Schögel, M., Tomczak, T. and Belz, C. (eds.): Roadm@p to E-Business - Wie Unternehmen das Internet erfolgreich nutzen, Festschrift zum 75. Geburtstag von Prof. Dr. Heinz Weinhold-Stünzi, St. Gallen, pp. 344-360.

Emerson, R. [1962]: Power – Dependence Relations. In: American Sociological Review, Vol. 27 (February), pp. 31-41.

Ennew, C. [1995]: Developing marketing strategy. In: Ennew, C., Watkins, T. and Wright M. (eds.) [1995]: Marketing Financial Services, 2nd edition, Butterworth-Heinmann, pp. 60-85.

Ennew, C. [1995a]: Product Strategy. In: Ennew, C., Watkins, T. and Wright, M. (eds.) [1995]: Marketing Financial Services, 2nd edition, Butterworth-Heinmann, pp. 96-112.

Ennew, C., Watkins, T. and Wright M. (eds.) [1995]: Marketing Financial Services, 2nd edition, Butterworth-Heinmann.

Eschke, S., Bölscher, J. and Schulenburg, J.-M. Graf v. d. [2001]: Customer Relationship Management in der Versicherungwirtschaft, Band 2, Hannoveraner Reihe zur Versicherungs-informatik, 1. Aufl., Göttingen.

Eversheim, W., Eickholt, J. and Müller, M. [1995]: QFD - Methode der Qualitätsplanung. In: Pressmass, D. (eds.): TQM I, Schriften zur Unternehmensführung Band 54, Wiesbaden, pp. 62-75.

Farny, D. [2001]: Allfinanzprodukte für private Haushalten. In: Ackermann, W. (ed.): Financial Services- Modelle und Strategien der Wertschöpfung, Band 1, Institut für Versicherungswirtschaft der Universität St. Gallen, St. Gallen, pp. 39-49.

Fenton, J. and Williams, C. [2003]: Finding 'Economic Value' in Distribution. In: Emphasis, No. 2, pp.14-7.

Finsinger, J. and Schmid, F. A. [1994]: Prices, Distribution Channels and Regulatory Intervention in European Insurance Markets. In: The Geneva Papers on Risk and Insurance, No. 70, January 1994, pp. 22-36.

Fischer, K. [1999]: Vertriebswege-Management – Aufbau integrierter Geschäftssysteme. In: Versicherungswirtschaft, No. 21, pp. 1627-1631.

Fischer, T. [1998]: Multibranding vs. einheitliche Markenphilosophie im Vertriebswege-Mix. In: Multi Channel Distribution im Banking: Tagungsband zum 6. Basler Bankentag, November 19, 1998, Basler Bankenvereinigung: Bern, Stuttgart, Wien, pp. 89-111.

Flur, D., Mendonca, L. and Nakache, P. [1997]: Personal Financial Services: A question of channels. In: McKinsey Quarterly, No. 3, pp. 116-125.

Frazier, G. [1999]: Organizing and Managing Channels of Distribution. In: Journal of the Academy of Marketing Science, Vol. 27, No. 2, pp. 226-240.

Frazier, G. and Antia, K. [1995]: Exchange Relationships and Interfirm Power in Channels of Distribution. In: Journal of the Academy of Marketing Science, Vol. 23, No. 4, pp. 321-326.

Frenkel, S. and Donoghue, L. [1996]: Call Centres and Service Excellence: Design and Management Challenges to Support a Service Excellence Strategy - A Knowledge Worker Case Study, CCC Papper, No. 066, University of New South Wales, Sydney.

Friedman, L. and Furey, T. [1999]: The Channel Advantage – Going to market with multiple sales channels to reach more customers, to sell more products, make more profits, Oxford.

Fritz, W. [1999]: Marketing und Vertrieb in der Versicherungsbranche an der Schwelle zum 21. Jahrhundert, Technische Universität Braunschweig, Braunschweig.

Fröhner, R. [1969]: Lebensversicherung der Assekuranz, Versicherung auf dem Weg zum Marketing. In: Die Absatzwirtschaft, No. 5, pp. 17-24.

Fromme, H. [2004]: Allianz weicht Bankstrategie auf. In: Financial Times Deutschland, 5 April 2004.

Fuchs, H. J. [1998]: Netzwerke und Szenen: Wie man in Kundennetzwerken Empfehlungsgeschäfte simuliert. In: Belz, C. et al.: Management von Geschäftsbeziehungen: Konzepte – Integrierte Ansätze – Anwendungen in der Praxis, St. Gallen, Wien, pp. 135-142.

Galliers, R. D. [1991]: Choosing Appropriate Information Systems Research Approaches: A Revised Taxanomy. In: Nissen, H. E., Klein, H. K and Hirschheim, R. (eds.): Information Systems Research: Contemporary Approaches and Emergent Traditions. Elesevier Science Publishers (Nort-Holland), pp. 327-345.

Gaski, J. F. [1984]: The Theory of Power and conflict in Channels of Distribution. In: Journal of Marketing, No. 3/84, pp. 9-29.

Gerhardt, M. and Doerfner, O. [2002]: Ertragsorientierte Vergütung als Steuerungsinstrument im Kommen - aber noch schwierig zu berechnen. In: Versicherungswirtschaft, No. 4, pp. 277-9.

Gericke, S. H. [2001]: Customer Relationship Management in der Assekuranz unter besonderer Berücksichtigung neuer Verfahren und moderner Informationstechnologien – Ziele, Nutzen, Inhalt und Umsetzung, Karlsruhe.

Gilham, B. [2000]: Case Study Research Methods, London and New York.

Goedeckemeyer, K.-H. [2004]: Europäische Retailbanken im Vergleich. In: Bankmagazin, No. 3, pp. 26-28.

Goldman Sachs [2003]: Insurance Europe - European Insurance Market Profiles.

Grönroos, C. [1990]: Relationship Approach to marketing in Service Contexts: The Marketing and Organizational Behavior Interface. In: Journal of Business Research 20, pp. 3-11.

Grönroos, C. [1991]: Strategic Management and Marketing in the Service Sector, Lund.

Grönroos, C. [1993]: From Marketing Mix to Relationship Marketing. Toward a Paradigm Shift in Marketing, Swedish School of Economics and Business Administration, Working Papers, No. 263.

Grönroos, C. [1994]: From scientific management to service management. In: International Journal of Service Industry Management, Vol. 5, No. 2, pp. 5-20.

Grönroos, C. [1995]: Relationship Marketing: The Strategy Continuum. In: Journal of the Academy of Marketing Science, Vol. 23, No. 4, pp. 252-254.

Grönroos, C. [2000]: Service Management and Marketing – a Customer Relationship Management Approach, 2nd edition, Chichester.

Gronover, S. and Bach, V. [2000]: Kundensegmentierung, Bericht No. BE HSG/CCC CRM/12, Version 1.0, 31.03.2000.

Gronover, S. [2003]: Multi-Channel Management - Konzepte, Techniken und Fallbeispiele aus dem Retailbereich der Finanzdienstleistungsbranche, University St. Gallen, St. Gallen.

Gross, P. [1994]: Die Multioptionsgesellschaft, Frankfurt a. M.

Gruner & Jahr [1995]: Dialoge 4. Gesellschaft, Wirtschaft, Konsumenten, Hamburg.

Gulati, R. and Garino, J. [2000]: Get the Right Mix of Bricks & Clicks. In: Harvard Business Review, May-June 2000, pp. 107-114.

Gutenberg, E. [1979]: Grundlagen der Betriebswirtschaft, Zweiter Band, Der Absatz, 16. Auflage, Berlin/Heidelberg/New York.

Haertsch, P. [2000]: Wettbewerbsstrategien für Electronic Commerce: Eine kritische Überprüfung klassischer Steuerungskonzepte, Lohmar, Köln.

Haller, M. [1986]: Funktionen-Marketing - zur Bewältigung der "Financial Services (R)Evolution"? In: Belz, C. (ed.): Realisierung des Marketing, Festschrift zum 60. Geburtstag von Prof. Dr. H. Weinhold-Stünzi, St. Gallen, pp. 1097-1124.

Haller, M. [1992]: Financial Services auf dem Weg ins Jahr 2000. In: Bankkaufmann, No. 1, pp. 34-6.

Haller, M. and Ackermann, W. [1992]: Versicherungswirtschaft - kundenorientiert, Zürich.

Hannemann, S. [1993]: Vertrieb von Finanzdienstleistungen: Einsatz von Maklern, Handelsvertretern und Franchise-Systemen, Wiesbaden.

Hardock, P., Wübker, G. and Lauszus, D. [2003]: Multi Channel Management: Mit richtigem Pricing zum Erfolg. In: Die Bank, No. 2, pp. 100-103.

Hardy, K. and Magrath, A. [1988]: Marketing Channel Management. Strategic Planning and Tactics, Gleview, IL.

Harrison, T. [2000]: Financial Services Marketing, Financial Times, Prentice Hall.

Harvard Business School [1999]: Charles Schwab Corporation (A), Case Studies, September 9, No. 9-300-024.

Harvard Business School [1999a]: Charles Schwab Corporation (B), Case Studies, September 9, No. 9-300-025.

Hayden, J. [2000]: Managing Multiple Channels. In: Best's Review, April, pp. 44-46.

Hayes, T. and Dove, D. [1997]: Developing a blueprint for distribution management, US Banker, Vol. 107, No. 12, pp. 46-9.

Heinrich, D. [2002]: Erfolgsfaktoren für Bankdienstleister. In: Ahlert, D., Evanschitzky, H. and Hesse, J.: Exzellenz in Dienstleistung und Vertrieb – Konzeptionelle Grundlagen und empirische Ergebnisse, Wiesbaden, pp. 89-123.

Heinsen, A. [2001]: Privatkundenprodukte im Multikanal-Vertrieb, Karlsruhe.

Henning-Thurau, T. and Hansen, U. (ed.) [2000]: Relationship Marketing – Gaining Competitive Advantage Through Customer Satisfaction and Customer Retention. Berlin.

Herzog, M. and Panzer, J. [2003]: Die Strategischen Schwachstellen der Finanzdienstleister. In: Die Absatzwirtschaft, October, pp. 48-50.

Hesse, J. and Huckemann, M. [2002]: Erfolgsfaktoren des Vertriebs. In: Ahlert, D. , Evanschitzky, H. and Hesse, J.: Exzellenz in Dienstleistung und Vertrieb – Konzpetionelle Grundlagen und empirische Ergebnisse, Wiesbaden, pp. 60-88.

Hientzsch, R. and Bormann, S. [2003]: Die Vertriebswege neu ausrichten. In: Die Bank, No. 11, pp. 744-8.

Hilger, H. and Beers, M. [1999]: Alternative Distributionswege im Wertpapiergeschäft des genossenschaftlichen Finanzverbundes. In: Zeitschrift für das Kreditwesen, pp. 958-962.

Holland, D. and Coleman, M. [2000]: Enabling Multichannel Distribution. In: Best's Review, October, p. 185.

Holmsen, C., Palter, R., Simon, P. and Weberg, P. [1998]: Managing Competition among your own channels. In: The McKinsey Quarterly, 1/1998, pp. 83-92.

Homburg, C. and Bruhn, M. [1998]: Kundenbindungsmanagement – Eine Einführung in die theoretischen und praktischen Problemstellungen. In: Bruhn, M. and Homburg, C. (ed.): Handbuch Kundenbindungsmanagement – Grundlagen – Konzepte – Erfahrungen, Wiesbaden, pp. 3-35.

Homburg, C., Schaefer, H. and Scholl, M. [2002]: Wie viele Absatzkanäle kann sich ein Unternehmen leisten. In: Absatzwirtschaft, No. 3, 2002, pp. 38- 41

Hoock, R. and Lüer, C. [2002]: Hat der Außendienst ausgedient. In: Versicherungswirtschaft, No. 13, p. 980.

Hösly, B., Bärtschi, D. and Campell, D. [1996]: Integrierte Marktbearbeitung am Beispiel eines Direktversicherers. In: Thexis Heft, 3/96, pp. 7-11.

Hougaard, S. and Bjerre, M. [2002]: Strategic Relationship Management, Berlin, Heidelberg, New York.

Howes, G. [1999]: The channel investment challenge. In: US Banker, New York, October, Vol. 109, No. 10, p. 27.

HSBC Trinkhaus & Burkhardt [2003]: Deutsche Finanzdienstleister - Branche in der Warteschleife, Analyst Research Report, June.

Hughes, T. [2001]: Market orientation and the response of UK financial services companies to changes in market conditions as a result of e-commerce. In: The International Journal of Bank Marketing, Vol. 19, Issue 6, pp. 222-231.

Hummel, T. (1998): Jüngere Entwicklung im Kostenmanagement - Target Costing und Prozesskostenrechnung. In: Steinle, C., Bruch, D. (eds.): Controlling, Stuttgart.

Hunt, S. [1997]: Competing Through Relationships: Grounding Relationship Marketing in Resource-Advantage Theory. In: Journal of Marketing Management, No. 13, pp. 413-445.

Hurth, J. [2001]: Multi-Channel-Marketing: Novum oder Phrase? In: Wirtschaftswissenschaftliches Studium, Vol. 30, No. 9, pp. 463-469.

Hypovereinsbank [2001]: Privatkunden-Vertriebskonzepte und Allfinanz in Deutschland, Equity Research, Branchen Analyse, June.

Instenberg-Schiebeck, G. [1999]: Multi Channel Banking – die Wege zum Kunden. In: Die Bank, Nr. 09/99, pp. 602- 607.

Insurance Advisory Board [2003]: Supporting Agents with Lead Generation, Corporate Executive Board, Catalog No. IAB114ROX.

Järvinen, R. [1998]: Service Channel Relationships – The Dyadic Relationships between Service Producers and Service Intermediaries, University of Tampere, Tampere.

Kastenmüller, S. [2002]: Die Marke im Spannungsfeld der Konvergenz. In: Schögel, M., Tomczak, T. and Belz, C. (eds.): Roadm@p to E-Business - Wie Unternehmen das Internet erfolgreich nutzen, Festschrift zum 75. Geburtstag von Prof. Dr. Heinz Weinhold-Stünzi, St. Gallen, pp. 596-618.

Kendl, E. [1997]: Reengineering im Versicherungsmarketing, Wiesbaden.

Kernstock, J., Brockdorff, B. and Schubiger, N. [2002]: Crossover Branding - Ein Bezugsrahmen zur medien- und kanalübergreifenden Markenführung. In: Schögel, M., Tomczak, T. and Belz, C. (eds.): Roadm@p to E-Business - Wie Unternehmen das Internet erfolgreich nutzen, Festschrift zum 75. Geburtstag von Prof. Dr. Heinz Weinhold-Stünzi, St. Gallen, pp. 582-594.

Kirsch, W. [1991]: Grundzüge des Strategischen Managements. In: Kirsch, W. (ed.): Beiträge zum Management strategischer Programme, München, pp. 3-38.

Klein, W. A. [1997]: Integration der Vertriebswege im Strukturwandel. In: Versicherungswirtschaft, No. 19, pp. 358-363.

Koch, G. and Köhne, T. [2000]: Die virtuelle Versicherung und ihre informationstechnologischen Grundlagen. In: Zeitschrift für Versicherungswesen, No. 4, February, pp. 95- 102.

Köhne, T. [1998]: Auf dem Weg zum kundenindividuellen Marketing: Erfolgsfaktoren des Target Marketing in der Assekuranz. In: Versicherungswirtschaft, No. 20, pp. 668-676.

Kollat, D., Blackwell, R. and Robesons, J. [1972]: Strategic Marketing, New York.

Krings, M. [2002]: Multi-Channel-Retailing MCR – Zukunftsstrategien für den Einzelhandel. In: Stölzle, W. and Garies, K. (eds): Integrative Management- und Logistikkonzepte, Wiesbaden, pp. 411-426.

Krotsch, S. [2002]: Wachstum durch Customer Relationship Management. In: Linn, N., Riese, C. and Krotsch, S.: Banken in der Wertfalle, FAZ-Institut, pp. 117-133.

Kühlmann, K. et. al. [2000]: Marketing und Vertrieb, first edition, Wiesbaden.

Kurtenbach, W., Kühlmann, K., Käßer-Pawelka, G. [1995]: Versicherungsmarketing – eine praxisorientierte Einführung in das Marketing für Versicherungen und ergänzende Finanzdienstleistungenen, 4th revised and extended edition, Frankfurt a. M.

Kurzmeyer, H. [1999]: Internet Banking – Konzpetes und Marktstrategien der CREDIT SUISSE. In: Multi Channel Distribution im Banking: Tagungsband zum 6. Basler Bankentag, November 19, 1998, Basler Bankenvereinigung: Bern, Stuttgart, Wien, pp. 125-139.

Ladwig, F. [2002]: Multi-Channel-Commerce im Vertrieb – Anforderungen, Lösungen und Perspektiven, Wiesbaden.

Lammenett, E. und Meister, G. [2003]: Kommunikationskanäle: Optimieren und verzahnen? In: Versicherungswirtschaft, No. 2, pp. 102-3.

Lang, B. and Colgate, M. [2003]: Relationship quality, online banking and the information technology gap. In: International Journal of Bank Marketing, Vol. 21, No. 1, pp. 29-37.

Layr, W. and Dahlem, C. [2001]: Gelebte Kundenpartnerschaft - die alten, neue Philosophie im Privatkundengeschäft der Bank. In: Schmoll, A. and Ronzal, W. (eds.): Neue Wege zum Kunden - Multi-Channel-Vertrieb im Bankgeschäft, pp. 54-78.

Lebalnce, G. [1990]: Customer Motivations: Use and Non-use of automated banking. In: The International Journal of Bank Marketing, Vol. 8, No. 4, pp. 36-40.

Leichtfuss, R. and Mattern, F. [1996]: Best Practices: What Retail Banks Can Learn From Each Other. In: Perspective, Vol. 18, Winter, pp. 41-51.

Lehmann, A. [1990]: Alternative Vertriebsformen im Wettbewerb – Neue Optionen für die Assekuranz? In: Lehmann, A. (Publ.): Tagungsband zur 19. Schwerpunkttagung der I-VW Management, 23. Oktober 1990, Zürich, pp. 3-16.

Lehmann, A. [1995]: Dienstleistungsmanagement – Strategien und Ansatzpunkte zur Schaffung von Servicequalität, 2nd edition, Stuttgart.

Lehmann, A. [1998]: Qualität und Produktivität im Dienstleistungsmanagement – Strategische Handlungsfelder im Versicherungs- und Finanzdienstleistungswettbewerb, Wiesbaden.

Lehmann, A. [2001]: Dienstleistungsmanagement – Transformation und Entwicklungsschritte. In: Maas, P. (ed.): Integriertes Dienstleistungs-Management: Auf dem Weg zum Customer Value, Band 3, Institut für Versicherungswirtschaft der Universität St. Gallen, St. Gallen.

Leitzmann, C.-J. and Keese, O. [2000]: Der systematische Kampf um den profitablen Kunden. In: Versicherungswirtschaft, Heft 15, pp. 1142-1143.

Lewis, B. [1995]: Customer care and service quality. In: Ennew, C., Watkins, T. and Wright M. (eds.): Marketing Financial Services, 2nd edition, Butterworth-Heinmann, pp. 193-211.

Li, F. [2002]: Internet banking: from new distribution channel to new business models. In: International Journal of Business Performance Management, Vol. 4, No. 2/3/4, pp. 136-160.

Liebmann, H.-P. and Zentes, J. [2001]: Handelsmanagement, München.

Lindstrom, M. [2002]: Clicks, Bricks & Brands, revised edition, London, Great Britain.

Linn, N., Riese, C. and Krotsch, S. [2002]: Banken in der Wertfalle, FAZ-Institut.

Lipke, D. [2000]: Mystery Shoppers. In: American Demographics, Vol. 22, No. 12, pp. 41-43.

Llewellyn, D. and Drake, L. [1995]: Pricing. In: Ennew, C., Watkins, T. and Wright M. (eds.): Marketing Financial Services, 2nd edition, Butterworth-Heinmann, pp. 138-173.

Lockett, A. and Littler, D. [1997]: The Adoption of Direct Banking Services. In: Journal of Marketing Management, No. 13, pp. 791-811.

Macchi, M. [2002]: Multikanal-Management – Wertgenerierung durch effiziente Vertriebsmodelle. In: Linn, N., Riese, C. and Krotsch, S.: Banken in der Wertfalle, FAZ-Institut, pp. 117-133.

Macneil, I. [1980]: The new Social Contract: An Inquiry into Modern Contractual Relations, New Haven.

Mallen, B. E. [1977]: Principles of Marketing Channel Management, Lexington, Mass.

Margrath, A. and Hardy, K. G. [1987]: Avoiding the Pitfalls in Managing Distribution Channels. In: Business Horizons, No. 5/88. pp. 29-33.

Maynard, P. [2001]: Integrated Channels: Customer Access for the 21st Century, May, LIMRA Europe Ltd.

Mawn, P. [2001]: How Hancock is Managing The Multichannel Challenge. In: National Underwriter Life & Health, Financial Services Edition, July 23, p. 10.

McDonald, L. [1999]: Managing Channel Conflict, In: Mortgage Banking, Vol. 60, No. 1, pp. 88-99.

McKechnie, S. and Harrison, T. [1995]: Understanding consumers and markets. In: Ennew, C., Watkins, T. and Wright M.: Marketing Financial Services, 2nd edition, Butterworth-Heinmann, pp. 33-59.

McKinsey [2000]: Multi-Channel Marketing – Making "Bricks and Clicks" Stick, McKinsey Marketing Practice.

Meffert, H. [1992]: Marketingforschung und Käuferverhalten, second edition, Wiesbaden.

Meffert, H. [2000]: Marketing, Grundlagen marktorientierter Unternehmensführung Konzepte – Instrumente – Praxisbeispiele, 9th edition, Wiesbaden.

Meffert, H. and Bruhn, M. [2000]: Dienstleistungsmarketing: Grundlagen – Konzepte - Methoden, mit Fallbeispielen, 3th edition, Wiesbaden.

Meffert, H. and Schleusener, M. [2001]: Markenführung im Dienstleistungsbereich - klassische und E-Branding im Spannungsfeld. In: Maas, P. (ed.): Integriertes Dienstleistungs-Management: Auf dem Weg zum Customer Value, St. Gallen, pp. 136-150.

Meidan, A. [1996]: Marketing Financial Services, London.

Mols, N. [1999]: The Internet and the banks' strategic distribution channel decisions. In: International Journal of Bank Marketing, Vol. 17, No. 6, pp. 295-300.

Morgan, R. and Hunt, S. [1994]: The Commitment-Trust Theory of Relationship Marketing. In: Journal of Marketing, No. 58, July, pp. 20-38.

Moriarty, R. and Moran, U. [19990]: Managing Hybrid Marketing Systems. In: Harvard Business Review, Vol. 68, No. 6, pp. 146-155.

Müller, H. [1993]: Marktsegmentierung im Privatkundengeschäft von Versicherungsunternehmen, Karlsruhe.

Müller-Peters, H. [1998]: Schock oder Chance? Das Verhalten der Kunden im Jahre vier nach der Deregulierung. In: Versicherungswirtschaft. pp. 1250-1251.

Muther, A. [1999]: Electronic Customer Care: Die Anbieter-Kunden-Beziehung im Informationszeitalter, Berlin, Heidelberg.

Muthers, H. and Muthers-Haas, H. [2001]: Ver-rückte Zeiten brauchten ver-rückte Banken - Auf der Such nach den erfolgsversprechenden Geschäftsfeldern von morgen. In: Schmoll, A. and Ronzal, W. (eds.): Neue Wege zum Kunden - Multi-Channel-Vertrieb im Bankgeschäft, pp. 19-40.

Neske, R. [2003]: Deutsche Bank Investor Day: Our Profile, Business Model and Strategy, How we plan to grow, London, September 4, 2003.

Neubert, M. [1998]: Computer Aided Selling – Informations- und Kommunikationssysteme der Vertriebssteuerung von Versicherungsunternehmen, Bayreuth.

Nevin, J. [1995]: Relationship Marketing and Distribution Channels: Exploring Fundamental Issues. In: Journal of the Academy of Marketing Science, Vol. 23, No. 4, pp. 327-334.

Nevries, P. and Segbers, K. [2003]: Ganzheitliche Controlling-Konzeption im E-Business, Unpublished Notes, University of Muenster, Germany.

Nieschlag, R., Dichtl, E. and Hörschgen, H. [1997]: Marketing, 18th edition, Berlin.

Österle, H. [1999]: Prozeßportale bei Banken: Vom Finanzdienstleister zum "Rundumservice". In: Bank und Markt, No. 12, Dezember 1999, pp. 33-36.

Ouchi, W. [1980]: Markets, Bureaucracies, and Clans. In: Administrative Science Quarterly, March, pp. 129-141.

Patton, M. [1990]: Qualitative Evaluation and Research Methods. Newyberry, Park. CA.

Pauluhn, B. [1999]: Kundensegmentierung und differenzierter Vertrieb im Privatkundengeschäft. In: Eichhorn, F.- J. und Hein, M. (eds): Neue Vertriebsformen für Finanzdienstleistungen im Privatkundengeschäft, Stuttgart, pp. 133-162.

Peitsmeier, H. [2003]: Alle Zeit der Welt: Bei der Citibank können Berater beraten - Duisburg sei Dank. In: Frankfurter Allgemeine Zeitung, 26 July, p. 17.

Peppers, D. and Rogers, M. [1997]: Enterprise One-to-one, New York.

Peter, S. [1997]: Kundenbindung als Marketingziel: Identifikation und Analyse zentraler Determinanten, Wiesbaden.

Peterson, R.; Balasubramanian, S. and Bronnenberg, B. [1997]: Exploring the Implications of the Internet for Consumer Marketing. In: Journal of the Academy of Marketing Science, Vol. 25, No. 4, pp. 329-326.

Pfeiffer, H. [1999]: Ziemlich viel Chaos. In: Die Zeit, No. 6, p. 24.

Popp, S. [1990]: Absatzwege für Bankdienstleistungen – Ansätze zur Analyse und Gestaltung der bankbetrieblichen Distribution, Studienreihe der Stiftung Kreditwirtschaft an der Universität Hohenheim, Hohenheim.

Porter, M. [1985]: Competitive Advantage, The Free Press, New York.

Porter, M. [1996]: What is Strategy? In: Harvard Business Review, November-December, pp. 61-78.

Porter, M. [1998]: Competitive Strategy: Techniques for Analysing Industries and Competitors, New York.

Porter, M. [2001]: Strategy and the Internet. In: Harvard Business Review, Vol. 79, No. 3, pp. 62-78.

Ramsay, J. and Smith, M. [1999]: Managing customer channel usage in the Australian banking sector. In: Managerial Auditing Journal, Bradford, Vol. 14, Iss. 7, p. 329.

Rasch, S., Lintner, A. and Mogelvang, S. [2003]: Überlegene Multikanal-Strategien sind gefragt. In: Zeitschrift für Betriebswirtschaft, No. 1, pp. 113-120.

Ravara, C. [2001]: Das nachfrageorientierte Management im Financial Services Bereich. In: Maas, P. (ed.): Integriertes Dienstleistungs-Management: Auf dem Weg zum Customer Value, St. Gallen, pp. 105-120.

Redwitz, G. [1999]: Konsequenzen der sozio-demographischen Veränderungen für den Handel. In: O. Beisheim (ed.): Distribution im Aufbruch - Bestandsaufnahme und Perspektiven , München, pp. 259-279.

Regan, L. (1999): Expense ratios across insurance distribution systems: an analysis by line of business. In: Risk Management and Insurance Review, Vol. 2, No. 2, pp. 44-59.

Regan, L. and Tzeng, L. [1999]: Organisational form in the property-liability industry. In: Journal of Risk and Insurance, pp. 253-273.

Reichheld, F. and Sasser, W. [1990]: Zero Defections: Quality Comes to Services. In: Harvard Business Review, No. 68, No. 5, pp. 105-111.

Reindl, E. and Blum, R. [2003]: Bei der Vergütung das Controlling nicht vergessen! - Neue Impulse durch wertorientierte Vergütungs- und Karrieremodelle. In: Versicherungswirtschaft, No. 19, pp. 1490-2.

Renggli, C. [1997]: Strategische Kontrollen - empirische Studien und eine Erhebung in Schweizer Unternehmen, Bern.

Rimpler, G. [1995]: Absatzkanal-Management, Linz.

Robicheaux, R. and Coleman, J. [1994]: The Structure of Marketing Channel Relationships. In: Journal of the Academy of Marketing Science, Vol. 22, No. 1, pp. 38-51.

Roesler, S. and Dettenbach, J. [2003]: Mehr als nur eine Nummer. In: bankmagazin, No. 1, pp. 36-38.

Salmen, S.-M. [2002]: Individualisierung von Kunden-Bank-Beziehungen durch den Einsatz von Electronic Relationship – Das Beispiel des Private Internet Banking, Kassel, Dissertation.

Sarel, D. and Marmorstein, H. [2002]: Migrating customers to new distribution channels: The role of communication. In: Journal of Financial Services Marketing, Vol. 6, pp. 254-266.

Schierenbeck, H. [1999]: Die Vertriebskanäle der Zukunft im Privatkundengeschäft. In: Multi Channel Distribution im Banking: Tagungsband zum 6. Basler Bankentag, November 19, 1998, Basler Bankenvereinigung: Bern, Stuttgart, Wien, pp. 3-50.

Schmidt-Kasparek, U. [2003]: AXA Vertriebsstrategie: Duale Produktwelt soll Erfolg bringen. In: Versicherungs-Magazin, 1 February.

Schmoll, A. and Ronzal, W. (eds.) [2001]: Neue Wege zum Kunden - Multi-Channel-Vertrieb im Bankgeschäft, Wiesbaden.

Schneider, G. [1997]: Multi-Channel-Management bei Banken. In: Bierbaum, D. und Feinen, K.: Bank- und Finanzwirtschaft: Strategien im Wandel, Festschrift für Hans E. Büschgen zum 65. Geburtstag, Wiesbaden, pp. 353-387.

Schnetzer, R. [1999]: Megatrends für den Vertrieb. In: Versicherungskaufmann, No. 12, pp. 14-18.

Schögel, M. [1997]: Mehrkanalsystem in der Distribution, Wiesbaden.

Schögel, M., Tomczak, T. and Belz, C. (eds.) [2002]: Roadm@p to E-Business - Wie Unternehmen das Internet erfolgreich nutzen, Festschrift zum 75. Geburtstag von Prof. Dr. Heinz Weinhold-Stünzi, St. Gallen.

Scholl, M. [2004]: Mulit Channel Management - Gestaltung, Steuerung und Erfolg von Multi Channel Vertriebssystemen, Universität Mannheim, Mannheim.

Schramm-Klein, H. [2003]: Multi-Channel-Retailing: Verhaltenswissenschaftliche Analyse der Wirkung von Mehrkanalsystemen im Handel, Wiesbaden.

Schüller, S. and Riedl, M. [2000]: Multi-Channel-Management – die Vertriebsherausforderungen im Retail Banking. In: Die Bank, No. 12, pp. 828-832.

Schultz, D. [1996]: The Inevitability of Integrated Communications. In: Journal of Business Research, Vol. 37, No. 3, pp. 139-146.

Schwanitz, J. [2001]: Web-Controlling in der Multikanal-Vertriebssteuerung. In: Die Bank: Zeitschrift für Bankpolitik und Bankpraxis, No. 8, pp. 589-595.

Schwanitz, J. and Krugmann, B. [2002]: Selbstbewusste Kunden wollen alles - und zwar sofort. In: Versicherungsbetriebe, No. 3, pp. 20-2.

Schwanitz, J. and Ahr, H. [2002]: Multikanalvertrieb: Kunden-Tracking als Steuerungsinstrument. In: bank und markt, No. 3, pp. 26- 28.

Sharma, A. and Dominguez, L. [1992]: Channel Evolution: A Framework for Analysis. In: Journal of the Academy of Marketing Science, Vol. 20, No. 1, pp. 1-15.

Shemwell, D. and Yavas, U. [1998]: Seven best-practices for creating a sales culture: transitioning from an internally-focused, transaction-oriented culture to a customer-focused, sales-oriented culture. In: International Journal of Bank Marketing, Vol. 16, No. 7, pp. 293-298.

Sheth, J. and Sisodia, R. [1997]: Consumer Behavior in the Future. In: Peterson, R.: Electronic Marketing and the Consumer, California, USA, pp. 17-37.

Sherden, W. A. [1992]: A new way to deliver products: by reengineering their distribution channels, insurers can gain a marketing advantage in an increasingly costly and competitive aspect of the business. In: Best's Review Life/Health, Vol. 93, No. 5, pp. 27-32 and p. 122.

Shumrak, H. M. [1996]: Matching Distribution Systems to Markets Spells Success. In: Best's Review Life /Health, June, pp. 69-70 and pp. 102-103.

Silberberger, H. [2002]: Der Kunde von heute - eine multidimensionale Herausforderung. In: Direkt Marketing, No. 8, pp. 52-56.

Sohler, M. [2003]: Erfolgreiches Multi Channel Banking: Von der Transaktions- zur Vertriebsank. In: Die Bank, No. 10, pp. 670-674.

Späth, P. [2000]: Strategische Vertriebswegeplanung von Universalbanken, Wiesbaden.

Specht, G. [1992]: Distributionsmanagement, 2nd edition, Stuttgart.

Stern, L. W. and Reve, T. [1980]: Distribution channels as political economies: a framework for comparative analysis. In: Journal of Marketing, Vol. 44, Summer, pp. 52-64.

Stern, L. W., El Ansary, A. I. [1992]: Marketing Channels, 4th edition, Engelwood Cliffs.

Stern, L. W., El Ansary, A. I. and Coughlan, A. [1996]: Marketing Channels, 5th edition, Engelwood Cliffs.

Stern, L. and Sturdivant, F. [1987]: Getting Things Done: Customer-Driven Distribution Systems. In: Harvard Business Review, July-August 1987, pp. 34-45.

Stern, L. and Weitz, B. [1997]: The Revolution in Distribution: Challenges and Opportunities. In: Long Range Planning, Vol. 30, No. 6, pp. 823-829.

Stone, M., Hobbs, M. and Khaleeli, M. [2002]: Multichannel customer management: The benefits and challenges. In: Journal of Database Marketing, Vol. 10, pp. 39-52.

Stummeyer, C. [2002]: Das Internet als ein Vertriebskanal im Rahmen einer Multikanal-Strategie. In: Gabriel, R. and Hoppe, U. (eds.): Electronic Business: Theoretische Aspekte und Anwendungen in der betrieblichen Praxis – Festschrift für Jörg Biethahn, Heidelberg.

Süchting, J. [1984]: Unternehmensführung in Banken und Sparkassen. In: Deutscher Sparkassen- und Giroverband (ed.): Standortbestimmung: Entwicklungslininen der deutschen Kreditwirtschaft, Stuttgart, pp. 307-325.

Surminski, M. [1998]: Der Vermittler und der Kunde der Zukunft. In: Zeitschrift für Versicherungswesen, No. 14, pp. 395-400.

Surminski, M. [2002]: Vertrieb im Umbruch? – Neue Herausforderungen für die Versicherungswirtschaft. In: Zeitschrift für Versicherungswesen, No. 15, August 2002, pp. 447-456.

Sydow, J. [1999]: Management von Netzwerkorganisationen – Zum Stand der Forschung. In: Sydow, J. (ed.): Management von Netzwerkorganisationen: Beiträge aus der Managementforschung. Wiesbaden, pp. 279-314.

Swoboda, U. [1996]: Die Bedeutung und Zukunft der modernen Konsumentenbank: Bankbetriebliche Erfolgsfaktoren mit Hilfe der Delphi-Expertenbefargung, Frankfurt a. M..

TECTEM [2001]: Benchmarking-Projekt Multi Channel Marketing, Screening Report, August 2001, St. Gallen.

TECTEM [2001a]: Benchmarking-Projekt Multi Channel Marketing, Review-Meeting, November 2001, St. Gallen.

TECTEM [2002]: Benchmarking Project – Multi Channel Marketing, Final Report, May 2002, St. Gallen.

Thibaut, J. and Kelley, H. [1959]: The Social Psychology of Groups, New York.

Tomczak, T. [1992]: Forschungsmethoden in der Marketingwissenschaft – ein Plädoyer für den qualitativen Forschungsansatz. In: Marketing ZFP, No. 2, 2nd quarter, pp. 77-87.

Tomczak, T. [1992]: Das Management indirekter Distributionssysteme. Unpublished Habilitation, Hochschule St. Gallen, St. Gallen.

Tomczak, T. and Reinecke, S. [1999]: Der aufgabenorientierte Ansatz als Basis eines marktorientierten Wertmanagements. In: Grüning, R. and Pasquier, M.: Strategisches Management und Marketing, Berlin, Stuttgart, Wien, pp. 293-327.

Tsay, A. and Agrawal, N. [2002]: Modelling conflict and coordination in multi-channel distribution systems: a review. In: Simchi-Levi, D. Wu, D. and Shen, M. (eds.): Supply Chain Analysis in the eBusiness Era, International Series in Operations Research and Management Science, Kluwer, pp. 1- 56.

Ulrich. H. [1970]: Die Unternehmung als soziales System. Grundlagen der allgemeinen Unternehmungslehre, Institut für Betriebswirtschaftslehre an der Hochschule St. Gallen, Band 1, 2. überarbeitete Auflage, Bern, Stuttgart.

Umbau, G. [2003]: Vergütungssystem für die Versicherungsvermittlung im Wandel, Karlsruhe.

Waescher, D. [2000]: Kundenorientierung und Kundenbindung im Fokus des Vertriebscontrolling. In: Controller Magazin 5/2000, pp. 403-406.

Walser, M. [2002]: Multi Channel Commerce – Herausforderung für Vertrieb und Marketing. In: Direkt Marketing, No. 9, pp. 52-58.

Weigand, R. E. [1977]: Fit products and channels to your markets. in: Harvard Business Review, No. 1/77, pp. 95-105.

Weigele, O. [1983]: Strategische Unternehmensplanung in Universalbanken, Schriftenreihe des Instituts für Kredit- und Versicherungswirtschaft, Abteilung Bankbetriebslehre, Vol. 1, Wien.

Weigelt, O. and Engler, K. [2003]: Effiziente Vertriebssteuerung nur mit aussagekräftigen Kennzahlen: nur wenige Unternehmen verfügen über die notwendigen Benchmarks. In: Versicherungswirtschaft, No. 4, pp. 282-284.

Wein, T. H. [1997]: Der deregulierte Versicherungsmarkt aus der sicht der Vermittler und Versicherer. In: Versicherungswirtschaft, No. 19, pp. 244-246.

Weinhold-Stünzi, H. [1994]: Vertriebsmanagement – Distributionsmanagement. in: Thexis, No. 3/93, pp. 2-8.

Weitz, B. and Jap, S. [1995]: Relationship Marketing and Distribution Channels. In: Journal of the Academy of Marketing Science. Vol. 23, No. 4, Fall, pp. 305-320.

Wellborn, J. [2000]: Financial Services Integration Drives the Way Agents are Paid. In: National Underwriter, March 23, p. 23 and 26.

Wheeler, S. and Hirsh, E. [1999]: Channel champions: how leading companies build new strategies to serve customers, San Francisco.

Wiedmann, K.-P.; Buckler, F. and Siemon, N. [2004]: Erträge steigern mit wertvollen Kundenbeziehungen. In: Bankmagazin, pp. 50-1.

Williamson, O. [1985]: The Economic Institutions of Capitalism. New York.

Wilson, A. [1997]: The culture of the branch team and its impact on service delivery and corporate identity. In: International Journal of Bank Marketing, Vol. 15, No. 5, pp. 163-8.

Wings, H. [1999]: Digital Business in Banken: Informationstechnologie – Erfolgsfaktor für die strategische Positionierung, Wiesbaden.

Winkelmann, P. [2000]: Vertriebskonzeption und Vertriebssteuerung: die operativen Elemente des Marketing, München.

Wirtz, B. [2002]: So binden Sie Ihre Kunden auf den richtigen Weg. In: Absatzwirtschaft, No. 4, pp. 48-53.

Wirtz, B., Schilke, O. and Büttner, T. [2004]: Channel-Management "Multi oder Mono?" - das ist nicht mehr die Frage: Absatzwirtschaft, No. 2, pp. 46-49.

Wright, M. and Howcroft, B. [1995]: Bank Marketing. In: Ennew, C., Watkins, T. and Wright M. (eds.): Marketing Financial Services, 2nd edition, Butterworth-Heinmann, pp. 212-235.

W. A. [2001]: Insurers See Technology As Driving Dramatic Change. In: Best's Review, December, p. 119.

W.A. [2004]: Die Vertriebsrevoluion findet nicht statt, In: Zeitschrift für Versicherungswesen, pp. 128-130.

Yin, R. K. [1994]: Case Study Research – Design and Methods, Applied Social Research Methods Series, Vol. 5, 2nd edition, Thousand Oaks, CA, USA.

Yulinsky, C. [2002]: Multichannel delivery with an eye on bottom line. In: American Banker, New York, May 9, Vol. 167, Issue 89, p. 14.

Zeithaml, V. and Bitner, M. [1996]: Services Marketing, Singapore.

Ziegenbein, K. [2002]: Controlling, 7th edition, Ludwigshafen.

GPSR Compliance

The European Union's (EU) General Product Safety Regulation (GPSR) is a set of rules that requires consumer products to be safe and our obligations to ensure this.

If you have any concerns about our products, you can contact us on ProductSafety@springernature.com

In case Publisher is established outside the EU, the EU authorized representative is:

Springer Nature Customer Service Center GmbH
Europaplatz 3
69115 Heidelberg, Germany

Batch number: 10725993

Printed by Printforce, the Netherlands